Pensions and the Economy

Pension Research Council Publications

A complete listing of PRC publications appears in the back of this volume.

Pensions and the Economy

Sources, Uses, and Limitations of Data

Edited by Zvi Bodie
and Alicia H. Munnell

Published by

Pension Research Council
Wharton School of the University of Pennsylvania

and

University of Pennsylvania Press
Philadelphia

The chapters in this volume are based on papers presented at the Wharton School Pension Research Council Spring Conference, "Pensions and the U.S. Economy: The Need for Good Data," Philadelphia, Pennsylvania, March 22–23, 1990.

© Copyright 1992 by the Pension Research Council of the Wharton School of the University of Pennsylvania

Library of Congress Cataloging-in-Publication Data
Pensions and the economy : sources, uses, and limitations of data / edited by Zvi Bodie and Alicia H. Munnell.
    p.   cm.
    "Based on papers presented at the Wharton School Pension Research Council Spring Conference . . . Philadelphia, March 22–23, 1990."—Verso t.p.
    "Pension Research Council publications."
    Includes bibliographical references and index.
    ISBN 0-8122-3118-X
    1. Pension trusts—United States—Congresses. 2. United States—Economic conditions—1981– —Congresses. I. Bodie, Zvi. II. Munnell, Alicia H. III. Wharton School. Pension Research Council. Spring Conference (1990 : Philadelphia, Pa.)
HD7105.45.U6P45   1992
331.25'2—dc20   91-45276
                                                                       CIP

Printed in the United States of America

Anna M. Rappaport, F.S.A., Managing Director, William M. Mercer, Inc., Chicago

Sylvester J. Schieber, Director of the Research and Information Center, The Wyatt Company, Washington, DC

Ray Schmitt, Specialist in Social Legislation, Congressional Research Service, Library of Congress, Washington, DC

Richard B. Stanger, National Director, Employee Benefits Services, Price Waterhouse, Washington, DC

Marc M. Twinney, Jr., F.S.A., Manager, Pension Department, Ford Motor Company, Dearborn, MI

Jack L. VanDerhei, Associate Professor of Risk and Insurance, Temple University

L. Edwin Wang, Past President, Board of Pensions of the Lutheran Church in America, Minneapolis, MN

Howard E. Winklevoss, President, Winklevoss Consultants, Inc., Greenwich, CT

Howard Young, F.S.A., Adjunct Professor of Mathematics, University of Michigan, Ann Arbor

Purpose of the Council

The Pension Research Council of the Wharton School of the University of Pennsylvania was created in 1952 for the purpose of sponsoring objective research in the area of private pensions. It was formed in response to the urgent need for a better understanding of the private pension movement. Private pensions have experienced a phenomenal growth during the last three decades, but their economic, political, and social implications are yet to be explored. They seem destined to play a major role in the quest for old-age economic security, but the nature of that role can be ascertained only on the basis of more enlightened evaluation of the capabilities and limitations of the private pension mechanism. It was to conduct an impartial study into the facts and basic issues surrounding private pensions, under the auspices of an academic and professional group representing leadership in every phase of the field, that the Council was organized.

Projects undertaken by the Council are broad in scope and predominantly interpretive rather than technical in nature. In general, attention is concentrated on areas which are not the object of special investigation by other research groups. Its research studies are conducted by mature scholars drawn from both the academic and business spheres. Research results are published from time to time in a series of books and monographs.

Pensions and the Economy: Sources, Uses, and Limitations of Data

Introduction

Zvi Bodie and Alicia H. Munnell

The expansion of employer-sponsored pension plans has been one of the most significant economic developments in the United States during the postwar period. These plans now affect the income security of millions of people, influence the employment and mobility of half the work force, affect the saving rate of individuals and of the nation, play a major role in financial markets, and have a significant impact on the federal budget.

Because of pensions' growth and importance, policy makers need to know the ways in which their provisions affect economic activity, and how changes in these provisions might alter behavior. Sorting out the links between employer-sponsored pensions and economic activity requires good information about the plans themselves, the firms that sponsor them, and the employees who are covered. Currently, data on pensions are scattered and few researchers are aware of all the available information.

The conference on which this volume is based was conceived as the first step toward developing a major, centralized source of information for pension research. The terrain was divided into five key areas where pensions interact with the economy: provision of retirement income, labor force activity, individual and national saving, financial markets, and the federal budget. Experts in each of these areas were asked to summarize the significant ways in which pensions might affect outcomes, to identify the information required to test the relevant hypotheses, and to highlight the extent to which the data are available. The result of this effort is a complete inventory of the major issues relating to pensions and economic activity, a compendium of the data available to explore these issues, and a listing of the most significant gaps in information. A sixth chapter assesses the issues and adequacy of information for foreign pension plans.

I. How Good a Job Are Pensions Doing in Providing Retirement Income?

The goal of federal tax policy since 1942 has been to encourage, through favorable tax provisions, the use of tax-qualified pension plans to ensure greater retirement income security for all employees. Pension plans, however, are just one part of a three-tiered system of retirement income maintenance that has developed in the United States. This system consists of (1) welfare programs such as the supplemental security income (SSI) program, which provides a minimum guaranteed income to the needy elderly; (2) a compulsory public contributory program—namely, Social Security; and (3) private provisions for retirement, which include individual saving as well as supplementary employer-sponsored pension plans.

Numerous approaches exist for evaluating the adequacy of retirement income produced by this multi-tiered system. The procedure adopted by Emily Andrews and Michael Hurd begins with a comparison of the per capita income of the elderly with that of the nonelderly. The authors find that without any adjustments the income of the elderly is only slightly below that of the nonelderly; making modest adjustments for income in kind, such as Medicare benefits, and for documented underreporting on the part of the elderly produces roughly equivalent incomes for the two groups; adjusting fully for income in kind and underreporting makes the elderly appear substantially better off.

This relationship between the incomes of the elderly and the nonelderly is also reflected in their poverty rates; without adjustments the two are virtually identical, with adjustments the poverty rate for the elderly is substantially lower than for the nonelderly. Poverty rates for the elderly have declined dramatically since the late 1950s, and the authors attribute most of this improvement to the Social Security program.

Andrews and Hurd note that despite the general improvement in the economic status of the elderly, some groups such as elderly widows still have extraordinarily large numbers living below the poverty line. Moreover, many older people reach retirement with few assets beyond their home, Social Security benefits, and a claim on Medicare; even though they may not actually be in poverty, they have few resources beyond housing equity to cover large, unanticipated expenditures.

Nonetheless, the authors interpret the equivalence in income levels and poverty rates between the elderly and nonelderly as an indication that retirement income is adequate. They also confirm that the income of the elderly is not, contrary to public perceptions, vulnerable to inflation. They then try to discern the extent to which this favorable determination can be attributed to pension plans. The answer is probably not very much. Data reported on the sources of income indicate that only 26 percent of those age 60 and over received any private pension income, and within this group pension income amounted to less than 20 percent of total income in more than half the cases. Moreover, the inflation protection stems primarily from fully indexed Social Security benefits rather than from private pensions, where partial inflation adjustments are provided only on an ad hoc basis. The lack of indexing of private pension benefits remains a major policy issue.

On the other hand, the data on the sources of income show the role of pensions had increased noticeably since the early 1970s when only 17 percent of the elderly were receiving pension benefits. In an effort to assess the importance of this source in the future, the authors explore the evidence on trends in pension coverage. Several sources of data indicate that pension coverage has remained virtually constant since the mid-1970s; moreover, the evidence on the determinants of pension coverage suggests that, because of permanent shifts in industry structure, the percentage of the work force covered by pension plans in the future is unlikely to increase. The fact that only half the work force is covered by a supplementary pension plan raises concerns about both equity and adequacy of the system. The authors urge research to determine the need for more extensive coverage and the merits of alternative ways of achieving that goal.

Future retirement income depends not only on the number of people covered, but also on the likelihood that participants will receive benefits and on the size of those benefit amounts. Data on types of plans reveal a shift from defined benefit plans to defined contribution plans, but little information is available about contribution rates under the defined contribution plans. In terms of the likelihood of receiving benefits, the introduction of five-year vesting, as a result of the Tax Reform Act of 1986, has increased the probability of receiving a benefit in retirement. On the other hand, the greater prevalence of defined contribution plans has contributed to the payment of more lump-sum pension cashouts; to the extent that these cashouts are spent rather than saved, this will reduce the likelihood of pension receipt.

The size of the benefit amounts under defined benefit plans depends not only on the specific plan provisions but also on the work patterns of the participants. Mobile employees receive significantly lower benefits as a result of changing jobs than they would have received from continuous coverage with one employer. The difference arises because final earnings levels determine pension benefits. Workers who remain with a plan receive benefits related to earnings just before retirement, but mobile employees receive benefits based on earnings at the time they terminate employment. The implication of this lack of portability for adequacy of retirement income, however, is not well understood.

Employer-provided health insurance has become an important component of the retirement benefit package. While several sources provide information about the prevalence of retiree health insurance, none covers the specifics of the various plans. In order to assess fully the economic well-being of older people, Andrews and Hurd argue that data are needed to provide estimates of the asset value of retiree health insurance benefits similar to those derived for Medicare and Medicaid.

The authors conclude with a list of the data requirements to assess the economic status of the elderly and explore the implications of alternative policy options. They place a high priority on longitudinal data to conduct research on life-cycle retirement income issues. Second, they urge periodic cross-section surveys, including matches with employer records, to determine the trends in pension plan provisions. Finally, they reiterate their call for more information on retiree health benefits.

Andrews and Hurd's first discussant, Laurence Kotlikoff, accepts their description of the income and wealth of the elderly, but questions their measure of income adequacy. Kotlikoff argues that defining adequacy in terms of income levels raises the question whether a sudden increase in the real wages of young workers due to productivity improvements would mean that the income of the elderly would suddenly become less adequate. He urges the authors to adopt a replacement rate concept such that adequacy would be defined as the ability to maintain their previous standard of living.

Kotlikoff also speculates that the current well-being of the elderly may be only temporary; the 1983 Social Security amendments reduced future benefits, and today's workers appear to be saving very little on their own. He urges more research on the issue of the income and consumption of the future elderly.

In his comments on the Andrews-Hurd paper, Sylvester Schieber endorses their call for better data to evaluate the effects of government policies on the adequacy of retirement income. In particular, Schieber expresses concern that short-run federal budgetary considerations are endangering the future of pension and retiree health benefits, and governmental agencies are not compiling and providing the data needed to evaluate the effects of these policies. He also points out the substantial barriers to access of the proprietary data bases maintained by benefits consulting firms.

II. How Do Pensions Affect Labor Market Activity?

Pensions have transformed the way workers are compensated in the labor force; as a result, they have the potential to affect the price of labor, the quantity of labor supplied, and the quality of the labor effort. In their review of the literature on pensions and labor market activity, Alan Gustman and Olivia Mitchell synthesize what is known about the form and function of employer-provided pensions and identify areas where further information is needed.

The first issue addressed is the nature of the pension promise: to what extent are pensions part of a short-term spot contract as opposed to a long-term contract between the firm and the workers? The issue has important implications for measuring pension accruals and for exploring the wage-pension tradeoff. In a spot market, pension promises would be valued on the basis of work to date; in the context of a long-term contract, accruals would also be contingent on the course of work and pay in the future. The authors believe that the available evidence indicates that pensions should be viewed as part of a long-term employment relationship.

Because of the long-term nature of the employee-employer relationship, one should not expect a dollar-for-dollar tradeoff of pension accruals for wages at any moment in time. Yet, whether or not such a tradeoff occurs is important in determining who bears the cost of pensions and who would be affected by pension reform. Although economists generally assume that workers pay for their pensions through reduced wages, such an offset has been difficult to document empirically. Part of the problem may be the long-term contract, part may be the appropriate definition of pension accrual, but even if these two issues could be resolved the lack of adequate data on firm wage payments makes it impossible to confirm a tradeoff between cash wages and pensions.

The second issue pertains to pensions and retirement. Here enormous strides have been made in constructing structural models where retirement decision making takes place in an intertemporal setting. The evidence shows clearly that pension reward structures powerfully affect older workers' decisions about when to leave their career employment. The typical pattern for most defined benefit plans is for the value of pension wealth to rise until the age of first eligibility for benefits and to decline thereafter. In the case of Social Security, pension wealth tends to peak at age 65 and then turn down. This means that after a certain age, the change in workers' pension wealth is actually negative if they stay on the job. Losses in Social Security and pension wealth are the same as pay cuts, and the evidence shows that people frequently respond to these pay cuts by retiring from their jobs. On the other hand, workers will tend to defer retirement when they are offered pension rewards for doing so.

Even here where significant progress has occurred, data limitations are a problem. Researchers rarely have access to accurate descriptions of pension formulas facing retiring workers. Analysts using the Retirement History Survey have nationally representative worker data but must rely on self-reported pension data and then impute accrual rates. On the other hand, a few studies have obtained actual pension formulas, but then the data sets have not been representative of the entire universe. This limits the usefulness of the results for policy analysis.

The third issue pertains to the relationship between pension coverage and mobility. On the whole, the empirical studies demonstrate that pensions not only affect mobility as workers approach retirement but also are associated with reduced turnover among younger people. The usual explanation for the pension-mobility relationship is that pension accruals tend to be backloaded; that is, pension accruals rise more than proportionately as retirement approaches. This phenomenon, however, would be unlikely to affect turnover among younger workers. Moreover, one study showed that persons covered by defined contribution plans, where backloading does not exist, also tend to change jobs less frequently. Hence, the apparent negative relationship between pension coverage and job mobility may reflect the effects of an omitted variable, with pensions taking credit for the effects of an unmeasured wage premium. Once again, firm-level data are needed to understand whether pensions have been designed to affect mobility and to understand whether such policies have been motivated by a desire to economize on hiring and training costs.

The fourth issue addressed is the relationship between pensions and productivity. The contract view of the labor market is based on the notion that in order to increase productivity over a worker's lifetime it may be desirable for workers and firms to enter into long-term contracts under which younger workers are paid somewhat less than the value of their marginal product and older workers paid somewhat more. This means that older workers have a lot to lose if they begin to shirk. Such a scheme, however, also requires older workers to leave at a certain time or the firm will be paying more compensation than it receives in work product. No direct tests have been formulated to validate this model, but several indirect pieces of evidence bear on its empirical applicability. Broadly speaking, most plan characteristics, accrual profiles, and the historical association of pension coverage and mandatory retirement are consistent with the contract view of the labor market. More proof must await longitudinal data on the firms offering pensions through time, with careful documentation of the plans, the firms' characteristics, and information about the employees.

The fifth issue pertains to the relationship between labor market outcomes and the employee's demand for insurance and saving. Pension activity takes place in an uncertain environment. To the extent that workers value the annuity features of defined benefit plans because of uncertainty about length of life, then pensions will reflect both basic labor market considerations and the demand for annuities derived from saving and insurance motivations. This combination of factors makes it even harder to model the demand for pensions. Pensions also exist in a world of capital market imperfections. Some workers who are unable to borrow may feel that pensions and Social Security allocate too much consumption to retirement; these individuals find that their retirement and saving decisions are inextricably intertwined.

Gustman and Mitchell conclude by reiterating what they see as the major unmet data needs in the area of pension and labor market activity. Their goals are ambitious: they call for a nationally representative panel of pensions with ongoing information on changes in plan provisions; a nationally representative data set centered around the firm, with matched information on employee characteristics, the pension plan, and firm financial and production information; and, finally, supplemental longitudinal information on the individuals covered in the national sample.

In her comments, Anna Rappaport stresses the difficulties of creating a data base like the one recommended by Gustman and Mitchell to help researchers who are interested in the labor market impacts of pension plans. As a benefits consultant with many years of experience, she believes that it would be a very complex undertaking and, if feasible at all, very costly. As a practical alternative, Rappaport suggests that researchers could learn a great deal about the incentive effects of pension plans by conducting carefully constructed interviews with plan sponsors and their advisors.

John Turner, the second discussant for the Gustman-Mitchell paper, shifts the focus from defined benefit plans and, following the outline developed by the authors, suggests a parallel research agenda for defined contribution plans. On the nature of the pension promise, Turner suggests that using data on defined contribution plans would avoid the problems of measuring pension accruals, since accruals under these plans clearly are valued on a spot basis. Turner believes that a study using data on defined contribution plans may help establish that a wage-pension tradeoff exists.

In the area of pensions and retirement, Turner argues that the relationship between mortality risk and lifetime income biases estimates of pension wealth and increments to pension wealth from postponing retirement; hence, this relationship could potentially bias the effect of these variables on the retirement decision. Using defined contribution pension wealth would avoid this bias.

Regarding the issue of pensions and mobility, Turner finds it difficult to believe that pensions, which account for only 5 percent of the compensation package, can have an important effect on turnover among younger workers. Moreover, even though defined contribution plans would not be expected to have any effect, they are often lumped together with defined benefit plans. Separating the two types of plans in the analysis will help clarify the relationship between pensions and mobility.

In terms of pensions and productivity, Turner contends that defined contribution plans may have a direct effect on productivity, especially among employees of small firms where a portion of their compensation is tied to the profitability of the company. Finally, regarding the interdependence of the saving and retirement decisions caused by the inability to borrow against defined benefit plan accruals, Turner again suggests looking at defined contribution plans. Frequently individuals can borrow against their defined contribution accounts, thereby allowing the researcher to eliminate one element of complexity from the analysis.

In short, while defined benefit plans tend to receive the most attention, researchers should note the growing importance of defined contribution plans; careful study of the impact of these plans on economic activity may help clarify many of the issues raised by Gustman and Mitchell.

III. What Is the Impact of Pensions on Saving?

Alicia Munnell and Frederick Yohn lay out a series of questions that need to be answered in order to determine the impact of pension plans on saving, highlight those aspects of pensions that may complicate the analysis, summarize the available empirical research, and finally make recommendations for improvement in the data. The saving issue is important both at the individual level, where the extent to which participants reduce their own saving in anticipation of pension benefits could affect the adequacy of their retirement income, and at the national level, where the behavior of individuals and the sponsoring firms determines the amount of money available for investment.

According to the simplest version of the life-cycle saving model, aggregate saving will be unchanged by the introduction of pension plans if (1) employees and employers correctly perceive the increase in future income encompassed by pension promises and correspondingly reduce wages by an equivalent amount, (2) employees reduce their direct personal saving by the increased value of future pension benefits, and (3) the firm transfers to the pension fund or some other firm investment an amount equal to the pension promise. Alternatively, if the firm chooses not to invest, the "no-effect" conclusion can still hold if the shareholders recognize that the dividend payments they receive reduce the net worth of the firm due to the increase in unfunded pension liabilities.

Munnell and Yohn note that both the real world and pensions are more complicated than the notions incorporated in the simple model, and these complicating factors make it impossible to determine a priori the effect of pensions on saving. For example, the illiquidity of pension promises and uncertainty about the value of future benefits in an inflationary environment raise a question as to whether individuals reduce their other saving dollar-for-dollar in response to promised future benefits. On the other hand, even if individuals do undertake fully offsetting behavior, the link between pensions and retirement behavior may increase aggregate saving in a growing economy, and, in a world of uncertain lifetimes, the fact that pensions are paid as annuities may reduce national saving. Finally, the introduction of taxes and in particular favorable tax provisions for compensation in the form of deferred pension benefits further complicates the analysis; does the higher net rate of return for pension saving cause employees to increase their total saving? And to the extent that increased saving occurs, does it compensate fully for the loss in government revenues from the favorable provisions? The authors then review the evidence relating to each of the questions.

To what extent do individuals reduce their own saving? Most of the empirical work has addressed this issue, and the bulk of the evidence provides some support for the prediction of the simple life-cycle model that individuals reduce their own saving in anticipation of benefits provided through public and private pension plans. However, with the exception of studies based on the 1983 Survey of Consumer Finances, none employs a good measure of anticipated pension benefits. Moreover, most of the studies focus on the retirement behavior of older men for whom retirement is the primary saving motive; little progress has been made in terms of assessing the impact on saving for the entire population. All that can be said is that some offset occurs and that it is less than dollar-for-dollar.

To what extent do employers carry out direct saving? Almost no progress has been made toward answering this question in any precise way. The problems are twofold. First, assessing the extent to which firms are saving in advance for pension commitments requires some measure of the annual increase in firms' pension liabilities; although considerable progress has been made in the area of pension accounting, the improved measures have only recently been put in place. Second, even with accurate measures of pension liabilities, the answer to whether firms are saving directly cannot be found by looking simply at the change in their pension fund accumulations; the relevant focus is the entire company and the amount by which the pension fund and the general treasury have increased their saving. In other words, no saving will have occurred if the firm puts $1,000 in its pension fund and simultaneously uses $1,000 of existing cash to pay *additional* dividends. Nevertheless, the accumulation of nearly $2 trillion in private pension fund assets has generally been interpreted to mean that firms have undertaken massive amounts of direct saving, and reported unfunded liabilities have been accepted as the measure of the shortfall in providing for promised pension payments.

To the extent that firms do not undertake adequate direct saving, do shareholders alter their personal saving? On the assumption, presumably, that the firm does not take offsetting action in the non-pension area, a series of studies have examined the relationship between unfunded liabilities and share prices; a reduction in share prices is the necessary trigger for individuals to adjust their own saving to compensate for the failure to save at the firm level. The evidence clearly shows that shareholders view a shortfall in pension assets relative to pension liabilities as a reason to lower the price they are willing to pay for a company's stock. The question still remains, however, whether the decline in stock prices induces increased saving on the part of shareholders.

Finally, does the increased saving resulting from the favorable tax provisions compensate for the government's revenue loss? Two pieces of information are required to answer this question. The first is the size of the government's revenue loss; this number is not currently available since the cash-based estimate currently published by the Treasury and the OMB does not appropriately account for tax concessions where tax payments are deferred. The second piece of needed information is the response of individuals to changes in the rate of return to saving created by the favorable tax provisions; the economics profession has not reached much of a consensus on the direction, much less the magnitude of this response. Very rough calculations suggest, however, that any conceivable increase in saving falls far short of the revenue loss. If these results persist upon closer scrutiny, the favorable tax provisions may well be contributing to lower national saving.

Munnell and Yohn offer two major conclusions. First, very little is known about the impact of pensions on saving beyond the fact that individuals tend to reduce their own saving in response to anticipated pension benefits and the offset tends to be less than dollar-for-dollar. Second, the relationship between pensions and saving is an area where the data, or lack thereof, have driven the analysis. Here the major problem appears not to be the microdata sets, where significant strides have been made, but rather the national accounts. The authors call for three major improvements. The first is the need to distinguish between defined benefit and defined contribution plans. The second issue is the need to use consistent, accrual-based accounting for the measurement of pension wealth. The current period increment in wealth outstanding is the relevant component of national saving, rather than the flow of benefit payments from these plans or the employer contributions and investment income inflows to these plans. Finally, the accounting of the current and capital accounts must be integrated.

Robert Avery, the first discussant, notes that analyzing the impact of pensions on saving behavior necessitates measuring both variables, which is a formidable task. On the savings side, few good household panel surveys have been completed and even these suffer from problems: they may miss the saving and dissaving associated with changes in household structure arising either from new formations or from dissolutions due to divorce or death, and, with the exception of the Survey of Consumer Finances (SCF), they have not adequately sampled the upper tail of the wealth distribution where most savings and wealth are found. Wealth surveys also typically suffer from problems of missing data.

On the pension side, Avery concurs with the authors that good individual pension data are hard to find. Avery notes that researchers need to determine just what information households have about their pensions, and how to turn this information into quantifiable measures of pension quality. Avery finds some hope for future investigators in the 1989 SCF, which overcomes many of the pitfalls in measuring saving, wealth, and pension benefits.

The second discussant for this paper, Robert Parker from the U.S. Bureau of Economic Analysis (BEA), concentrates his remarks on macrodata issues. Parker agrees that differentiating between defined benefit and defined contribution plans would be useful and would not require any fundamental change in the National Income and Product

Accounts (NIPA). On the other hand, he has serious reservations about valuing the pension part of personal income and saving as pension accruals. He sees several problems: this would diverge from current definitions whereby the non-wage part of employee compensation is measured as cost to the employer, not value to the employee; business income would be required to reflect contingent liabilities, which is not currently done; finally, accrual-based data are not available for all businesses, and when available are frequently subject to revisions.

Parker thinks that the proposal for an integrated set of capital and current accounts has the greatest potential for providing more useful data; these accounts would show both the cash and accrual-based contributions without changing the present NIPA measures. These accounts could also serve as a core of a satellite account, which cuts across sectors and focuses on specific areas of economic activity. The BEA already has such an account for pollution and is considering ones for other areas including pensions. The balance sheet for a pension satellite account would provide detail on different types of pension plans and would feature revaluation accounts, which capture the impact on household wealth of changing asset values. The integrated current account would show different measures of income and saving. In addition, this satellite account could include a microdata base that would provide comparable information on the income and wealth of individuals, their occupations, and demographic characteristics. In short, Parker agrees with the authors that the time is right for improving the data on pensions in the national accounts.

IV. What Are Appropriate Pension Funding Strategies and How Do They Affect the Economy?

Zvi Bodie and Leslie Papke examine the effect of the funding and investment policies of defined benefit plans on the security of employee benefits and on capital markets. The authors begin by clarifying the way in which funding matters. Bodie and Papke point out that, even without funding, accrued benefit promises are guaranteed by the sponsoring firm; participants have a claim on the plan sponsor similar to that of other creditors. If the plan sponsor is a good credit risk, the promised benefits are secure; if not, a large portion of the promised benefits can be guaranteed by a third party like the Pension Benefit Guaranty Corporation (PBGC). In other words, the benefits are fairly certain, and the benefit claims are the economic component that enters into individual saving and spending decisions. Funding has only an indirect impact on benefit security. First, it can somewhat reduce the risk of default by backing the claims with a more diversified portfolio of assets. Second, to the extent that funded assets perform well, the sponsor may be willing to increase benefits.

This notion that good pension fund performance will lead to benefit enhancements reflects the authors' concept of the sponsor's pension liability. Specifically, they view a guaranteed floor, measured by the accountant's accumulated benefit obligation (ABO), as the correct target for funding and investment standards. The authors cite for support the fact that both Congress and the Financial Accounting Standards Board have adopted the ABO as the appropriate measure of a corporate sponsor's pension liability. This liability is fixed in nominal terms, since it contains no projections of benefits based on future salary increases. The authors contend, however, that benefits as defined by the ABO should be viewed as the minimum that participants can expect to receive; the benefits can be enriched from time to time at the discretion of management. A good example of such initiatives is the ad hoc cost-of-living adjustments provided to retirees. Thus, defined benefit pension plans can be viewed as participating annuities.

In order to minimize the costs of providing the guaranteed benefits, the sponsor has a strong incentive to hedge the ABO by investing in fixed-income securities with a matching duration, that is, to immunize it. Any other strategy introduces risk of a shortfall, which will have to be guaranteed by the sponsor; this guarantee has an economic cost that should be avoided. The incentive to immunize the ABO is strongest when the plan is fully funded. If the plan is overfunded, sponsors will want to pursue a policy of contingent immunization, investing in high-yield, high-risk equities and shifting back to fixed-income securities as the assets drop toward 100 percent funding. If the plan is underfunded, sponsors may want to pursue a high-risk investment strategy and exploit the guarantee provided by the PBGC.

The desire to immunize liabilities has had an impact on capital markets by creating a demand for fixed-income instruments with a guaranteed duration. The authors contend that many of the innovations of the last ten years, such as zero-coupon bonds, guaranteed investment contracts, and interest rate futures contracts, can be viewed as the market response to this demand. These products all offer ways of eliminating duration uncertainty from traditional bonds and mortgages. Immunization strategies have also created a market for index options and futures contracts as a way of converting equities into short-term, fixed-income investments. The authors also argue that the lack of demand for CPI-linked bonds reflects a consensus that the pension liability is a nominal commitment.

The authors review the empirical work on pension finance to determine the extent to which their views are borne out in the data. In terms of funding, some evidence indicates that the health of the corporation influences its funding and asset allocation policies. Specifically, the profitability of the firm appears to affect the interest rate used to value liabilities, so that more profitable firms can make larger pension contributions. On the other hand, only 10 percent of the plans appear to be invested solely in fixed-income securities as theory would suggest. But the majority of underfunded plans whose sponsors are in financial distress do invest a smaller proportion in fixed-income securities than their healthy counterparts.

Like the other authors, Bodie and Papke conclude that better data could help resolve some of the remaining issues in pension fund finance. With regard to funding strategy, pension plan sponsors could be asked directly whether their funding target is the ABO, the ABO with implicit cost-of-living adjustments, or something else. With regard to investment policy, it would be useful to obtain information about goals, strategies, and tactics. Are they employing immunization strategies? If so, how are they implementing them? Why are they investing in equities? These questions could be added to existing government forms, so the information could be attained efficiently.

Irwin Tepper, Bodie and Papke's discussant, raises questions about each of the main themes put forth by the authors. He begins with a discussion of determining the correct liability target. Tepper agrees that it may be reasonable not to anticipate ad hoc cost-of-living adjustments in measuring liabilities, but suggests that ignoring future expected pay increases may be less correct. Proponents of using the projected benefit obligation (PBO), which includes expected future pay increases, argue that both the employer and the employee know that pay will rise and with it the accrued benefit. Those who oppose the use of the PBO emphasize that the future pay increases are contingent upon the employee continuing to work and numerous other factors, including the survival of the firm. If one were interested in contingent claims, it is unclear why the PBO would be a logical stopping point; perhaps the definition of liability that includes future pay increases should also include future service.

Whatever measure of liability is adopted, Tepper asks whether a hedge strategy is always the minimum cost approach. For a company that views termination as remote, but believes that some of the pension surplus will be captured by the participants, the gains and losses from investment policy are asymmetrical. In this case, the sponsor would want to reduce the participants' potential claim by reducing the variability of investment, so the authors' ABO hedge strategy would be optimal. For the sponsor who believes that the level of benefits is independent of the fund's performance, the gains and losses are symmetrical and the minimum-risk hedge strategy does not dominate all other policies.

Tepper contends that the questions about which liability to target and whether or not to hedge would be moot, if it were relatively certain that equities would outperform bonds over the relevant horizon for the plan, and the plan sponsor were willing to absorb interim volatility along the way. The empirical support for the superiority of equities is that they have outperformed bonds over virtually all time horizons of ten years or more since 1926. Some advocates, as discussed by Bodie and Papke, also base the case for equities on an incorrect application of the law of large numbers to demonstrate that the risk from investing in stocks declines as the investment is held for longer time periods. If the returns are statistically independent from one year to another, no such decline will occur. Proponents of the "dominance of equities" contend, however, that the demonstrated superiority of performance is due to the fact that returns are not independent; government takes actions to reverse negative developments and ensure that owners of capital are compensated over the long term. In short, Tepper raises a number of questions that demonstrate continuing controversy even in this relatively well-researched area of pension fund finance.

V. What Are the Implications of Pensions for the Federal Budget?

David Lindeman and Kathleen Utgoff summarize the nature of the tax preference for qualified pension plans, discuss the appropriate way to estimate the revenue loss associated with this preference, catalog instances in which the current cash-based calculation has misled policymakers, and sketch out the modeling and data requirements to perform the correct calculation. As long as income, as opposed to consumption, is the basis for personal taxation in the United States, the favorable treatment accorded compensation paid in the form of deferred pension benefits results in a revenue loss. According to the authors, this loss consists of two components; one is the value of deferral, and the other pertains to the likelihood of a lower rate in retirement, which can be considered either part of the preference or part of lifetime averaging provisions.

By allowing the deferral of taxes until retirement, the current treatment of pensions is equivalent to what would occur under a cash-flow consumption tax. This treatment offers two advantages over strict income taxation. First, the full dollar of pension contribution, without any reduction for income tax, is available for investment during the employee's working years—in contrast to income taxation where the employee would have only the after-tax dollar to invest. Second, no tax is currently paid on the investment income from accumulated pension assets, whereas under strict income taxation interest is taxed as it accrues. This portion of the tax advantage can be summarized as the differences in the present values of $(1 - t)W(1 + r)^n$ and $(1 - t)W(1 + (1 - t)r)^n$.

The second advantage, which the authors refer to as income averaging, could occur under either an income tax or a cash-flow consumption tax. The advantage arises because, under a progressive rate structure, when benefits are distributed in retirement they are likely to be taxed at a lower marginal rate than if they had been taxed as they accrued to the employee.

The problem is that the tax expenditure estimates currently published by the U.S. Treasury and the OMB are not the appropriate numbers to consider when making pension policy. These estimates consist of two parts—the revenue loss from exempting this year's employer contributions and pension fund earnings from current taxation, and the revenue gain from currently taxing this year's payments of pension benefits. Their limitations can be seen clearly by considering a situation in which (1) pension contributions and plan earnings exactly equal benefit payments and (2) workers face the same tax rate in retirement as they do during their working years. Under these assumptions, the revenue loss would be zero according to the government figures, yet individuals covered by pension plans would continue to enjoy the benefits of deferral.

The real danger is that current pension policy is being driven by this cash-receipt accounting. The authors contend, for example, that the reduction in funding limits imposed in 1987 under the Omnibus Budget Reconciliation Act was designed simply to raise revenues under cash accounting. Similarly, in the area of asset reversions, the authors argue that the lack of any effort to limit reversions is due to the fact that employers pay excise and income taxes on reversion amounts; anything that restricts reversions loses revenues. Finally, the authors cite the efforts to redesign individual retirement accounts so that the tax deduction comes at withdrawal, rather than at deposit, as another example of legislators responding to cash-based accounting.

To calculate the value of the tax expenditure perfectly would require a simulation model that projects the population and the pension system into the future. Maintenance of the large models has been hindered, however, by lack of information on wage histories and detailed firm and plan information. On the other hand, in the absence of a major modeling effort, simple estimates of the annual revenue loss resulting from deferral could be made by calculating the difference for the average covered employee between (1) the present discounted value of the revenue from current taxation of employer contributions and pension fund earnings as they accrue over the employee's working life and (2) the present discounted value of the taxes collected when employer contributions and investment returns are taxable after retirement. To make this estimate would require assumptions about the average age of covered workers, the typical retirement age, life expectancy at retirement, the rate of earnings on pension reserves, the appropriate discount rate, and marginal tax rates for workers and retirees. These assumptions are attainable and the estimate produced from them, while far from perfect, would be superior to the cash-based calculation currently driving pension policy.

Lawrence Thompson emphasizes a key point made by the authors that, in policy debates, the conceptual framework is as important as the actual numbers and provides an example to supplement this opinion. Thompson presents budget deficit figures in a variety of ways (the unified budget deficit as typically displayed, deficit by fund type, and deficit by expenditure type) to illustrate that the framework used can dramatically affect the perceived problem and, thus, the proposed solutions. This exercise underscores Utgoff and Lindeman's point that the conceptual framework is just as important as the actual numerical estimates in shaping policy debates.

Gary Burtless, the other discussant for the Lindeman-Utgoff paper, agrees that a present-value calculation is needed to reflect the revenue loss from deferral. He notes that the authors have no behavioral response built into even their idealized system, but does not find this troubling. Rather, he offers a rationalization for this no-response assumption. Namely, the income of the individuals and the firms is predictable, and the tax code simply defines how that income is divided between the government, on the one hand, and the tax-filing units (workers and firms) on the other. A reform in the tax code changes the way income is divided between the government and filing units; the goal of the present value calculations is to discount the change in each year to the present. Burtless's main concern is that the authors do not provide sufficient detail about the data requirements to make a full-fledged present-value calculation.

VI. What Can We Learn from International Private Pension Statistics?

In their paper, Lorna Dailey and John Turner present a progress report on the U.S. Department of Labor's project to collect and analyze international private pension statistics. The project is designed to shed light on virtually all of the issues raised in this volume by examining the experience of other countries. The countries specifically discussed in the chapter are Australia, Canada, France, Japan, the Netherlands, Switzerland, the United Kingdom, and Germany.

In many of these countries, the role of private pensions in providing retirement income to the elderly is much smaller than in the United States. Instead, they rely on a combination of government and family provision. In countries where private pensions have developed, however, problems similar to those in the United States have also emerged. Countries could learn much from each other about how to address these problems if better and more comparable pension statistics were available.

Dailey and Turner summarize the key characteristics of foreign plans based on the international statistics that they have been able to compile. They note that pensions provided by private employers in France and Switzerland are mandatory, while those in the other countries are voluntary. In terms of coverage, the percentage of the labor force participating in a private plan varies enormously. Coverage rates in 1986 were 48 percent in the United States, 30 percent in the United Kingdom, 27 percent in Canada, and 22 percent in Australia. In all of these countries coverage is more prevalent for higher-paid workers and for those who work for large or unionized firms.

The proportion of people age 65 and older receiving pension benefits has been increasing in all countries for which beneficiary data are available. In some countries, like Japan and Australia, private retirement benefits are taken primarily in the form of a lump sum rather than an annuity. Protecting retirement benefits against inflation is a policy concern in all of the countries, but post-retirement inflation adjustments of private pension annuities appear to be voluntary and only partial in most of them.

Funding of private pensions differs greatly across countries. The pension systems of France and Germany are largely unfunded, in the sense that no separate designated pool of pension assets is set aside from which benefits will eventually be paid. In Japan retirement benefits are only partially funded. In Japan and Germany, however, the present values of accruing retirement benefits are recorded on the sponsor's books as they are earned and constitute a recognized liability of the plan sponsor.

In the United States, Canada, and the United Kingdom, where the law mandates minimum funding levels, pension fund asset management is a policy concern. Plan sponsors can and often do pass on some of the investment risk to insurance companies or, in the case of defined contribution plans, to the plan beneficiaries. Defined benefit plans are by far the most common type of plan around the world. Only in the United States and Australia are defined contribution plans common.

In all countries, employer pension contributions exceed employee contributions as a source of funding. The employer's share is highest in Japan, where it is typically 100 percent. The United States has the next highest employer share.

The tax treatment of private pension plans varies considerably across countries. In all countries except Australia and New Zealand, tax deductions are allowed for employer contributions to tax-qualified pension plans. In Japan and Germany, a tax deduction is allowed even when no contributions are made, so long as the newly accrued liability is recognized on the company's books.

In most countries the earnings on pension fund assets are tax exempt. Japan, however, has a tax of 1.173 percent on pension assets and Australia has a 15 percent tax on certain pension investment earnings. Many countries limit the amount of advance funding permitted to sponsors in order to prevent abuse of the tax advantages provided under the law.

For anyone interested in studying the subject of pensions and retirement-income policy in other countries, Dailey and Turner append to their Chapter 7 an extensive bibliography.

In his discussion of the Dailey and Turner paper, Robert Clark endorses their basic premise that international comparisons of private pensions are an important method of understanding the economic effects of pensions and are useful for considering changes in existing public policies. He stresses that one must use caution in interpreting the data, because in many countries public provision of retirement income is much more important than private pensions. Furthermore, many countries make no clear distinction between severance payments and retirement benefits.

Clark would like to see an international data base that links information on all sources of retirement income. He thinks that only by looking at private pensions in the broader context can we make meaningful comparisons for public policy purposes.

VII. Conclusion

Pensions are institutions that affect all aspects of the economy: they contribute to retirement income; they influence individual and national saving; they help determine the quality, quantity, and price of labor; they are significant players in the capital markets; and they constitute the major tax expenditure in the federal budget. Because of their broad impacts, analyzing pensions requires a variety of disciplines within the economics profession. Until this volume, those interested in, say, pension fund finance have traveled in different circles from those concerned about the labor market aspect of pensions. It is herein demonstrated that the experts in the various disciplines have much to learn from each other; they can contribute both analytical insights and information about isolated data sources. In short, this volume has confirmed the need for and the potential benefits that can be derived from a major centralized source for pension research.

Chapter 1
Employee Benefits and Retirement Income Adequacy: Data, Research, and Policy Issues

Emily S. Andrews and Michael D. Hurd

Summary

Retirement income is generally expected to consist of individual savings, employer pensions, and Social Security. Findings on the overall economic status of the elderly are reviewed first, and the contribution of particular sources of income is discussed thereafter. Regardless of the exact measures used, the elderly are found to be as well off as the nonelderly. In addition, the poverty rate of the elderly is now below that of the nonelderly. While pensions have become a more important source of income, the future role of pensions depends on the benefit packages provided by employers. Pension participation rates have at most remained constant since the mid-1970s, while pensions have shifted towards defined contribution plans and away from defined benefit plans. Nonetheless, more pension plan participants have vested benefits, and more participants receive lump-sum distributions. To address future research and policy issues related to the economic status of the elderly (including retirement income adequacy, pension coverage, pension portability, and the treatment of retiree health benefits), new data are needed in specific areas. Longitudinal data are needed to conduct research on life-cycle retirement income issues. Periodic cross-section surveys, including matches with employer records, are needed to determine trends in pension plan provisions. Information on retiree health benefits should also be expanded, and private-sector sources of benefit information explored.

I. Introduction

Society has paid considerable attention to the economic status of the elderly, because for much of this century the elderly have faced high poverty rates. Furthermore, the elderly have fewer options than the nonelderly to deal with costly unanticipated expenditures. The most important public policy measure to improve the ability of the elderly to meet their economic needs was the establishment of Social Security and Medicare. Both programs increased retirement income and reduced financial uncertainty.

Although Social Security has become the most important source of income for a majority of the elderly, from its inception the expectation was that private savings and employer-sponsored pensions would also play an important role. These privately provided sources can be tailored to the particular requirements of workers in certain jobs and industries, whereas Social Security is aimed at the elderly as a whole. Thus, the three kinds of retirement income offer different benefits and probably ought to be part of the portfolio of each retiree.

The first goal of this chapter is to review findings on the economic status of the elderly in order to determine whether their retirement income is adequate. Adequacy is, of course, hard to define and measure, but one measure is whether the (adjusted) income of the elderly is as high as the income of the nonelderly. The second goal is to examine the role of pensions in providing retirement income. Of particular interest are trends and levels of pension coverage and pension characteristics. Retiree health insurance is considered as well. Some recent public policy issues are reviewed including concerns about retirement income, pension coverage, portability, and retiree health insurance. The chapter concludes with a section on future research and data needs.

II. Retirement Income Adequacy

One method of determining retirement income adequacy is to compare the income of the elderly to the income of the nonelderly. For many years the income of elderly households grew faster than the income of the rest of the population.[1] For example, between 1970 and 1986 the average household income of the elderly grew by 20 percent in real terms, compared to just 9 percent for the entire population. As a result, by 1987 the average household income of the elderly was 64 percent of the household income of the nonelderly. This comparison has a number of defects, however, as a measure of consumption opportunities. It does not take into account household size, taxes, underreporting of income, or income-in-kind. Household size, in particular, is important because the elderly live in much smaller households than

1. An elderly household has a household member over the age of 65.

TABLE 1   Mean Household Income of the Elderly Relative to
the Nonelderly, 1986

Income concept	Poverty line	Budget share
Gross money income	0.79	0.91
After-tax money income	0.84	0.99
After-tax money income plus housing	0.90	1.04

Source: Authors' calculations from U.S. Bureau of the Census (1988).

the nonelderly. In 1986, for example, the average size of elderly house-holds was 1.9 persons and the average size of nonelderly households was 2.9. If income were measured on a per capita basis, rather than on a per household basis, in 1986 the income of the elderly would have been only about 3 percent below the income of the nonelderly.

No adjustment for household size is universally accepted, but a common method is based on the poverty line: household income is divided by the poverty line for that household (after normalization) to produce a measure of income per adult equivalent (Smeeding, 1989). For example, if a single elderly person is assigned an adult equivalent weight of 1.0, in the poverty-line scaling an elderly couple is assigned a weight of 1.26 and a nonelderly three-person household a weight of 1.47. Therefore, if each household had an income of $20,000, the poverty-line scaling would assign the single elderly household an in-come of $20,000, the elderly couple an income of $15,873, and the three-person household an income of $13,605. This scaling implies large returns to scale in consumption: a couple needs only 26 percent more income than a single person.

An alternative to the poverty-line scaling is one based on observed consumption behavior. An example is a budget-share scaling estimated from the 1972–73 Consumer Expenditure Survey (van der Gaag and Smolensky, 1982). This scaling implies more modest returns to scale, since a couple needs 37 percent more income than a single person. This alternative has a firmer foundation than the poverty scaling because it is based on observed behavior rather than on arbitrary assumptions. Therefore, at least in principle, it is superior to the poverty-line scaling.

The ratio of size-adjusted income of the elderly to size-adjusted income of the nonelderly in 1986 for the poverty-line scaling and the budget-share scaling is shown in Table 1.

The ratio of elderly to nonelderly income is 0.79 under the poverty-line scaling and 0.91 under the budget-share scaling. Because the elderly pay lower taxes than the nonelderly, an adjustment for taxes increases the ratio further. The last adjustment adds an imputed re-turn to housing equity, which increases the income of the elderly more than the income of the nonelderly because the elderly hold more housing equity. By the budget-share scaling, in 1986 the elderly had incomes about 4 percent higher than the nonelderly. The adjustments are probably not controversial, and by the budget-share scaling show that the incomes of the elderly and nonelderly were about the same in 1986.

According to a validation study of the 1973 Current Population Survey, the elderly underreport their incomes by 37 percent and the nonelderly by 3 percent because of the underreporting of financial asset income. Were income to be adjusted for underreporting by these factors, the income of the elderly would be somewhat greater according to the poverty-line scaling and substantially greater by the budget-share scaling than the income of the nonelderly. Because financial assets are very highly concentrated, an adjustment for underreporting might be valid for mean incomes but would not reflect the economic status of most households.

Adjusting for nonmoney transfers (income in kind) is also controversial; but as the transfers are large and surely of value to the recipient, they should be taken into account when assessing consumption opportunities. The most common method of valuing income in kind is market valuation, the cost to the provider. Some people object that recipients value in-kind transfers, particularly Medicare, at less than the market value.[2] An alternative method which, although arbitrary, has some plausibility assigns a "fungible value" to in-kind transfers. The fungible value is zero if the household income is so low that it cannot purchase the minimum necessary amounts of food and clothing. At higher income levels, income in kind frees money income that would have otherwise been spent on the good that has been transferred. This liberated income can then be spent as desired, so it is valued as ordinary money income, and is the fungible value of the in-kind transfer. Fungible value probably understates the value of the transfer to the average recipient because it places no value on the transfer for households with low income levels.

In 1986, according to the fungible value measure, the elderly received $2,560 in nonmoney transfers, mostly Medicare. This was 12 percent of their pretax, unadjusted household income. The nonelderly had nonmoney transfers of $886, which was just 3 percent of their pretax, unadjusted household income. The fungible value for the elderly is substantially below the market value of the transfers. Even so, if the fungible value of nonmoney transfers were added to the income

---

2. If the recipients do value the transfers at less than market value, the transfers are inefficient: the recipients would be better off at less cost if the transfers were in cash.

TABLE 2   1986 Poverty Rates (Percent)

Income concept	Elderly	Nonelderly
Measured income	12.4	13.8
Adjusted income	5.7	10.9

Source: U.S. Bureau of the Census (1988).

of the elderly and nonelderly, the elderly would be better off under the poverty-line measure.

The conclusion of the comparison of income levels is that, regardless of the exact magnitudes of the adjustments made for underreporting and the value of nonmoney transfers, on average the elderly were as well off as the nonelderly in 1986. Making modest adjustments for underreporting or income in kind implies they were at least as well off under poverty-line scaling and better off under budget-share scaling. Adjusting fully for underreporting and income in kind makes them substantially better off under either scaling.[3]

It should be emphasized that the full income comparisons are not utility comparisons. The adjustment for nonmoney transfers puts a monetary value on the transfers to an individual that yields a monetary measure of the economic position of the individual. It aims to answer the question: what money income would make the individual as well off as the combination of actual money income and nonmoney income transfers? Although actual measurement may pose difficulties, the concept is clear. A substantial difficulty, however, arises in comparing incomes (whether adjusted for income in kind or not) across individuals or households, because such a comparison would require that the utility functions of the individuals be the same. This is unlikely, particularly because the elderly and nonelderly have such different needs, especially different medical needs. The difficult issue is not, as some people believe, the valuation of nonmoney transfers, but rather the use of an income measure to make cross-person or cross-household welfare comparisons.

Income Distribution Among the Elderly

From the point of view of policy, the most important aspect of income distribution is the number of people living below the poverty line. The poverty rates of the elderly and the nonelderly in 1986 are shown in Table 2.

3. Adjusting for underreporting, market value of nonmoney transfers, and taxes gives an income ratio of 1.48 for the budget-share measure (Hurd, 1989).

TABLE 3 Percentage Distribution of Sources of Income of Persons 55 and Older

Source	1967	1976	1984	1986
Earnings	29	23	16	17
Social Security	34	39	38	38
Pensions and other retirement	15	16	15	16
Assets	15	18	28	26
Public assistance	4	2	1	1
Other	3	2	2	2
Total	100	100	100	100

Source: U.S. Congress (1987) and U.S. Bureau of the Census (1987).

Adjusted income includes capital gains, nonmoney income (measured as fungible value), and taxes. Even as calculated by measured income, the poverty rate of the elderly was lower than that of the nonelderly. This is a considerable social accomplishment, since in 1959, 35.2 percent of the elderly were in poverty. Social Security can take much of the credit for the improvement. For example, in 1984, 78 percent of the income of households in the lowest income quintile came from Social Security. Although the poverty rate of the elderly is lower than that of the nonelderly, in 1986, 21 percent of elderly widows were in poverty. This high proportion of impoverishment remains a matter of social concern.

Sources of Income

The fraction of income from earnings has fallen sharply since 1967, reflecting the trend toward early retirement (Table 3). On average the most important increase has come from asset income, but because assets are distributed very unequally, the average is a misleading guide to the experience of most households. Social Security has increased modestly as a fraction of total income. The category "other" includes transfers from relatives, including children, which are not an important source of income for the elderly.

The percentage of families receiving specific fractions of income from different sources has changed in recent years (Table 4). For example, in 1971, 31 percent of elderly households had income from earnings and 15 percent had more than half their income from earnings. By 1986 only 19 percent of elderly households had any earnings. The importance of Social Security can hardly be exaggerated: 57 percent of households had more than half their income from Social Security, and 24 percent had 90 percent or more of their income from Social Security. Although the income from private pensions has in-

TABLE 4   Percentage Distribution of Elderly Households by
           Importance of Income Source

	1971	1980	1986
A. *Earnings*			
Total percent	100	100	100
0	69	78	81
1–49	16	12	11
50–100	15	10	8
90–100	5	2	2
B. *Social Security*			
Total percent	100	100	100
0	13	9	8
1–49	38	32	35
50–100	49	59	57
90–100	17	23	24
C. *Private Pensions and Annuities*			
Total percent	100	100	100
0	83	79	74
1–19	6	10	13
20–49	8	9	11
50–100	3	2	2
D. *Government Pensions*			
Total percent	100	100	100
0	94	89	87
1–49	3	7	8
50–100	3	4	5
E. *Income from Assets*			
Total percent	100	100	100
0	51	41	40
1–19	27	33	30
20–49	15	17	18
50–100	7	9	12

Source: Income of the population aged 60 and older, *Social Security Bulletin*,
various years.

creased, by 1986 only 13 percent had more than 20 percent from
pensions, a slight increase from 1970. Even if it is assumed that no one
has both a private and a government pension, only 39 percent of
elderly households had pension income in 1986, up from 23 percent in
1971.

Inflation Vulnerability

The elderly are often believed to live on fixed incomes that decline in
real terms with inflation. In fact, this has not been the case: their

TABLE 5   1898–1902 Cohort Real
Income

Year and age	Mean income	Median income
1967: 65–69	10,730	7,820
1972: 70–74	11,360	8,330
1977: 74–79	11,210	8,060
1982: 80–84	11,560	8,560

Source: Radner (1986).

incomes have been effectively indexed. Table 5 gives before-tax real money income (1982 dollars), adjusted for household size, of the cohort born in 1898–1902.

The stability observed between 1967 and 1972 is not a reliable indicator of income indexing but rather the result of two countervailing changes: a reduction in earnings because of retirement, with an increase in Social Security benefits due to retirement and to changes in the benefit schedule in the early part of the 1970s. On the other hand, the stability between 1972 and 1982, when the CPI increased by 130 percent, indicates effective indexing. Just why income should be indexed is not apparent from the distribution of income by source. Only part of pension income and part of asset income are indexed, so that total income is not completely indexed. Detailed study of income in the Retirement History Survey (RHS), however, confirms that incomes of individuals were stable during the 1970s, a period of high and variable inflation (Burkhauser, Holden, and Feaster, 1988). Apparently the unindexed portions of income were small and concentrated among a few individuals.[4]

The conclusion is that the elderly are not particularly vulnerable to inflation.[5] The indexing of Social Security is responsible for a considerable part of this stability.

Wealth

Fully inclusive wealth measures have been developed using the 1975 and 1979 RHS (Table 6). Medicare and Medicaid wealth is measured as the expected present value of transfers valued at market cost to the government. It is probably an overestimate for some elderly, although the fact that many retirees have additional private medical insurance

4. A method of measuring inflation vulnerability based on income and wealth holdings in the RHS leads to similar conclusions (Hurd and Shoven, 1985).

5. See Clark et al. (1984) and Burkhauser, Holden, and Feaster (1988) for a similar conclusion.

TABLE 6　Average Household Wealth and the Distribution of Wealth[a] by Source, 1975 and 1979 RHS Sample

	1975		1979		Lowest wealth decile 1979	
	Wealth	Percent	Wealth	Percent	Wealth	Percent
Housing	22.4	14	26.9	18	1.4	4
Business and property	11.0	7	11.6	8	1.1	3
Financial	23.2	15	22.5	15	0.7	2
Pensions	23.2	15	18.0	12	1.6	4
SSI, welfare and transfers	2.7	2	2.3	2	3.6	10
Medicare–Medicaid	15.8	10	17.7	12	11.9	34
Social Security	48.4	31	44.0	30	14.2	40
Future earnings	9.6	6	3.9	3	1.0	3
Total	156.3	100	146.7	100	35.5	100

[a] Wealth in thousands of 1979 dollars. Based on 7,483 (1975) and 6,610 (1979) observations from the RHS. Farm families and farm wealth excluded.
Source: Hurd and Shoven (1985).

indicates that it is accurate for many. Future earnings are the expected present value of labor earnings.

The wealth levels are roughly consistent with fully inclusive income measures derived from the CPS (Hurd, 1989) and confirm that on average the elderly are reasonably well off. Only 36 percent of the saving was done by households in 1975 (Table 6). Other saving was undertaken on behalf of households by firms (in the form of pensions) and by society (in the form of Social Security, Medicare, and Medicaid). The table shows that a substantial fraction of the elderly reach retirement age with very few assets beyond a claim on Social Security, Medicare, and Medicaid. Households in the lowest wealth decile had practically no private saving.

About 42 percent of the RHS households had pension income in 1979, when the heads of the households would have been about 68 to 73. Pensions accounted for 15 percent of total wealth in 1975. The decline in pension wealth between 1975 and 1979 is due to aging of the RHS population, which causes the discounting for mortality to increase, and to an increase in the inflation rate, which raises the discounting of nominal pensions.

A good comparison to the RHS is the 1983 Survey of Consumer Finances (SCF). The SCF has two samples: the first is a self-weighting sample of 3,665 households; the second is a special high-income supplemental sample of 438 households. The aim of including the supplemental sample was to learn more about the upper part of the wealth distribution. Including the supplement has little effect on median wealth but large effects on mean wealth, as shown in Table 7.

TABLE 7   Wealth of the Elderly in the
1983 SCF (dollars)

Type of average	Without supplement	With supplement
Mean	118,700	250,100
Median	51,000	51,900

Sources: SCF with supplement: Avery and Elliehausen (1986); SCF without supplement: calculations from the SCF data.

The SCF included many questions designed to elicit information about pension recipiency and the structure of pension plans. Pension coverage of the relevant age group in the SCF (65 to 74) and pension wealth were about the same as in the RHS.

TABLE 8   Pension Wealth and Coverage: 1983 SCF

Age	Mean pension wealth ($)	Percent of total wealth	Percent covered
55–64	73,900	27.3	61.0
64–74	24,900	10.1	45.2
75+	7,300	5.8	28.7

Source: McDermed, Clark, and Allen (1989).

Mean pension wealth among 64- to 74-year-olds was $24,900 (1983 dollars), which is $18,146 in 1979 dollars. This compares with mean pension wealth in the RHS of $18,000 in 1979 (when most of the heads of the RHS households would have been 68 to 73).

III. Pension Coverage and Participation

Over the past decade, several data series have documented the extent to which the work force is covered by and participates in employer-sponsored pension plans.[6] Data are available on the number of workers

6. The terms "coverage" and "participation" have proved confusing for many not involved in the public policy debate. In this chapter, workers are deemed covered by a pension plan if their employer sponsors a plan for any employee. Workers participate in the plan if they are included in the plan. Workers may be excluded from the plan either because they have not met the plan's age and service standards for participation (as allowed under the Employee Retirement Income Security Act of 1974) or because their jobs are not covered by a pension. The legal use of the term "covered workers" refers to those employees who are eligible for plan participation after they have met appropriate age and service standards. The difference in use stems, in part, from the inability of survey data to distinguish satisfactorily between these two categories of participation.

TABLE 9   Private-Sector Defined Benefit and Defined Contribution Pension
Plan Participation, Selected Years, 1975–1985 (millions)

Plan type	1975	1980	1981	1982	1983	1984	1985
Primary plan participants	30.7	35.5	36.9	37.5	39.0	39.7	40.5
Defined benefit	26.8	29.7	29.7	29.4	29.6	29.8	28.9
Defined contribution	3.9	5.8	7.2	8.1	9.4	9.9	11.6
Secondary plan participants[a]	7.6	13.1	13.9	15.7	18.9	21.1	21.8
Defined benefit	0.4	0.4	0.4	0.4	0.4	0.4	0.1
Defined contribution	7.2	12.7	13.5	15.3	18.5	20.7	21.7

[a]All secondary plan participants also participate in primary plans.
Source: EBRI, *EBRI Issue Brief* (April 1989): U.S. Department of Labor tabulations of
Internal Revenue Service Form 5500 responses.

in plans and on the percentage of the work force included. Pension participation, which grew rapidly for the three decades following World War II (Yohalem, 1977), has leveled off and may actually be declining.[7]

According to U.S. Department of Labor tabulations of annual reports filed by all tax-qualified pension plans (Form 5500), the number of pension plan participants covered under one or more private-sector plans grew from 30.7 million workers in 1975 to 40.5 million workers in 1985 (Table 9). The growth in the number of plan participants included in more than one pension plan was dramatic. Secondary plans expanded nearly threefold from 7.6 million participants in 1975 to 21.8 million participants in 1985. Using these estimates, Beller (1989) calculates that about 46 percent of all private wage and salary workers participated in pension plans. He suggests that coverage rates have been relatively stable over the past fifteen years. While not strictly comparable, this figure is the same as that reported by Yohalem for 1975. In other words, pension plan participation has just kept pace with the growth in the labor force.

While the Form 5500 data provide the best estimates of the total number of participants,[8] they are wanting in other respects. In particular, plan filings include no information about the demographic characteristics of plan participants or about the types of plan provisions provided.

Since 1979 the Bureau of Labor Statistics (BLS) has collected data on employee benefits provided by medium and large employers. The survey has changed and expanded over the years, however, so that a

7. The historical coverage data series abruptly stops in 1975. Researchers at the Social Security Administration and elsewhere were only able to construct a comparable series for one year following the untimely death of Alfred M. Skolnik, who constructed the original series.
8. Studies have shown that self-reporting leads to at least some undercount of participation (Mitchell, 1988).

TABLE 10   Plan Participation Rates in Medium and Large Firms for Full-
Time Employees

Pension plan 1988	Employees in medium and large private firms							
	1979	1980	1981	1982	1983	1984	1985	1986
All retirement plans 86	a	a	a	a	a	a	91	89
Defined benefit pensions only 80	87[b]	84[b]	84[b]	84[b]	82[b]	82[b]	80	76

[a]Data not available.
[b]Includes money purchase pension, profit sharing, savings and thrift, stock bonus, and employee stock ownership plans in which employer contributions must remain in the participant's account until retirement age, death, disability, separation from service, age 59½, or hardship.
Source: EBRI (1979+).

consistent time series cannot be constructed. Based on earlier surveys, the pension participation rate among employers of medium-sized and large firms declined from 87 percent in 1979 to 82 percent in 1984 (Table 10). An expanded set of questions indicated that 91 percent of employees in medium-sized and large firms were retirement plan participants in 1985 compared to only 86 percent in 1988.[9] The BLS figures suggest that pension participant rates, while higher than originally estimated, declined precipitously in recent years.

A third series on pension participation, available from the U.S. Bureau of the Census since 1979, is based on the March Income Supplement to the monthly Current Population Survey (CPS). All survey respondents are asked whether they were ever included in a pension plan on their job during the previous year. According to that series, the pension participation rate for workers age 15 and older declined from 45 percent in 1979 to 43 percent in 1983 and 41 percent in 1987 (Table 11).

The pension supplements added to the May 1979, May 1983, and May 1988 CPS probably provide the best data on trends in pension coverage and participation rates.[10] Between 1979 and 1983, the pension coverage rate for nonfarm wage and salary workers decreased

9. This figure is based on the original BLS survey coverage. The definition of medium and large firms was expanded in 1988 to include smaller firms in a number of industries. Nonetheless, tabulations were published in 1988 according to both the old and new universe definitions.

10. An earlier CPS pension supplement was conducted in April 1972 but only surveyed full-time wage and salary workers. Findings from that survey are presented in Kolodrubetz and Landay (1973). The data tapes are no longer available.

TABLE 11 Pension Plan Participation Rates, Civilian Wage and Salary Workers, Aged 15 and Older, 1979–1987

1979	1980	1981	1982	1983	1984	1985	1986	1987
44.9%	44.9%	44.3%	43.8%	43.4%	42.4%	42.8%	42.6%	40.8%

Source: Employee Benefit Research Institute tabulations based on data from U.S. Bureau of the Census, March Current Population Surveys, 1980–1988.

TABLE 12 Pension Plan Coverage, Participation, and Benefit Entitlement Rates for Non-Farm Employees, May 1979, May 1983, and May 1988

Year	Percentage of workers covered	Percentage of workers participating	Percentage of participants entitled
1979	61	50	51
1983	56	46	55
1988	59	44	67

Source: Piacentini (1989).

from 61 percent to 56 percent (Table 12). One reason for this decline may have been the impact of the 1982 recession on employment (Andrews, 1985). The coverage rate appears to have rebounded in 1988 to 59 percent (Piacentini, 1989).[11] Nonetheless, part of the dip between 1979 and 1983 may have resulted from differences in the survey coverage question rather than from adverse economic conditions and layoffs in manufacturing.

By contrast, the pension participation rate declined consistently between 1979 and 1988 according to CPS pension supplement data (Table 12). The participation rate for nonfarm workers in 1979 was 50 percent. The rate declined to 46 percent in 1983 and 44 percent in 1988 (Piacentini, 1989).

A third dimension of pension coverage, type of plan and plan generosity, also affects future receipt of retirement income. The best overall statistics on plan type come from the 5500 forms. According to Beller (1989), the number of participants in defined benefit plans increased from 27.2 million in 1975 to 30.1 million in 1980. Subsequently, the total number of participants declined to 29.0 million in 1985. By contrast, the number of participants in primary defined contributions

11. Piacentini also presents data on an expanded definition of pension coverage. This definition includes those who additionally reported that they had a profit-sharing plan or additionally reported that they had a 401(k) plan. The expanded definition raised the coverage rate from 59 percent to 63 percent.

plans increased from 3.9 million in 1975 to 11.6 million in 1985. The number of participants in secondary defined contribution plans increased from 5.9 million in 1975 to 16.0 million in 1985 (excluding those with tertiary defined contribution plans).

This represents a significant shift in coverage. As a result of the shift toward defined contribution plans, the proportion of plan participants having primary coverage from a defined benefit plan fell from 87 percent in 1975 to 71 percent in 1985.

Specific pension plan provisions constitute another important aspect of pension coverage. While information is available on the prevalence of different types of defined contribution plans, little is known about plan contribution rates on a nationwide basis. The 1988 CPS pension supplement provides information about individual contributions to private-sector 401(k) plans, but these plans only represent part of the defined contribution universe.[12]

The only research on trends in defined benefit plan provisions was conducted by Mitchell and Luzadis (1988) for a very small number of plans. Presumably, shifts in defined benefit plan eligibility provisions and in benefit formulas could be traced based on the BLS Employee Benefit Surveys. But these files are difficult to work with, and the research has not been done.

Determinants of Pension Coverage

Studies have investigated the determinants of pension coverage and the growth in pension contributions as a share of total compensation. Both supply-side and demand-side arguments have been offered. On the demand side, theory would suggest that workers will sort themselves according to their preferences for deferred compensation provided on an after-tax basis. Demand-side arguments suggest that workers in higher marginal tax brackets and older workers will be more likely to be covered by a pension plan (Dorsey, 1982; Woodbury, 1983; Long and Scott, 1982). Supply-side arguments suggest that pensions are provided as an integral part of personnel policy in implicit long-term contracts (Kotlikoff and Wise, 1985; Andrews, 1989a).

Cross-section studies on pension coverage report generally consistent findings about the specific factors that influence pension coverage. Several studies base their findings on one of the CPS pension supplements (Dorsey, 1982; Andrews, 1985 and 1989b; Freeman, 1985).[13]

12. Some nationwide data are also available from the BLS on allowable contribution rates for contributory thrift and profit-sharing plans.
13. In addition, other studies have analyzed differences in pension participation rates purely from the standpoint of two-way tabulations. These studies include those of

Other cross-section data have been used as well, including the Survey of Consumer Finances (Gustman and Steinmeier, 1986), the BLS Expenditures for Compensation Survey (Freeman, 1985), and the National Federation of Independent Business (NFIB) benefits survey (Andrews, 1989a). Other studies use time-series data to estimate how the share of pension compensation has grown (Woodbury, 1983; Long and Scott, 1982; Woodbury and Huang, 1988). Because of data constraints, each of these studies omits one or more theoretically important variables.

Studies of coverage generally find that workers in larger firms, unionized workers, and workers with higher income and longer job tenure have higher pension coverage rates than others. Several researchers found that the effect of unionization is stronger for union members in small firms than for those working for larger employers (Andrews, 1985 and 1989b; Gustman and Steinmeier, 1986; Freeman, 1985).

While coverage rates also differ by industry, the relative ordering of industrial coverage tends to change depending upon the other variables entered into the equation (Allen and Clark, 1987; Andrews, 1989a). Andrews hypothesizes that this may reflect the effect of omitted variables such as the capital-labor ratio and firm profitability.

A number of studies found that differences in marginal tax rates influence pension contributions and coverage growth (Long and Scott, 1982; Woodbury, 1983; Barth, Cordes, and Friedland, 1984). Woodbury and Huang (1988) estimate that much of the decline in the importance of pension contributions in recent years relative to taxable compensation is a result of the lowering of marginal tax rates. Furthermore, since marginal tax rates are closely related to earnings, the greater propensity for those with higher earnings to have pension coverage may be related to tax incentives that defer income.

Nonetheless, those studies that include marginal tax rates (demand-side variables) in a reduced-form pension contribution or coverage equation omit a number of potentially important supply-side variables. For instance, in a study of small employers, Andrews (1989a) found that higher estimated administrative costs reduce the likelihood of pension coverage among small employers. Using tabulations from 1979 corporate tax records, she also found that corporate profitability and capital-labor ratios were related to the likelihood of coverage among particular firm-size industry categories. Unfortunately, no data set contains all the necessary variables to distinguish these effects.

Kolodrubetz and Landay (1973); Beller (1981); Schieber and George (1981); Piacentini (1989); and Woods (1989).

Several recent studies have investigated the determinants of the type of plan provided—be it defined contribution or defined benefit plan (Dorsey, 1987; Luzadis and Mitchell, 1989; Clark, Gohmann and McDermed, 1988). Dorsey uses data from the 1981 Form 5500 matched with information on earnings, education, age, and occupation from the 1970 census disaggregated to the 3-digit industry level. Clark, Gohmann, and McDermed use Form 5500 data for 1977 and 1983. Luzadis and Mitchell use the 1983 Survey of Consumer Finance (SCF) linked with information from plan sponsors.

All three studies find that employer size has an important impact, with smaller firms more likely to offer primary defined contribution plans. Woodbury and Mitchell find that unionization is related to defined benefit plan coverage. Woodbury also finds that defined benefit plans are more likely in industries in which workers are predominantly of one sex. Mitchell and Luzadis find that workers in more profitable firms and wealthier workers are more likely to have defined contribution plans than defined benefit plans. Clark, Gohmann, and McDermed conclude that, because of regulatory changes, defined benefit plans have become a less effective means of enforcing implicit contracts. The data indicate decreasing probabilities of starting defined benefit plans in recent years.

While these studies of plan type determination are suggestive, they suffer from the same problems as studies of pension coverage itself. No data set has all the supply-side and demand-side variables that would permit the estimation of a full reduced form equation.

Pension Vesting, Cashouts, and Portability Networks

Vesting rates can be tracked using the Department of Labor's Form 5500 and the three CPS pension supplements. According to the 5500 forms, among primary plan participants 56 percent were fully or partially vested (Beller, 1989).[14] Among supplemental plan participants, 90 percent were fully or partially vested (Beller, 1989). This represents a 12-percentage-point gain in vesting among primary plan participants from 44 percent in 1977. The 1977 vesting rate for supplemental plans was lower in 1977 as well, at 82 percent.

According to the CPS pension supplements, 51 percent of nonfarm wage and salary workers participating in a pension plan were vested in 1979. This figure rose to 55 percent in 1983 and 67 percent in 1988 (Table 12). Among private wage and salary workers 47 percent said they were entitled to benefits in 1979, 50 percent said they were entitled to benefits in 1983, and 65 percent said they were entitled to

14. This figure refers to those participants for whom vesting status is known.

benefits in 1988. This trend is generally consistent with that reported using Form 5500. Andrews (1985, 1989a) and Rogers (1981) used the CPS pension supplements to investigate factors influencing vesting. These studies found that tenure on the job was the most important variable.

The greater prevalence of defined contribution plans should contribute to the greater frequency of lump-sum pension cashouts. Grubbs (1981) reports that 93 percent of all defined contribution plans permit lump-sum distributions at retirement. Defined benefit plans provide cashouts as well. Atkins (1986) indicates that 39 percent of single-employer, primary defined benefit plans offer some type of lump-sum distribution. Within that category, 20 percent permit small amounts only, 9 percent provide the return of employee contributions, and 10 percent provide access to the full lump sum. Grubbs found more limited lump-sum options at retirement under defined benefit plans. Only 60 percent of all defined benefit plans and 23 percent of large defined benefit plans permitted some type of lump-sum distribution at retirement.

The Social Security Administration's 1982 New Beneficiary Survey indicated that nearly 10 percent of all men with pension coverage from any job reported receiving a distribution from their last job at retirement (Andrews, 1985). The median value of that distribution was $20,000. Another 4 percent of men received a distribution from their longest job averaging $10,000.

The 1983 and 1988 CPS pension supplements provide information on the recipiency of lump-sum distributions before retirement. In May 1983, a total of 8.5 million workers (7 percent of all workers) reported receiving at least one lump-sum distribution from prior pension plan participation. This represents an increase from the 6.6 million recipients who reported this type of distribution in 1983. Piacentini (1989) indicates that, based on the 1988 survey, 41 percent of those reporting a lump-sum distribution received their most recent cashout after 1984.

The reported value of these distributions averaged about $6,800 per recipient in constant 1988 dollars. The average size of the reported distribution increased by age of receipt, with cashouts received by workers between ages 25 and 35 averaging $4,100 and those received by workers between ages 55 and 60 averaging $26,000.

Both the May 1983 and May 1988 surveys asked how these distributions were used. Andrews (1985) found that 32 percent of all recipients reported saving their distribution in some form or another.[15] These estimates of saving were biased downward, however, because 63 per-

15. Savings included investment in a retirement program or insurance annuity, investment in housing, or investments in other financial instruments.

TABLE 13   How Lump-Sum Recipients Used Their Most Recent Lump-Sum
Distribution: May 1988[a]

Amount of most recent LSD	Received LSD from prior job (thousands)	Percentage of recipients using all their lump-sum distribution for:		
		Savings[b]	Consumption[c]	Mixed consumption & savings
$1–$499	1,042	50	49	1
$500–$999	955	59	37	3
$1,000–$2,499	1,627	56	38	5
$2,500–$4,999	1,220	62	31	5
$5,000–$9,999	1,114	67	25	7
$10,000–$19,999	660	67	20	13
$20,000 or more	495	70	19	12
Total	8,478	59	34	5

[a]For purposes of determining exclusive uses of LSDs, "don't know" and missing responses were taken as "no" responses.
[b]Includes all financial savings, purchase of a house, payment of a mortgage, and payment of loans or debts.
[c]Includes purchase of a car, education expenses, expenses incurred during a period of unemployment, and other uses.
Source: Piacentini (1990).

cent of all lump-sum recipients classified the use of their distribution as "other." For the year 1988, Piacentini found that 64 percent of recipients used their distribution for some type of savings (Table 13).[16]

Atkins (1986) used the 1983 CPS pension supplement data to analyze the use of lump-sum distributions. He found that the amount of the distribution and the age of the recipient affected whether that cashout would be invested or spent on current consumption. Those with higher education were also more likely to save their funds. Atkins also investigated factors influencing the decision to use different savings instruments.

A similar analysis has not yet been conducted using the 1988 CPS pension supplement. Further analyses might provide some insight into the impact of higher penalty taxes and expanded options for tax-favored savings on the likelihood of retaining a lump-sum distribution until retirement.

According to Meier and Basset (1981), three different studies conducted before and after the Employee Retirement Income Security Act of 1974 (ERISA) reported that between 45 and 50 percent of all

16. In this case savings included investment in an IRA, an annuity or retirement plan, in other financial savings, in the purchase of a house, payment of a mortgage, or payment of loans and debts.

multiemployer plans have some reciprocity.[17] Grubbs (1981) found that only 8 percent of single-employer plans had portability or reciprocity with unrelated employers. Most of these provisions appeared to be in the form of retirement or preretirement lump-sum distributions.

Grubbs found that only 2 percent of all participants were part of the ten centrally administered portability networks of unrelated employers. All had been established by 1963. The largest and best known was the Teachers Insurance and Annuity Association and related College Retirement Equities Fund (TIAA-CREF).

Trends in Retiree Health Benefits

Health insurance protection is increasingly considered an important component of retirement income. For this reason, both Medicare and Medicaid benefits for the elderly are included in measures of income and wealth. Retirees also receive benefits from employer-sponsored health insurance plans after retirement, but the asset value of these benefits cannot be estimated with available data.

Information on the prevalence of retiree health insurance coverage among workers in medium and large firms has been provided since 1981 in the BLS Survey of Employee Benefits.[18] In 1986, 75 percent of full-time workers in medium-sized and large firms had health insurance plans that continued coverage after early retirement. Sixty-eight percent were in plans that continued coverage after retirement at age 65.

In 1986, 64 percent of full-time workers had plans in which employers paid all or part of the plan costs for early retirees; 59 percent had plans with full or partial employer-financed coverage after retirement (Table 14). An estimated 41 percent of workers had health insurance plans in retirement in which the employer paid the full costs of coverage.

Employer plans typically provide benefits at the same level for retirees as those provided current workers. However, retiree plans typically integrate Medicare coverage into plan benefits. BLS data also indicate that the proportion of participants with reduced coverage increased from 15 to 18 percent for early retirees between 1985 and 1986.

Between 1981 and 1985, the number of workers with plans that provided employer-subsidized benefits after early retirement grew by

17. Much of this discussion is found in Andrews (1986).
18. This section is taken largely from Chollet (1989).

TABLE 14   Employer Retiree Health Insurance Plan Participation Rates for
Employees in Medium and Large Firms by Selected Benefit
Provisions and Age of Retiree, 1986

Benefit provision	Retirees under 65 (%)	Retirees 65 or older (%)
With employer contribution to retiree coverage	64	59
Effect of retirement on benefit level		
no change	50	46
reduced coverage	12	10
increased coverage	1	1
Retiree share of cost		
partial cost	23	17
no cost	41	41
No retiree coverage[a]	32	38
Provision not determinable	2	2
Retiree policy not established	1	1
Other[b]	1	1

[a]Includes plan participants who pay the full cost of plan.
[b]Includes employees who participate only in the employer's dental insurance plan and
for whom health insurance coverage provisions are unknown.
Source: Chollet (1989).

more than 14 percent. The number of workers with plans that continued coverage after age 65 grew by 18 percent.

According to tabulations of the Survey of Income and Program
Participation (SIPP), 30 percent of retirees age 65 and older and 17
percent of retirees under age 65 reported having health insurance
coverage from a past employer (Chollet, 1989). A recent study by the
National Center for Health Services Research (NCHSR) (Monheit and
Schur, 1989), however, found that half of all retired persons age 55 and
older in 1987 had health-care benefits provided by former employers.
The findings were based on data from the NCHSR's National Medical
Expenditure Survey (NMES) covering the civilian noninstitutional
population, the nursing home population, and persons in facilities for
the mentally retarded. Unlike evidence about pension coverage and
pension recipiency, the findings on retiree health insurance coverage
are not consistent.

Morrisey and Jensen (1988) have investigated variations in retiree
health insurance provision by firm size and industry using the BLS
Employee Benefits Survey. Once again, large employers are found to
be much more likely to furnish continuing benefits to their retirees.
Whether this is due to supply or demand considerations is not known.
Presumably retiree health insurance costs are greater for small em-

ployers as they are in the case of medical insurance and pension plans in general.

IV. Policy Issues

Retirement Income

For many years an important policy issue was whether retirement incomes were adequate. The answer seems to be "yes" on average, if the standard of comparison is incomes of the nonelderly. However, the distribution of income among the elderly remains a matter of social concern. Many reach retirement with few assets beyond housing equity, Social Security, and a claim on Medicare, so although they may not actually be in poverty, they have only a small financial cushion to cover large unanticipated expenditures. The poverty rate of widows remains high. The 1984 Retirement Equity Act addressed the poverty of widows by encouraging the choice of a pension with joint survivorship rights. In simulations using RHS data, the average income of widows would have been substantially higher had all couples receiving pensions had survivorship rights, but the impact on poverty rates would have been small: because of the high correlation between pension rights and other economic resources, most of the poor widows would have had no pension claims even with survivorship rights. Because pension coverage does not seem to be increasing, the poverty rates of widows will probably not be greatly affected by a change in survivorship rights. High poverty rates among women remain a public policy concern.

Although the elderly as a group apparently were not substantially affected by the high and variable rate of inflation in the 1970s, the effective indexing of their incomes could change as their portfolio of assets and their particular circumstances change over time. For example, as pension income becomes a more important income source, policymakers may want to address the issue of inflation protection of pension benefits after retirement. Although private pensions were adjusted to the increase in inflation of the 1970s on an ad hoc basis (Clark et al., 1984), society may not want to rely on the goodwill of firms to protect pension income.

Pension Coverage and Participation

One of the long-standing issues in the area of pension policy has been the perception that retirement income goals are perhaps not being met because less than half the labor force participates in an employer-sponsored pension plan. Proposals to increase pension coverage range from the use of additional tax incentives for small employers to the mandating of pension plans for all employers.[19] Other proposals, such as the extension of Simplified Employee Pensions, also aim at the increase of pension coverage.

Economic analysis is needed to determine both the need for increased pension coverage and the effectiveness of different policy proposals. Determining the need for increased pension coverage requires information about the proportion of future retirees who will not receive pensions and an evaluation of the adequacy of the rest of their retirement income relative to their lifetime earnings. Determining the effectiveness of alternative policy proposals requires an evaluation of the impact of those proposals on the retirement income of future retirees and on the labor market and the economy.

Pension Portability

Pension portability is the one retirement income issue that has received the greatest attention in the last few years. During the late 1980s several legislative proposals introduced in Congress contained the word "portability" in their titles.[20]

Several concerns motivate the portability debate. Perhaps the foremost is the realization that retirement benefits received by workers holding more than one lifetime job will be less than the hypothetical benefit received by a worker concluding a full career under only one employer. Portability losses occur upon job change under defined benefit plans when vested benefits are calculated as a percentage of some measure of final salary per year of service under the plan. With final salaries frozen at the point of job change, the multiple-job worker's pension does not reflect real-wage growth or inflation.

A secondary concern about portability has been raised in recent years as a corollary to concerns about flagging U.S. productivity and decreased international competitiveness. The argument is made that nonportable pensions tend to reduce worker mobility precisely when greater work force mobility is needed to adjust to shifts in demand. A further argument has been made that portability losses may have increased in recent years because the work force has become more

19. A tax credit for small employers was proposed in the Small Business Retirement and Benefit Extension Act of 1987. Mandating was proposed by the 1981 Carter Commission on Pension Policy.

20. These include the Pension Portability Act of 1987, the Portable Pension Plan Act of 1987, and the Pension Portability Improvements Act of 1987. For details see Andrews (1989a) and an update in Piacentini (1989).

mobile. Data on job tenure, however, do not confirm this hypothesis (Andrews, 1989a).

Theoretically, three separate kinds of portability losses can be distinguished. First, employees who leave their jobs before they are vested will lose future retirement benefits. The Tax Reform Act of 1986 effectively reduced vesting standards from ten years to five years to reduce portability losses of this type.[21]

Andrews and Chollet (1988) and Andrews (1987b) used ICF Inc.'s PRISM microsimulation model to estimate the impact of five-year vesting on different cohorts in the future and found that, for workers born during the early years of the baby boom, five-year vesting would increase both benefit recipiency and benefit levels. This effect was particularly large for women.

Recent portability proposals have focused on a second type of portability loss—the loss in benefits when employees spend cashouts from pension plans received upon job change prior to retirement. Simulations conducted by Andrews (1987a) suggest that if a worker with continuous coverage under defined benefit plans consumed all cash distributions except that from the last (and longest) job, a reduction in retirement income of approximately 35 percent would result.[22]

A study by Hay/Huggins and Mathematica Policy Research (1988) estimated the potential size of increased portability losses resulting from the consumption of lump-sum distributions.[23] According to the Hay/Huggins model, if all workers who are currently permitted to take cashouts from their primary plans spend those distributions, the average portability loss would increase from 15 to 21 percent of full-career benefits.

The third type of portability loss—the loss from restrictions on service credit portability—is the primary culprit reducing benefits for those who hold multiple lifetime jobs. Portability would be enhanced if plans acted as if employees were credited for years of service and salary as if they had never changed jobs. According to findings from the Hay/Huggins model, if all employers were required to index vested benefits for price inflation, the overall portability loss would be reduced from

21. While other vesting standards are enumerated, ten-year cliff vesting was the most popular before the Tax Reform Act of 1986 and five-year cliff vesting is now likely to take its place.

22. Losses due to job change under defined benefit plans were simulated as well, based on a model developed by Clark and McDermed (1987). Two other 1987 studies simulated policy losses for defined benefit plans—one by Rappaport et al. for the American Association of Retired Persons and one by the Congressional Budget Office.

23. The model is based on a set of work histories designed to represent job change and tenure patterns observed in the 1983 Survey of Consumer Finance and focuses on full-time employees entering the work force at age 20 and retiring at age 65.

15 to 5 percent. Indexing deferred vested benefits to real-wage growth would virtually eliminate the portability loss.

As in the case of pension coverage, statistics assessing the need for further legislation, and information about how specific policy proposals will affect retirement income and the economy, are needed to evaluate the desirability of enhanced pension portability.

Health Insurance for Retirees

Retiree health insurance is an emerging issue in a policy environment in which the definition of retirement income has been expanding to include health benefits as well. Unlike employer-sponsored pension plans, the ability to prefund retiree health insurance is extremely limited. Conservative estimates of unfunded liabilities for current workers range from $100 billion to $300 billion (Chollet, 1989).

Current options to fund retiree health insurance are not attractive, particularly as expected cost increases due to inflation cannot be prefunded with qualified contributions. For many years, health care costs have been rising more rapidly than consumer prices in general.

Retiree health insurance issues are connected to broader concerns about our health-care system related to access and health-care cost inflation. Both issues are potentially explosive for early retirees who are not yet eligible for Medicare benefits. To date, proposals to address the issue of retiree health insurance have been modest. The primary recommendation has been to permit overfunded pension plans to deposit excess assets in a fund to pay for the health-care costs of future retirees. Nonetheless, informal discussions have taken place about the need to regulate eligibility standards in return for more favorable funding provisions.

Consequently, statistics are needed to assess the extent of coverage employers provide their retired workers and the scope of benefits provided. Ideally, the value of these benefits to retirees should be estimated to assess the role that these benefits play in comparison to Medicare and Medicaid. Such information would enable policymakers to assess the balance between public- and private-sector insurance for future retirees.

V. Data and Research Needs

The Economic Status of the Elderly

The RHS has provided much of our information about retirement and the economic status of the elderly. But the 1970s was an unusual decade: average Social Security benefits at retirement roughly doubled, inflation over the decade averaged about 7.5 percent per year, retirement ages fell sharply, and many women entered the labor force. Furthermore, the RHS has no detailed information on the structure of pensions, very important because even the choice of retirement age seems to respond strongly to specific plan provisions. A new longitudinal data source similar to the RHS is badly needed to verify findings from the RHS and explore the consequences of the changes since the 1970s. The new data source should have details of pension coverage and pension characteristics.

More research is needed about life-cycle effects as the retired age. Because the RHS ended when the maximum age of the original heads of households was 73, it provided no information about the eventual economic status of the RHS population. Cross-section data sources can be very misleading about life-cycle effects because of the historical experience of each cohort and because of differential mortality by economic status. A very useful data set would be one that would reinterview the RHS population.

Although the Survey of Income and Program Participation (SIPP) may be of some use in identifying life-cycle behavior, the panels are too short to study retirement income issues fully because many changes in economic status take place over more than a decade.

Pension Plans and Plan Participation

The best data to analyze pension coverage and participation come from the three May CPS pension supplements. The clearance from the Office of Management and Budget (OMB) for the 1988 survey indicated that this was the last supplement the OMB intended to authorize. OMB suggested that the SIPP would be able to fill the role of the pension supplement. It cannot, however, in part because it is not timely, it is more difficult to use, and it does not include all the necessary data. For instance, if support is no longer provided for another CPS pension supplement, no detailed analysis can take place on pension plan cashouts prior to retirement.

The 1988 CPS pension supplement is itself less valuable than earlier surveys because the firm-size variable has been topcoded at 100 employees to preserve confidentiality. Such topcoding was not considered necessary for the 1979 or 1983 surveys. Firm size is perhaps the single most important determinant of pension coverage and plan type.

While the U.S. Department of Labor's processing of Form 5500 may be on a steadier track than in prior years, compilation and cleaning of these tapes still continues with a significant lag.

The BLS program of collecting data on plan provisions for private sector plans has also been curtailed. Data are now collected every two years rather than annually, and staffing is not available for the provision of full technical assistance to the users of a very complicated survey. While a survey of small employers was proposed at one point, this effort may not take place. The new survey of state and local benefit plans, however, has been a positive addition to the BLS surveys.

Both research and policy analysis on coverage and portability issues require more than the simple maintenance of basic data collection efforts. Both efforts require matched data sets containing information about the employee, the firm, and the pension plan provisions. Several approaches are possible. The first is to ensure that the next Survey of Consumer Finances (or similar survey) is again sent to employers to add data on plan provisions. Efforts might also be made to match data from the 1988 BLS Employee Benefits Survey to the 1988 CPS pension supplement. This type of match was done for pension benefits by Allen, Clark, and McDermed (1986) and is being done by RAND again under contract to the Department of Labor. Research should be done to determine the validity of this type of statistical match and to provide such data to users on an ongoing basis.

Finally, the policy analysis of many pension issues requires the continued development of microsimulation models, which have traditionally been expensive and difficult to develop and update. Modeling requirements would be well served by a match between the CPS pension supplement and Social Security earning records. But such a match has been proscribed since the 1978 match.

Retiree Health Benefits

Discussions of retiree health benefit issues have taken place virtually without data or analysis. Recent changes in the BLS definition of medium-sized and large employers and changes in the tables make current comparisons more difficult. For many reasons, most health economists working with these data prefer to do their own tabulations rather than using BLS analysis. Consequently, the findings from these surveys are fully available to only a few researchers. Furthermore, data are not available for small employers.

In 1988, the Labor Department funded an add-on to the August Current Population Survey focusing on retiree health insurance. These data will provide the first opportunity to analyze the prevalence of such plans according to individual worker characteristics. Information about employees matched with plan data would also be desirable. Ultimately, data are needed to provide estimates of the asset value of retiree health insurance benefits comparable to figures derived for Medicare and Medicaid.

Private Sector Alternatives

Attention is usually focused on public-use data provided by the government. A number of private-sector organizations also publish data about plan provisions. These data, often gathered from client surveys, represent an important segment of the employer universe. They can provide insights into the growth of benefits such as 401(k) plans and the increasing prevalence of lump-sum distributions. To date, such information has been of limited importance to researchers because only published tabulations have been available.

While private-sector sources undoubtedly have confidentiality considerations equal to, if not greater than, those of the government, the use of such microdata by researchers on a confidential basis could play an important role in expanding our basic understanding of the way in which employers change plan provisions and plan sponsorship in response to changes in regulation and changes in the economy.

References

Allen, Steven G. and Robert L. Clark. 1987. "Pensions and Firm Performance." In Morris Kleiner, Richard Block, Myron Roomkin, and Sidney Salsburg, eds., *Human Resources and the Performance of the Firm*. Madison, WI: Industrial Relations Research Association, 1987, pp. 195–242.

Allen, Steven G., Robert L. Clark, and Ann A. McDermed. 1986. "Job Mobility, Older Workers and the Role of Pensions." Final report for U.S. Department of Labor, Contract no. J-9-M-5-0049, October 1986.

Andrews, Emily S. 1985. *The Changing Profile of Pensions in America*. Washington, DC: Employee Benefit Research Institute, 1985.

———. 1986. "Pension Portability and Benefit Adequacy." *EBRI Issue Brief* 56 (July 1986).

———. 1987a. "Pension Portability and What It Can Do for Retirement Income: A Simulation Approach." *EBRI Issue Brief* 65 (April 1987).

———. 1987b. "Changing Pension Policy and the Aging of America." *Contemporary Policy Issues* (September 1987): 84–97.

———. 1989a. *Pension Policy and Small Employers: At What Price Coverage?* Washington, DC: Employee Benefit Research Institute, 1989.

———. 1989b. "Factors Affecting Coverage, Participation and Vesting: Preliminary Findings, May 1988." Paper prepared for the Employee Benefit Research Institute.

Andrews, Emily S. and Deborah J. Chollet. 1988. "Future Sources of Retirement Income: Whither the Baby Boom." In Susan M. Wachter, ed., *Social Security and Private Pensions: Providing for Retirement in the Twenty-First Century*. Lexington, MA: Lexington Books, 1988.

Atkins, G. Lawrence. 1986. *Spend It or Save It? Pension Lump-Sum Distributions and Tax Reform.* Washington, DC: Employee Benefit Research Institute, 1986.

Avery, Robert B. and Gregory E. Elliehausen. 1986. "Financial Characteristics of High-Income Families." *Federal Reserve Bulletin* 72, 3 (March 1986): 163–75.

Barth, James R., Joseph J. Cordes, and Robert B. Friedland. 1984. "Some New Evidence on How Taxes Affect the Wage-Fringe Tradeoff." Discussion paper, Department of Economics, George Washington University (D-8416), 1984.

Beller, Daniel J. 1981. "Coverage Patterns of Full-Time Employees under Private Retirement Plans." *Social Security Bulletin* 44 (July 1981): 3–11.

———. 1989. "Coverage and Vesting Pattern in Private Pension Plans, 1975–1985." In John A. Turner and Daniel J. Beller, eds., *Trends in Pensions.* Washington, DC: U.S. Government Printing Office 1989. pp. 39–67.

Burkhauser, Richard, Karen C. Holden, and Daniel Feaster. 1988. "Incidence, Timing, and Events Associated with Poverty: A Dynamic View of Poverty in Retirement." *Journal of Gerontology* 43, 2 (March 1988): S46–S52.

Chollet, Deborah. 1989. "Retiree Health Insurance: Trends and Issues." In *Retiree Health Benefits: What Is the Promise?* Washington, DC: Employee Benefit Research Institute, 1989. pp. 19–36.

Clark, Robert L., Stephen F. Gohmann, and Ann A. McDermed. 1988. "Declining Use of Defined Benefit Pension Plans: Is Federal Regulation the Reason?" Unpublished manuscript, April 1988.

Clark, Robert L., George Maddox, Ronald Schrimper, and Daniel Sumner. 1984. *Inflation and the Economic Well-being of the Elderly.* Baltimore: Johns Hopkins University Press, 1984.

Clark, Robert L. and Ann A. McDermed. 1987. "Portability and Pension Wealth." Unpublished manuscript.

Dorsey, Stuart. 1982. "A Model and Empirical Estimates of Worker Pension Coverage in the U.S." *Southern Economic Journal* (October 1982): 506–20.

———. 1987. "The Economic Functions of Private Pensions: An Empirical Analysis." *Journal of Labor Economics* 5, 4 Part 2 (October 1987): S171–S189.

Employee Benefit Research Institute. 1979+. *Employee Benefits in Medium and Large Firms,* 1979–88. Washington, DC: U.S. Government Printing Office, 1980–89.

———. 1989a. "Questions and Answers About Employee Benefits." *EBRI Issue Brief* (February 1989).

———. 1989b. "Pension Participation Declines as Pension Recipiency Increases." *Employee Benefit Notes* (May 1989): 4–7.

Freeman, Richard B. 1985. "Unions, Pensions and Union Pension Funds." In David A. Wise, ed., *Pensions, Labor, and Individual Choice.* National Bureau of Economic Research. Chicago: University of Chicago Press, 1985.

Grubbs, Donald S., Jr. 1981. "Study and Analysis of Portability and Reciprocity in Single-Employer Pension Funds." Final Report prepared for U.S. Department of Labor. Washington, DC: George S. Buck Consulting Actuaries, Inc., July 1981.

Gustman, Alan L. and Thomas L. Steinmeier. 1986. "Pensions and Unions." Report submitted to U.S. Department of Labor, Office of the Assistant Secretary for Policy, May 1986.

Hay/Huggins Company, Inc. and Mathematica Policy Research. 1988. "The

Effect of Job Mobility on Pension Benefits." Department of Labor Contract J-9-P-7-0044, Task Order #4, July 1988.

Hurd, Michael D. 1989. "The Economic Status of the Elderly." *Science* 244 (May 1989): 659–64.

———. 1990. "Research on the Elderly: Economic Status, Retirement, and Consumption and Savings." *Journal of Economic Literature* XXVII, 2 (June 1990): 565–637.

Hurd, Michael D. and John B. Shoven. 1985. "Inflation Vulnerability, Income, and Wealth of the Elderly, 1969–1979." In Martin David and Timothy Smeeding, eds., *Horizontal Equity, Uncertainty, and Economic Well-Being.* Chicago: University of Chicago Press, 1985. pp. 125–72.

Kolodrubetz, Walter W. and Donald M. Landay. 1973. "Coverage and Vesting of Full-Time Employees Under Private Retirement Plans." *Social Security Bulletin* (November 1973): 20–36.

Kotlikoff, Laurence J. and David Wise. 1985. "Labor Compensation and the Structure of Private Pension Plans: Evidence for Contractual versus Spot Labor Markets." In David Wise, ed. *Pensions, Labor, and Individual Choice.* Chicago: University of Chicago Press, 1985.

Lawrence, Helen H. 1989. "Trends in Private Pension Plans." In John A. Turner and Daniel J. Beller, eds., *Trends in Pensions.* Washington, DC: U.S. Government Printing Office, 1989. pp. 69–93.

Long, James E. and Frank A. Scott. 1982. "The Income Tax and Nonwage Compensation." *Review of Economics and Statistics* (May 1982): 211–19.

Luzadis, Rebecca A. and Olivia S. Mitchell. 1989. "A Multinomial Logit Model of Pension Outcomes." Unpublished manuscript (July 1988, revised).

McDermed, Ann, Robert Clark, and Steven Allen. 1989. "Pension Wealth, Age-Wealth Profiles, and the Distribution of Net Worth." In Robert E. Lipsey and Helen Stone Tice, eds., *The Measurement of Saving, Investment and Wealth.* Chicago: University of Chicago Press, 1989 pp. 689–731.

Meier, Elizabeth L. and Preston C. Bassett. 1981. Chapter 16 in *Technical Papers.* President's Commission on Pension Policy. Washington, DC: U.S. Government Printing Office, 1981.

Mitchell, Olivia S. 1988. "Worker Knowledge of Pension Provisions." *Journal of Labor Economics* (January 1988): 212–39.

Mitchell, Olivia S. and Rebecca A. Luzadis. 1988. "Changes in Pension Incentives Through Time." *Industrial and Labor Relations Review* 42, 1 (October 1988): 100–108.

Monheit, Alan C. and Claudia L. Schur. 1989. *Health Insurance Coverage of Retired Persons.* NMES Research Findings 2, DHHS Publication (PHS) 89–3444, 1989.

Morrisey, Michael A. and Gail A. Jensen. 1988. "Employer-Sponsored Post-Retirement Health Benefits: The State of Knowledge and Some Unresolved Issues." Working Paper, University of Alabama at Birmingham, September 1988.

Piacentini, Joseph S. 1989. "Pension Coverage and Benefit Entitlement: New Findings from 1988." *EBRI Issue Brief* (February 1989).

———. 1990. "An Analysis of Pension Participation at Current and Prior Jobs, Receipt and Use of Lump-Sum Distributions, and Tenure at Current Job." Draft report prepared for the U.S. Department of Labor, Pension and Welfare Benefits Administration, Office of Research and Economic Analysis.

Radner, Daniel. 1983. "Adjusted Estimates of the Size Distribution of Family Money Income." *Journal of Business and Economic Statistics* 1 (April 1983): 135–46.

———. 1986. "Changes in the Money Income of the Aged and Nonaged, 1967–1983." U.S. Department of Health and Human Services, 1986.

———. 1987. "Money Incomes of Aged and Nonaged Family Units, 1967–84." *Social Security Bulletin* 50, 8 (August 1987): 9–28.

Rappaport, Anna et al. 1987. "Pension Portability Analysis." Report prepared for the American Association of Retired Persons, December 1987.

Rogers, Gayle Thompson. 1981. "Vesting of Private Pension Benefits in 1979 and Changes from 1972." *Social Security Bulletin* 44 (July 1981): 12–29.

Schieber, Sylvester J. and Patricia M. George. 1981. *Retirement Income Opportunities in an Aging America: Coverage and Benefit Entitlement.* Washington, DC: Employee Benefit Research Institute, 1981.

Smeeding, Timothy. 1989. "Full Income Estimates of the Relative Well-Being of the Elderly and the Nonelderly." In D. Bloom and D. Slottje, eds., *Research in Economic Inequality, Vol. 1.* Greenwich, CT: JAI Press 1989, pp. 83–122.

U.S. Bureau of the Census. 1987. "Income of the Population 55 and Over, 1986." *Current Population Reports.* Washington, DC: U.S. Department of Commerce, 1987.

———. 1988. "Measuring the Effect of Taxes and Income on Poverty: 1986." *Current Population Reports* P-60, 164-RD-1. Washington, DC: U.S. Department of Commerce, 1988.

U.S. Congress. 1987. House of Representatives. Committee on Ways and Means. *Retirement Income for an Aging Population.* Washington, DC: U.S. Government Printing Office, 1987.

———. 1987. Congressional Budget Office. *Tax Policy for Pensions and Other Retirement Savings.* Washington, DC: U.S. Government Printing Office, 1987.

U.S. Department of Labor. Bureau of Labor Statistics. *Employee Benefits in Medium and Large Firms, 1979–88.* Washington, DC: U.S. Government Printing Office, 1980–1989.

van der Gaag, Jacques and Eugene Smolensky. 1982. "True Household Equivalence Scales and Characteristics of the Poor in the U.S." *Review of Income and Wealth* 28 (March 1982): 17–28.

Woodbury, Stephen A. 1983. "Substitution Between Wage and Nonwage Benefits." *American Economic Review* (March 1983): 166–82.

Woodbury, Stephen A. and Wei-Jang Huang. 1988. "The Slowing Growth of Fringe Benefits." Paper presented at the Eastern Economic Association Annual Convention, Boston, March 10–12, 1988.

Woods, John R. 1989. "Pension Coverage Among Private Wage and Salary Workers: Preliminary Findings from the 1988 Survey of Employee Benefits." *Social Security Bulletin* 52 (October 1989): 2–19.

Yohalem, Martha Remy. 1977. "Employee-Benefit Plans, 1975." *Social Security Bulletin* 40 (November 1977): 19–27.

Comments by Laurence J. Kotlikoff

The chapter by Emily Andrews and Michael Hurd provides an excellent survey of information on the distributions of income and wealth by age as well as the role of pensions in affecting these distributions. The chapter delivers the following punch lines: (1) the mean income of the elderly is close to, if not larger than, that of the nonelderly; (2) poverty rates of the elderly are close to, if not less than, those of the nonelderly; (3) the resources of many of the elderly are highly annuitized; that is, many of the elderly have very little in the way of liquid assets; (4) pension wealth is a small but important component of total resources of the elderly; (5) the growth of pension coverage has slowed or stopped, implying that the growth of pension income in the future will slow or stop. In the short run, however, the growth of pension income among new retirees will continue because the fraction of near-term retirees covered by private pensions exceeds the fraction of current retirees who were covered by private pensions during their working years; and (6) the real incomes of the elderly are less inflation-sensitive than many observers might have expected.

In addition to documenting these points with a range of data, the authors mention several problems confronting the private pension system. These include (1) concerns about limited portability of pensions and the associated "locking-in" of employees; (2) concerns about the very strong retirement incentives of many/most defined benefit plans; (3) potentially massive unfunded employer-retiree health benefit liabilities; and (4) paucity of data sets that can be used to study private pensions.

The paper covers much interesting material, but the authors should reconsider the appropriate definition and measurement of income adequacy. To the authors, adequate income of the elderly appears to mean that the elderly have disposable incomes that are as large or larger than those of younger workers. But this standard makes little sense as a notion of adequate retirement income. If young workers suddenly experience an increase in their real wages because of productivity improvements, should we conclude that the elderly have simultaneously experienced a reduction in the adequacy of their retirement incomes?

The notion of retirement income adequacy is immediately directed to the question of whether the elderly have saved enough, privately or through the government, to maintain their pre-retirement standard of living. Hence, what is needed is not a comparison of income levels of the current elderly with income levels of the current young and middle-aged, but rather a comparison of the current consumption level of the elderly with the level of consumption they enjoyed when young. This definition of adequacy may lead to quite different conclusions and policy than that examined by the authors.

A related problem with the notion of adequacy proposed by the authors is the question of who should pay to improve the income adequacy of the elderly. Once one understands that more income adequacy (as defined by the authors) for the elderly means less income for some other generation, their whole notion of income adequacy degenerates into a value judgment about the intergenerational distribution of welfare.

If the authors were to consider the replacement rate concept of adequacy, they would be in a position to say something more interesting about the role of private pensions in ensuring that each generation that comes along does not overconsume when young. Pensions may help prevent overconsumption when young because they take the resources out of the hands of young workers and, from the workers' perspectives, save them. If young workers are liquidity-constrained, and many surely are, they are unlikely to be able to borrow against these savings to finance current consumption. Hence, private pensions may be changing the shape of the longitudinal age-consumption profile. This is an issue that should be explored with data; it is to be hoped that the authors will consider doing so in their future research.

Another concern with the chapter is that, while it provides a fine description of the income and wealth position of the current elderly, it does not provide the same for the future elderly. When the baby boom generation retires, their relative income position vis-à-vis other generations and their relative consumption position vis-à-vis their consumption when young and middle-aged may be much different than in the case of current retirees. For example, future Social Security benefits of baby boomers were cut in the 1983 Social Security Amendments by roughly 15 percent. In addition, the baby boom generation appears to be saving, on its own account, at very low rates. Added to these causes for concern is the continuing trend toward early retirement, the continuing expansion of life spans, and the U.S. government's current course of fiscal policy which appears to entail an implicit dissipation of the Social Security trust fund by adhering to the Gramm-Rudman-Hollings deficit targets which include the Social Security surplus. In sum, the income and consumption adequacy of the elderly may well be a transient phenomenon. Again, more study by the authors on the issue of the income and consumption position of the future elderly would be very welcome.

Comments by Sylvester J. Schieber

The chapter by Emily Andrews and Michael Hurd evaluates a host of issues related to employee benefits and retirement income adequacy. Its primary focus is on the cash benefits provided by Social Security and employer-sponsored pensions. Other income sources, including income from assets and public assistance, receive limited consideration and some of the benefits provided through retiree health insurance programs are discussed. The chapter concludes with a discussion of data requirements to help respond to unanswered policy questions and support future research, the purpose of this volume. Overall, the chapter points out that there is a patchwork quilt of information on retiree pension and health programs, but that many of the patches are missing.

The first stated goal of the chapter is to review findings on the economic status of the elderly in order to determine whether their retirement income is adequate. The authors combine a survey of the literature with their own tabulations of a variety of public-use data sets to accomplish this review. They show that currently the elderly are generally as well or better off than the nonelderly and document that the elderly have not been particularly vulnerable to inflation, primarily because of Social Security.

The second stated goal of the paper is to examine the role of pensions in providing retirement income. Again the authors combine their own analysis of extant data sets with the work of other authors in this endeavor. Based on their analysis of the 1979, 1983, and 1988 Current Population Surveys (CPS), they suggest that pension participation may be declining. The analysis of the public disclosure data (i.e., Form 5500 filings) suggests that coverage levels have stabilized, but the data are wanting. A shift from defined benefit to defined contribution plans is documented, but virtually no information is available on the implications of this shift for the income security of future retirees. None of the existing data sets allow adequate estimation of models explaining determination of pension coverage by plan type. Further, analysis on shifts in defined benefit plan provisions is, for all practical purposes, nonexistent.

The Form 5500 data sets provide concrete evidence that vesting levels are up, but no information allowing an evaluation of the distributional effects on benefits that have resulted. The CPS data also support the conclusion that vesting levels are up. Only sketchy information is available on the prevalence and utilization of lump-sum payments that occur when workers terminate employment with vested benefits under tax-qualified plans.

The authors note the importance of employer-sponsored health benefits plans in evaluating the retirement income security of the elderly, especially early retirees. They show that by comparing existing data sets, the findings on retiree health coverage are not consistent. They conclude that the value of employer-sponsored plans cannot be estimated with available data.

A number of policy issues requiring further analysis are identified in the chapter. The authors suggest that we should assess the need for increased coverage and the effectiveness of different policy proposals in accomplishing this goal. Also, the desirability of enhanced pension portability is mentioned as a current policy issue that deserves analysis. Finally, retiree health coverage and benefits should be evaluated so the proper balance between public- and private-sector programs for future retirees can be determined.

A policy story remains that the paper does not tell. During the 1980s, a number of new laws were enacted that had major effects on pension and retiree health benefits programs. Neither the costs nor the benefits of those policy changes can be assessed on a macro basis, because of the lack of evidence with which to assess them. All we know is that pension coverage has stabilized or slightly declined, and that a shift has occurred from defined benefit to defined contribution plans. The rest of the information we have is anecdotal. As we move into the 1990s, more policy changes are being considered that would further affect employee benefits. These new proposals, once again, cannot be evaluated on the basis of the relative merits of their costs and benefits.

On the data front, the authors are kinder and gentler than I would be in their assessment of the government's role in providing information that can be used to enlighten the policy deliberations. I understand the reluctance of researchers to criticize the government agencies when they depend on government data for their analyses, and sometimes on government financial support for their work. But, the issues being addressed in this chapter involve large and important stakes. Certainly, the current federal deficit levels are worrisome to many policy makers, but that does not warrant employee benefits policy being made blindly.

Policies affecting employer-sponsored pension plans may affect two-thirds to three-fourths of the workers the Employee Retirement Income Security Act (ERISA) was implemented to protect. Policies affecting employer-sponsored health benefits programs may affect a similar portion of the total population. The government has an obligation to track these programs and the effects of public policies on them. If policy researchers do not make this point, they should not expect policy makers to think of it on their own.

The separate relevant administrative agencies of government must be encouraged to collect useful information for analytic purposes. To the extent multiple agencies have information that can be more effectively used when combined, unnecessary privacy barriers that prohibit their working together should be eliminated. If new laws are needed to allow the combining of governmental data, such laws should be passed with provisions to assure that reasonable privacy protections are maintained. Any public-data user who attempts to use a combined data set of this sort to identify specific individuals should be subject to criminal penalties.

The authors close with a discussion of the need for access to privately developed data sets that can be used to provide insights into the prevalence of employee benefits plans and their provisions. Three hurdles must be overcome in order for this to happen.

The first relates to the competitive environment existing for firms that might be the source of the data being sought. Collecting the kinds of information being sought is expensive and is done for business purposes by those that collect it. If the Pension Research Council, or some other entity, is to serve as a clearinghouse for these kinds of data, assurances will have to be given that the information cannot be used for competitive purposes against the firm that collected the information in the first place.

The second hurdle relates to a language barrier that has to be broken. Academics, especially theoretical economists, and professionals in the employee benefits arena do not speak the same language. My own observation is that neither side seems disposed to solve the problem. If academic or policy researchers cannot explain why they want private firm data, and how they intend to use it, I believe it unlikely that any private firm will share its information.

The third hurdle relates to trust and is interrelated with the language problem. I believe many professionals in the employee benefits business are skeptical about the fairmindedness of many policy researchers. For example, there is a perception that many academic researchers have a strong predisposition toward defined contribution plans. There is also a perception that this predisposition can lead to biased analyses of the relative merits of defined benefit versus defined contribution plans. In order for benefits professionals to become more sanguine about the intentions of policy researchers, a dialogue covering a wide range of employee benefits issues must unfold. Such a dialogue will be impossible if the two groups cannot converse.

I believe the Pension Research Council can play a role in encouraging the development of public and private data sets that can be used to enlighten policy deliberations related to retirement income security programs. The Council can offer forums where benefits professionals and researchers can come together and explain their relative goals and methods of operation. The Council can begin a dialogue that will identify common interests and specific differences between theoretical and policy approaches to problems, and the pragmatic solutions that evolve in reality. If the dialogue is successful, some of the data needs identified by Andrews and Hurd may be filled through the evolution of the Council's role.

Chapter 2
Pensions and Labor Market Activity: Behavior and Data Requirements

Alan L. Gustman and Olivia S. Mitchell

Introduction

A revolution in U.S. pay practices has occurred since the end of World War II: while labor compensation consisted primarily of wage payments in the mid-1940s, non-wage benefits today account for over one-third of total compensation (U.S. Chamber of Commerce, 1989). Pensions have played a key role in this transformation of the way workers are paid.

Because pensions are an important part of compensation, and because they are exceedingly complex labor market institutions, employer-sponsored pension plans have commanded a great deal of attention from researchers and policy makers in the last ten years. This chapter reviews recent studies in order to highlight research findings about the role of pensions in the labor market. In doing so, our goal is to review and synthesize what is known, and to identify areas where further information is most needed, for increasing our understanding of behavior and for guiding the pension policies of the next decade in the U.S. and abroad.

A number of facts may be cataloged from the studies cited in this review:

1. More than half of all private-sector workers are covered by employer-provided pensions. Defined contribution plans offer work-

The order of the authors' names was determined alphabetically. Portions of this paper draw on the joint work of Alan Gustman and Thomas Steinmeier, and that of Olivia Mitchell and Gary Fields. Without implicating them, Fields's and Steinmeier's contributions are gratefully acknowledged as are the comments of Zvi Bodie, Robert Hutchens, Richard Ippolito, Andrew Oswald, Anna Rappaport, and Steve Venti. Views contained herein are solely those of the authors, and not those of the institutions with whom they are affiliated.

ers an important tax shield and opportunities for a retirement annuity; nevertheless, three-fourths of covered workers are covered by more complex defined benefit plans.

2. It might be thought that firms with pension plans would have to pay lower wages to offset having a pension, but there is almost no evidence supporting this view. It also might be thought that wages would fall at the point when workers vest in their plans and at the moment when they become eligible for retirement, but such dramatic wage changes are not observed once benefit entitlement occurs.

3. Workers with pension plans change jobs less often than do workers without pensions.

4. Pensions have a powerful influence on workers' retirement decisions. In defined benefit plans, retirement patterns are particularly responsive to incentives on qualifying for retirement benefits. This is due to accrual profiles which rise rapidly just before early or normal retirement, and exhibit sharp discontinuities just after reaching eligibility for retirement. There is some evidence that changes over time in defined benefit plans are moving to encourage even earlier retirement.

5. Within the set of defined benefit plans, pension provisions vary tremendously. Eligibility rules and retirement benefits vary along both age and years-of-service dimensions. Across firms there are also large differences in the position and pattern of benefit accrual profiles. There are many possible explanations for these differences, but no single theory explains them all.

6. Pensions are inherently uncertain promises because benefit receipt may be conditional on survival, turnover, retirement, investment performance, and inflation. Workers do not understand many of these inherent uncertainties, though there is evidence that some may obtain wage premiums offsetting riskier pension promises.

7. There is almost no direct evidence on pensions' effects on productivity, and what little evidence there is suggests only a negligible effect.

8. Pensions are more common in large firms and in unionized firms.

Some of these findings are inherently contradictory and must be resolved to produce a clearer picture of pensions' role and function in the labor market. As we will show below, some explanations are available in the literature, but others remain outside our grasp. What we emphasize throughout this chapter is that pensions are labor market institutions. As such, in order to better judge various rationales for what pensions do in the labor market, researchers and analysts need a more complete picture of how workers and firms benefit from pensions.

Our assignment in writing this chapter was to review what was known, and what was not, in order to develop recommendations for new data in the pension area. We believe that the strongest need is for a nationally representative data set in which the unit of observation is the firm, the establishment, or the pension plan. To understand how pensions alter the price, the quantity, and the quality of labor, more insight is required into how pensions affect compensation and employment outcomes. We believe it would be most useful to distinguish among leading theories that emphasize firms' motivations for pensions. To this end the most useful data set would contain information on the characteristics of a firm's (or firms') employees, their wages and turnover/retirement patterns, and their ages and seniority. Ideally this would be matched with information on other production inputs as well as outputs and firm financial data. Of even greater utility would be longitudinal data combining company-side information with employment and wage histories of the employees.

The discussion below is divided into five parts. Section I provides an overview of current theoretical and empirical research on the role of pensions in the labor market. Section II reviews in more detail five approaches to modeling what pensions do in the labor market. Section III reviews evidence on the impact of market structures and labor market institutions on pension outcomes. Section IV summarizes the discussion and offers recommendations for further research. Section V highlights data needs.

I. Overview of Theoretical and Empirical Issues

The Approach to Modeling

Our review of the role of pensions in the labor market is organized within a supply and demand framework, where references to the supply side should be understood as pertaining to workers supplying their labor, and references to demand pertaining to firms' demand for workers. Specifically, on the supply side, as workers evaluate different wage offers, non-wage benefit offerings, and job attributes when deciding which job to accept, they determine the rate at which they are willing to trade off pensions for wages. The framework also postulates that workers differ with respect to their tastes for pay and benefits, the sophistication with which they can process information about their benefit packages, and their views of other aspects of their jobs. Taking the firm's viewpoint, employers will offer a wage and benefit package in accordance with their anticipated effects on output and costs, aiming to maximize profits. Again, the model recognizes that firms differ in their perception of specific benefits: thus, a small employer might find it more expensive to provide a pension as compared to a larger firm which can spread fixed costs and risks, including those associated with pensions, across its larger work force. In addition, larger firms must be conscious of the effects of their actions on market prices.

In the general case, this framework explaining how pension outcomes are determined emphasizes that observed pension outcomes in the labor market are the joint product of workers' valuation of pensions, and firms' decisions about whether to provide pensions and, if so, how to structure them. By aggregating decisions made by individual workers and firms to the market level, it is possible to study how pensions affect three labor market outcomes of key interest: the *price of labor*, the *quantity of labor*, and the *quality of labor*. Importantly, our approach recognizes that these key outcomes are not determined in a static way, but instead span time, incorporate uncertainty on both workers' and firms' parts, and are in other ways complex.[1]

Much of the pension literature examines how pensions affect the *price of labor*. As we shall show in more detail below, measuring the price of labor when pensions are present is a complex task. For example, in a defined benefit pension plan, the pension promise is outlined in the pension formula specified by the sponsoring firm. This typically depends on past tenure, the worker's wage path over time, and the worker's retirement age. In a defined contribution plan, in contrast, the sponsoring employer specifies annual contributions to the plan, and retiree annuities depend strictly on annual contributions and the fund's investment performance.[2] Over time, an employee accrues a benefit entitlement based on past work, the value of which will depend on his plan specifics and, in a defined benefit plan, an expected future benefit accumulation to be delivered contingent on continued work at that firm. Valuing the pension also depends on other factors including

1. For introductory discussions on the economics of pensions see Ellwood (1985); Ippolito (1986a); McGill (1984); and Munnell (1982).

2. If the defined benefit plan were to terminate with insufficient funds to meet promised benefits, workers' accrued vested nominal pension benefits are guaranteed by the Pension Benefit Guaranty Corporation (PBGC). The PBGC is a federal pension insurance agency created under the 1974 Employee Retirement Income Security Act (ERISA), which guarantees benefits up to an annual maximum if a plan is terminated with insufficient funds. The agency charges an annual premium which is now less than fully experience-rated (Ippolito, 1989). Unlike the defined benefit plans, defined contribution plans' liabilities are by definition equal to assets. For this reason the PBGC is not required to insure defined contribution participants' benefits against plan termination.

tax laws which shelter benefit accrual, the risks and returns to pension investments, and funding practices.

Pricing the resultant pension annuity is central to determining how workers value their benefit promise, and also to understanding how companies evaluate pension costs. Interestingly enough, there appears to be a wedge between workers' valuation of pension promises and what their employers perceive as pension costs. This can arise for many reasons. For instance, firms often face economies of scale in financial markets, can pool risks, and can frequently reduce adverse selection for insurance or annuities, making it possible for employers to purchase pension annuities at a lower price than could individual workers acting alone in the private insurance market. In general, therefore, pricing labor when pensions are in the picture requires devising a thorough understanding of what the pension promise is worth to the firm, and also how much workers would be willing to trade off in terms of wages to receive more in pensions. In assessing this tradeoff, it is not sufficient to take a static one-period perspective; instead, pension accruals must be viewed in terms of their time path, and compared against the structure of wage payments over the worker's period of attachment to his or her firm.

Labor market analysts have also devoted some attention to understanding how pensions affect the *quantity of labor* employed. Along this line, labor market research investigates how pensions are used to attract and retain younger and middle-aged workers, and also how pensions act as a personnel tool to encourage older workers to retire. When these hiring and termination decisions are aggregated across workers in a firm, they determine the age and experience structure of firms' employee populations, the time remaining until workers leave their jobs, and the relation between active employees and the pool of retirees (and their benefits). In general, the literature concludes that pensions have a profound effect on employment patterns, particularly for older workers.

Analysts focus on the effects of pensions on *labor quality* because pensions are one method of influencing worker productivity. As we note below, however, researchers have been held back because data are often lacking with which to measure labor quality and output. Some dimensions of quality are readily observable, such as employees' levels of formal education.[3] Other worker characteristics are more difficult to

---

3. The distinctions among price, quantity, and quality outcomes are intended to provide a rough guide for the discussion. They are not sharp since some outcomes are difficult to classify into a particular category. For example, age and experience of the work force may be considered a dimension of quality rather than quantity. In that sense, the labor market flows, and especially retirement rates, may be thought of as a dimension

measure, however, including willingness to work, innate ability, and ability to make good long-range judgments. In addition, productivity may itself be affected by such things as the firm's hiring, training, and compensation structure. For this reason, labor market researchers have only just begun to pinpoint the effect of pensions on labor quality.

While employees' demand for and firms' supply of pensions are the primary factors affecting the observed patterns of pensions and their consequences, these do not operate in a vacuum. In particular, factors influencing *market imperfections and market structure* also play key roles in shaping observed pension outcomes. Information shortfalls are a prime example of how market imperfections can work. Pensions are instruments of sufficient complexity that both workers and their benefit administrators often have difficulty understanding the plan and its implications. For instance, studies show that workers in mid-career understand their plans only poorly.[4] Unless the margin of well-informed agents is sufficiently large to ensure efficiency in the market, misinformation could affect employee responses to incentives and limit a pension plan's effectiveness in raising productivity. Imperfections in other markets have just begun to be examined, along with their implications for pensions. For example, there is some suggestion that liquidity constraints and imperfections in annuity and insurance markets prevent workers from separating savings and retirement decisions.[5] As a result, work and pension profiles will tend to be adapted so as to better meet workers' desired consumption targets.

Other structural features of the labor market also affect pension outcomes. For example, where labor unions are present, pensions are more likely to be found and to differ in form and structure from pensions found in nonunion firms.[6] Firm size has also been shown to be important, in that large companies are more likely to offer pensions and are more likely to offer defined benefit pension plans as well.[7]

---

of quality. Similarly, work effort may be thought of as a dimension of labor quantity or quality. In addition, most of the prices are contingent on age of entry (Parsons, 1988), and on continued firm attachment (Lazear and Moore, 1988), and thus on the quantity outcomes.

4. However, there is evidence that workers nearer retirement age are better informed. See Mitchell (1988); Bernheim (1989); and Gustman and Steinmeier (1989a).

5. See Burtless and Moffitt (1984); Nalebuff and Zeckhauser (1985); and Robb and Burbidge (1989).

6. In the private sector, see Freeman (1985), Gustman and Steinmeier (1986c and 1989a), and Ippolito (1985c); in the public sector, see Mitchell and Smith (1989).

7. Large firms have been found to pay higher than expected wages. According to Brown and Medoff (1989), much of this differential is unexplained. Large firms are also more likely to offer pensions (Kotlikoff and Smith, 1983) than are small firms (Andrews, 1985; Luzadis and Mitchell, 1987). Evidence that large firms are also more likely to offer defined benefit plans is reported in Kotlikoff and Smith (1983), Dorsey (1987), Ippolito (1985c), and elsewhere.

Research also shows that some firms directly pursue a policy of paying higher-than-market wages which is not due to measured or unmeasured worker ability.[8] If this "efficiency wage" policy is designed at least in part to reduce shirking and to economize on hiring, turnover, and training costs, it would then raise worker productivity.[9] Alternatively, firms offering pensions might be sharing rents (profits higher than competitive returns resulting from market power), which would explain why their workers also are paid wages higher than they could receive elsewhere.

Regulatory policy also weighs heavily on and shapes the role and function of pensions in the labor market. First and foremost, worker and firm valuations of pension promises depend crucially on tax policy and related legislation, including laws governing the features of tax-qualified pension plans. Much research has concluded that tax laws permitting pension contributions and investment accruals greatly spurred the spread of pensions over the last four decades in the U.S. (Ippolito, 1986a). Laws also constrain formation and administration in myriad other ways, including the nondiscrimination regulations pursuant to the Employee Retirement Income Security Act (ERISA) and subsequent extensions of this bill. Last but certainly not least, the passage of the Age Discrimination in Employment Act (ADEA) virtually eliminated mandatory retirement and restricted other wage and pension payments linked to age. The effects of these and other constraints on behavior created by the tax and regulatory system are explored briefly in Section III.

Empirical Pension Studies: Distinguishing Their Approaches

Empirical pension studies have explored many of the price, quantity, and quality outcomes described above. In the remainder of this chapter we seek to highlight these findings, and draw lessons from their conclusions. Prior to doing so, however, it is necessary to outline the main empirical approaches if we are to reconcile some of their findings.

One approach to investigating pensions' role in the labor market is descriptive, with the goal being to explore the form and structure of one or many specific pension provisions. For example, cross-sectional plan characteristics and their correlates are explored extensively by Kotlikoff and Smith (1983), while pension accrual patterns as they differ across firms are examined by Kotlikoff and Wise (1985, 1987b).

---

8. See Katz and Summers (1989) and Krueger and Summers (1988).
9. See Akerlof and Katz (1989) and Holzer, Katz, and Krueger (1989).

The latter study also describes cross-firm variation in accrual profiles at vesting, early and normal retirement ages and relates these benefit value variables to the characteristics of pension benefit formulas.[10]

Another set of studies is more analytical, seeking to relate pension outcomes to the factors shifting labor supply and demand curves. Most commonly such studies take a "reduced form" approach, which means that one or another pension provision or some other price, quantity, or quality related outcome is viewed as determined by supply and demand working together. For example, a key component of quantity, such as the retirement or mobility rate, may be related statistically to vectors of worker, industry, and occupational characteristics (Luzadis and Mitchell, 1987). In reduced form analysis, the supply and demand curves themselves are not separately estimated, although in rare instances some more basic parameters may be identified in a reduced-form study.

A few researchers have taken yet a more challenging path, hoping to unravel employers' and employees' "structural" demand and supply functions. In a simple (non-pension) case, econometric techniques permit structural estimation of a supply curve by holding factors constant that affect supply, leaving the demand curve free to trace out the position of the curve being held fixed. This is accomplished by having a single price term appear on one side of the equation being estimated, and a single quantity term in another. In the pension context, however, special problems arise in undertaking structural analysis. This is primarily because it is not satisfactory to focus on one dimension of the complex price, quantity, and quality related outcomes. Thus, for example, in examining the price of labor, what matters is not just the level of a single wage, but rather the mix between wages and pension accruals over the worker's years at the firm. A further complication is that the structure of the pension promise, as reflected in plan provisions, affects the weights attached to current wages, future wages, deferred benefits for which payment is guaranteed, and the option value of the future pension, contingent on the course of continued employment and wages. Perhaps for these reasons, existing studies do not currently offer a full understanding of the simultaneous behavior generating pension outcomes. As a result, much empirical analysis "tests" partial explanations and accordingly includes only parts of the behavioral story, attempting to establish whether a single aspect of behavior is roughly consistent with available data. When only a part of the story is examined, the problem of omitted variable bias arises.

10. Other informative pension descriptions appear in Ippolito and Kolodrubetz (1986) and Turner and Beller (1989).

Nevertheless, not all the news is bad. Structural equations associated with individual workers have been estimated quite successfully in some cases, as in the retirement literature where clear evidence has emerged that pensions affect workers' retirement ages directly. This is possible because the dependent variable in individual-level data, namely the retirement age, is postulated to be influenced by the pension accrual rate (the independent variable). Because the right-hand-side pension term is taken to be determined outside any particular individual's decision problem, the retirement outcome can be formulated as a function of the net reward for continued work and simultaneous equations techniques need not be applied.[11]

A variety of empirical studies concerning pensions' role and function in the labor market are identified and discussed in more detail below. It must be stated at the outset, though, that we believe that structural analysis is of most value for predicting the effects of policy changes. Nevertheless, few structural studies currently exist in the pension literature. Producing more and better studies which can do what is needed in the pension arena requires better data than researchers currently have.

If analysts are to undertake further structural analysis in the pension area, it will be necessary to obtain data that permit careful measurement of the separate elements of firms' compensation packages as well as detail on both the worker side and the firm side. Three general types of data are currently available.[12] (1) Detailed plan provisions have been obtained in the form of cross-section surveys; these are limited in that they contain only partial information and, because they capture differences at only one moment in time, cannot be used to isolate the effects of unobserved variables. (2) National-level time series data have also been used to carry out pension analysis in some retirement research. However, aggregation across companies hides interesting cross-sectional differences in behavior, and bias often results when relationships that are nonlinear at the firm level are estimated at the aggregate level. (3) Finally, a few analysts have used microeconomic longitudinal data, especially valuable for analyzing specific workers' retirement patterns as they age. Nevertheless existing panels like this are inadequate in other ways, which will be spelled out in more detail below.

We turn now to a more detailed description of available studies.

11. Adjustments may be made, however, for initial job choice by those with different preferences for retirement (Fields and Mitchell, 1984).
12. For detail on existing data sets which contain pension variables, see the Data Appendix in preparation for the Pension Research Council.

II. Modeling the Role and Function of Pensions in the Labor Market

Our purpose in this section is to review what pensions do in the labor market. Specifically, we analyze the nature of the pension promise, the and the effects of pensions on work incentives; we finish with a discussion of interdependence in decisions determining pensions and other labor market outcomes. The subsequent section reviews the impact of market imperfections and labor market institutions on pension outcomes.

The Nature of the Pension Promise

Many people would probably agree that a primary function of employer-sponsored pensions is to help workers save for retirement. There are a number of reasons why pensions provide an attractive vehicle for savings. For instance, pensions offered at the workplace appear to help employees impose needed "self control," in that regular employer contributions directly to the pension plan eliminate the need for workers to make frequent (and difficult) saving decisions (Thaler and Shefrin, 1981). Group pensions also offer scale economies in investment and administrative costs, making a given dollar of contributions produce more in retirement income when the funds are invested on behalf of larger groups (Mitchell and Andrews, 1981). Advance commitment to workplace benefit plans reduces moral hazard and adverse selection, thus giving employees access to lower-cost group retirement benefits than those obtained individually (Bodie, 1989). The fact that most pension benefits are paid out in the form of an annuity also protects pension participants from outliving their retirement savings; this aspect of group pensions prevents risk-averse older persons from having to curtail consumption drastically so as to avoid outliving their incomes in old age (Kotlikoff and Spivak, 1981). Last but not least, tax law shields most pension contributions from income taxation until retirement, so that retirement savings carried out in a pension have a substantial tax advantage over non-pension savings alternatives (Blinder, 1981; Ippolito, 1985c, 1986a; Woodbury, 1983).

Some researchers focus on the risks inherent in pensions, and emphasize that workers might not actually receive promised pension benefits under some circumstances. For example, someone quitting a job prior to becoming vested loses pension rights, while even vested workers leaving their firm prior to retirement receive a benefit which is likely to be eroded by inflation. Such capital losses serve to focus attention on the uncertainties inherent in the pension promise.

The value of retirement savings to the covered worker and its cost to the providing firm depend on the course of future employment and wages. This value must therefore be discounted using an interest rate that takes account of both the deferred nature of the pension promise and the associated risk. In turn, the value of a pension promise depends on one's view of what pensions are doing. Specifically, the value of a promised pension and how much it costs a firm to offer a pension depend on the nature of the employment arrangement.

In a *spot market*, a firm pays workers according to the value of their productivity in the current period, while a worker's asking price is determined by his or her opportunity cost in the current period. The key feature of the spot labor market is that it clears on the basis of productivity and labor costs at each moment in time, and the worker's remuneration in each period equals the value of his or her marginal product in that period. When a pension figures as a component of labor compensation, spot market theory predicts that, holding the productivity profile constant, wages are lower for workers whose pension accrual is higher, with the value of the pension being measured by its current-period accrual rate.[13] Data on wages and pension accruals would be predicted to show that, for workers of a given productivity level, in any given year, higher pension accruals are offset by lower wages.[14]

In a spot market, the portion of costs attributable to a pension is valued by the accrual pattern specific to that particular pension plan. For example, if a plan is a defined contribution pension, the firm pays a part of labor compensation in the form of a wage and the rest in the form of an immediate contribution to a pension fund held in the worker's name. In this case (and ignoring taxes), the pension accrual will be valued at the employer's contribution amount (perhaps adjusted for risk associated with the portfolio investment). In the case of a defined benefit plan, where benefits are specified according to a particular formula, the worker's spot pension accumulation is equal to the increment to his pension present value based on seniority to date, on the assumption that the current period is his last period of employment. Specifically, the pension valuation method employed in this scenario ignores the (possibly non-zero) probability that a worker might remain with the firm in future periods.[15]

13. We abstract from other non-wage aspects of the job in this discussion.

14. If wages in period t are w_t, and the pension accrual P_t, the estimated tradeoff for a pension-covered worker is given by the coefficient a_p in the following equation: In w_t = as + a_p P_t + a_x X; see Ehrenberg and Smith (1987). The question we are discussing in this section is how P_t should be measured. As will be seen below, reliable estimates of a_p are still not available.

15. The spot calculation also ignores any discrepancy between productivity and compensation costs in future periods such as might arise in the presence of specific investment, or in the opposite direction from repayment of a bond posted by the worker

Some analysts argue that the spot market approach does not apply to pension-covered workers. Here, the view is that the employment relationship is closer to a *long-term contract*, recognizing that pension-covered workers are frequently attached to jobs for long periods of time. In this vein, workers generally have reason to expect to be employed at that same firm in the future with some non-zero probability. In this type of labor market, it is not sufficient to consider pension promises accrued on the basis of work to date. In addition, the worker in each period accumulates a pension option value which reflects the expected value of a deferred payment, contingent on the course of work and pay in the future.[16] In this more complex case, costing pensions must take into account compensation expectations reflecting value outside of the current period, and labor quantity measures should include expected attachment to the firm in future years.

It might be argued that, despite the prevalence of long-term attachment, the labor market for most employees operates as if it were a spot market. Indeed, if workers' pension option values are small, focusing on the year-by-year pension accrual rates may yield an adequate measure of pension accumulations. However, the evidence strongly challenges both versions of the spot market model. Pension accrual rates are quite uneven in many private sector defined benefit pensions, tracing steep peaks and valleys as workers vest in their plans or attain early and normal retirement (Bulow, 1981, 1982; Kotlikoff and Wise, 1985, 1987b). In the federal sector, pension plans with this trait are discussed by Leonard (1987): for instance, at twenty years of service there is a sharp spike in the accrual rate as the military worker becomes eligible for a pension. Increases in pension wealth are then reduced in the remaining years of work. We doubt the spot market model because wage levels do not appear to fall suddenly when pension accrual patterns take a sharp jump upward.[17] Indeed, given the specific role

---

to insure productivity. See Lazear and Moore (1988) for a recent discussion of these issues.

16. See Abowd and Manaster (1982); Lazear and Moore (1988); and Stock and Wise (1988b).

17. See Kotlikoff and Wise (1985). What would be needed for the spot market to hold in view of these discontinuous pension accrual patterns is sudden productivity changes with age, but there is no reason to suspect these hold true. Although available data sets do not directly measure whether and how productivity profiles change with age, there is also evidence that wage profiles for workers with defined benefit plans are at least as steep as those without a pension (Ippolito, 1987; Mitchell and Pozzebon, 1987). In other words, workers with backloaded plans do not have depressed wages in later life, contradicting the spot market theory.

A spot market approach does more than predict that formal wage structures would offset pension accrual spikes which coincide with vesting and qualification for early and normal retirement benefits. It also would predict that the offsetting wage spikes would of necessity be revalued with changes in the inflationary environment. This is because

played by age and service in positioning these spikes, one would expect to see these age and service requirements mirrored in the formal wage and salary structures adopted by larger firms, but no such evidence has been uncovered. These irregularities in pension profiles highlight the need for a model which recognizes that working an additional year makes available to an employee a pension option value of rather significant proportions.

In a parallel manner, the long-term contract approach suggests that understanding pensions' role in determining quantities of labor employed must recognize that long-term employment is the right outcome to observe.[18] Most models of employer demand for labor are theoretical thus far, and the few available empirical studies estimating structural labor demand equations are fundamentally flawed—at least for analyzing demand for pension-covered workers. This is because these analyses typically assume that accrued pay in a given year is equal to workers' productivity, an assumption which ignores the possibility that at any age or tenure productivity may not equal compensation calculated on a spot accrual basis.[19] For example, if compensation structures defer a portion of the reward on the assumption of long-term attachment, then measured compensation and implied productivity of younger workers would be systematically understated.

Pension valuation in both spot and long-term contexts

The following example highlights the key difference in pension values calculated using the spot market versus the long-term contract approach. We use data from the 1983 Survey of Consumer Finance, the only nationally representative U.S. survey to provide labor market and demographic information from individuals together with matched information obtained from their employers which also reports in detail the provisions of covered workers' pension plans.[20] In this sample,

---

pension spikes and backloading are highly sensitive to inflation. Hence formal wage and salary structures would have to be revised to mirror the changing importance of pension spikes as inflation varies. While there is some research on the effect of inflation on pensions (Allen, Clark, and Sumner, 1986), lack of data has precluded an analysis of changes in wage and pension structures with inflation.

18. In the case of long-term attachment, hiring and training costs are allocated over a number of periods. Just as the relation of per worker to per hour costs affects the optimal length of the work week, the size of hiring and training costs will affect the optimal length of attachment. This creates a bias against hiring older workers (Hutchens, 1986a).

19. However, productivity and compensation must match when aggregated over the full period of attachment (Lazear, 1979).

20. Efforts are underway by the BLS to combine the information on the labor market variables for the National Longitudinal Survey of Mature Women (and their spouses) with employer-provided information on their pension plans. The new Health and Retirement Survey will also attempt to provide joint information on covered workers

employees covered by defined benefit plans had on average $20,000 in accrued pension value (1983 dollars), counting from their date of pension eligibility to the survey date and assuming the worker terminated immediately. On an annual basis, the annualized spot market accruals thus computed averaged about 3.8 percent of earnings. In contrast, long-term projected benefits were much larger. For instance, if pension wealth was calculated on the assumption of continued work until retirement age, the average pension accumulation was $47,000 or almost 9 percent of annual earnings (Gustman and Steinmeier, 1989a).[21]

Analogous issues arise in calculating pension liabilities, which are most pertinent to pension funding patterns and how they appear on the sponsoring firm's balance sheet. For many years, corporate balance sheets specifically highlighted the spot market accrued liability, delegating projected liability to a footnote. In recent years, however, there has been increasing emphasis on funding for projected liabilities. Further, public policy has also focused on the importance of assuming prolonged attachment.[22] This is because covered workers are currently guaranteed only their accrued benefits (the spot market view). What this implies is that these workers bear the risk of not receiving their projected benefits, particularly in the event of mergers, takeovers, and company shutdowns.[23]

Several analysts employ hedonic models to evaluate whether and how pensions and wages offset each other in the compensation package. This approach is used to analyze the supply and demand for pensions at the market level by estimating the influence of worker- and firm-side factors influencing tradeoffs for pensions and wages. In the hedonic approach, some elements of the compensation package must appear on the left-hand side, while others appear on the right-hand

---

together with plan descriptions obtained from their employers. Neither survey will be representative of the full population, in each case focusing only on those nearing retirement age.

21. The accrued value of the pension is assumed to be proportionate to the fraction of pay from hire date until retirement, that the employee has earned to date. Further adjustments may be made to reflect likely turnover rates. See Barnow and Ehrenberg (1979).

22. A recent exception is the funding limitation in the Omnibus Budget Reconciliation Act of 1987, which links the funding limit to the accrued rather than the projected liability.

23. The rise of takeovers and such also raises questions about the strength of reputation effects which once were thought to insure workers against abrogation of implicit contracts. For a related analysis, see Pontiff, Schleifer, and Weisbach (1989). On the other hand, most terminations do not impose large pension capital losses on workers because new plans (or spinoffs) give workers past service credit (Ippolito, 1986b).

side of a structural equation (Brown and Rosen, 1982; Ehrenberg, 1980; Smith and Ehrenberg, 1983). Several of these empirical studies are reviewed by Mitchell and Pozzebon (1987), who conclude that there is no concrete evidence that wages and pensions are directly traded off in the compensation package. A recent paper by Montgomery, Shaw, and Benedict (1989) suggests that estimates are more sensible when pension values are measured assuming attachment is prolonged and lasts until retirement, as compared to assuming that the accrual is computed using a spot market concept.

Because very little firm-side information is used in the hedonic estimates derived to date, we cannot be sure that even the aggregate tradeoffs between pension and wages are reliably identified. More generally, the existing hedonic estimates do not yet incorporate what we know about how pensions influence productivity on the demand side. In this sense, the hedonic models estimated to date have almost been reduced-form in spirit.

Irrespective of whether pensions are being measured with a spot or a long-term contract view, limitations in available data present serious problems. Existing surveys of plan formulas often lack good data on wages paid in the offering firms. However, the SCF data suggest that information on plan descriptions can be used to estimate both the current-period accrual rates and the option value of pensions if wage profiles used are very close to actual wages in the firm's narrowly defined industry (Gustman and Steinmeier, 1989a). Distortions will result, however, if the wages used are not closely linked to wages in the industry in which the pension plan is found.

An alternative way of assessing pension values is to take information obtained from individual worker interviews and join it with pension statistics taken from a different source matched according to each covered worker's reported industry. Unfortunately, however, this approach cannot isolate the structure of supply and demand because more information is required on specific firms' wage structures, employment policies, and workforce characteristics. Researchers taking this tack have also been alerted to the fact that there is wide variation in pension plan provisions within industries (Kotlikoff and Wise, 1985, 1987b). Hence, great care is required in selecting appropriate criteria for choosing "representative" plans to match with covered individuals working in a given industry. One possibility is to evaluate each plan separately before matching, and to attribute the average of the accrual profiles within a given industry to all covered workers in that industry. The alternative of trying to find average values for all pension plan parameters is probably very imprecise. By ignoring correlations among plan characteristics and nonlinearities within each pension plan's rules, there is a greater possibility of distorting the description of the average accrual profile.

A different possibility is to measure pension values by the pension receipts of retirees. A serious problem with this strategy is that the group of recipients is inevitably biased toward those who retire early. Insofar as younger retirees receive different benefits from older ones, the benefits estimates will need to be corrected for (choice-based) sample selection. Moreover, lump-sum payments are likely to be missed entirely. In addition, given the rapid spread of pensions over the postwar period and the special treatment of those on board at start-up, pension payments received by current retirees may not be representative of those expected by currently active employees (Ippolito, 1989).

Two further points should be made about the calculation of pension values. First, it is worth noting that approaches which rely on plan descriptions provided by covered individuals have some important weaknesses, primarily because workers are often unable accurately to report their pension plans' provisions. This is taken up again below in the discussion of imperfections in information. Second, there is evidence that pension plan provisions, and the associated accrual profiles, change substantially over time (Ippolito, 1989; Mitchell and Luzadis, 1988a). Accordingly, it is inappropriate for researchers to assume that pension values are static, but rather must make specific allowance for the possibility that pension plans change over time. There currently exist no longitudinal nationally representative surveys of pension plans which would permit researchers to evaluate changes in pension values over time. Evidence on several dozen collectively bargained pension plans does show considerable fluidity (Mitchell and Luzadis, 1988a), and it would be extremely valuable to develop a more representative time series of pension plans over several decades.

Pensions and Retirement

In the last fifteen years, a vast retirement literature has progressed from reduced form studies, which established a simple linkage between pensions and retirement outcomes, to structural analyses more suitable for distinguishing firm-side incentives from employee preferences. Recent structural retirement models also recognize that retirement decision making takes place in an intertemporal setting, to the extent that workers weigh both current and future retirement opportunities when deciding when to leave their jobs.[24] For this reason, most

24. This point was first recognized by Burkhauser (1979), who devised an income maximizing model of retirement, and was incorporated in a utility maximization frame-

of these studies recognize the key role played by employer-provided pensions: most posit that in the neighborhood of the retirement age, pensions alter the rewards for continued work.

A great deal of empirical evidence has been amassed showing conclusively that pension reward structures powerfully affect older workers' decisions about when to leave their main jobs.[25] Specifically, this occurs when an employee's rewards for continued work fall below the value of his or her full-time leisure, or below the returns from work on an alternative job plus any change in the value of leisure as a result of the job change. Researchers have also found that workers with more generous pensions tend to retire earlier than do those with lower levels of pension benefits. Finally, workers tend to defer retirement when they are offered pension rewards for doing so; that is, employees continue to work when their pension plans provide them with higher benefit present values for continued work.

What these models have in common is that they posit that older workers formulate a sort of cost-benefit analysis, comparing the utility of continuing to work (including earnings) with the utility of retiring, where the latter is powerfully affected by Social Security and all relevant employer-provided benefits (including pensions). For instance, Social Security provisions such as the retirement earnings test are incorporated in the budget constraint formulated in a number of these studies. Proposed Social Security policy changes including the 1983 reforms, and ongoing proposals for crediting work after retirement on an actuarially fair basis, have also been simulated using these models (Burtless and Moffitt, 1984; Fields and Mitchell, 1984; Gustman and Steinmeier, 1985b, 1989d). One important element of the post-retirement budget constraint that has not yet been properly modeled is post-retirement health insurance, a benefit which is only recently being recognized as extremely costly to providing firms and tremendously valuable to retirees (Clark, 1987a; Rappaport, 1988, 1989). What is not clear is whether such non-pension benefits typically offset or exacerbate retirement incentives inherent in pension provisions. Future firm-specific data collection efforts must recognize all important pre- and post-retirement benefit plans including pensions, so as not erroneously to attribute behavioral patterns to one benefit when perhaps another might be more influential.

---

work by Gordon and Blinder (1980). Fields and Mitchell (1984) went further by paying serious attention to the institutional richness of the life-cycle budget constraint facing older workers, while Gustman and Steinmeier (1983, 1985a) analyzed retirement in the face of a minimum-hours constraint on the main job and reduced wage offers on partial-retirement jobs.

25. Earlier studies are surveyed in Mitchell and Fields (1982); Quinn, Burkhauser, and Myers (1990) review the more recent literature.

Many studies estimate retirement equations for samples of men, but only a few analysts have examined women's retirement patterns. An important early study by Anderson, Clark, and Johnson (1980) develops the framework for analysis, elaborating on interdependencies of retirement decisions within the family. Several empirical studies have been conducted on the determinants of women's retirement patterns for the cohort of women retiring in the 1970s, and suggest a coherent story. Wives' own economic variables appear to have a relatively weak effect on their retirement patterns, while "non-economic" variables such as having a husband in poor health play a much more important role.[26] Whether the dramatic changes in women's labor market attachment patterns observed over the last forty years in the United States will modify retirement patterns among future cohorts of women has yet to be seen.

Researchers continue to seek better ways of formulating more realistic behavioral models, relaxing assumptions about perfect foresight and allowing for the fact that retirees face changing circumstances and sometimes change their minds, leading to reverse flows out of retirement.[27] These models improve on the life cycle/perfect foresight framework which suffers from misspecification bias. Such extensions typically demand more detailed information than has generally been available in the past, including workers' savings and consumption patterns over time. Some new and provocative findings are emerging from these studies, especially regarding the inability of older workers to borrow against future income and the role that this type of liquidity constraint plays in the retirement process.[28]

There are problems with this new line of investigation, however. Incorporating information on consumption patterns may produce bias in retirement estimates if the consumption patterns of the aged are improperly modeled. Another problem is that savings and consumption measures are notoriously imprecise. Errors in measurement of consumption may spill over into the estimates of parameters underlying the retirement decision. Still another difficulty with recent studies on retirees' consumption patterns is that they typically ignore pensions' effects on retirement, partly because including pensions would be difficult econometrically, and partly because the authors use data sets which contain imprecise pension information. As a result, pension-

---

26. See for instance Hanoch and Honig (1983); Honig (1985); Hurd (1988); and Pozzebon and Mitchell (1989).

27. See for instance Berkovec and Stern (1988), and Rust (1988, 1989).

28. Questions about liquidity constraints, raised most recently by Robb and Burbidge (1989), have been explored by Burtless and Moffitt (1984, 1985) in an empirical retirement context.

covered workers have been eliminated from the sample, or else the effects of pension benefits are completely ignored in the analysis.[29]

Although econometric advances have been made in the pension/ retirement area, much empirical analysis has been limited in scope because of data problems. For instance, researchers rarely have access to accurate descriptions of the pension formulas covering retired workers. Analysts using the Retirement History Survey (RHS), for instance, have nationally representative worker data but woefully inadequate pension information, because pension data in the RHS are self-reported. Accordingly, although the level of benefits is known, analysts are forced to impute rates of accrual using industry averages (Gustman and Steinmeier, 1986a). However, as was mentioned earlier, this process is error ridden because there is wide variation in accrual rates among pension plans. Only three study teams have obtained actual pension formulas to analyze the effects of pension incentives on retirement behavior; they conclude that there is strong evidence linking pension incentives to workers' retirement ages. Fields and Mitchell (1984) use a longitudinal sample of retirees from fourteen firms, while Burkhauser (1979), Stock and Wise (1988a, b), and Kotlikoff and Wise (1989) use a single firm. Because the data sets used are not representative of the entire universe of pension-covered workers, empirical findings cannot be generalized. The consequence of this data problem is that estimates of the effects of pensions on retirement available for policy analysis are severely limited. Predictions must be derived using results drawn either from a nationally representative data set containing imprecise self-reported pension descriptions, or from a nonrepresentative sample containing good pension information. A high priority data need is a nationally representative longitudinal data set on workers as they near and enter retirement, linked with a clear and complete representation of their pension incentives over time.[30]

There are several other data needs in the pension/retirement area. First, there is only one technically sophisticated study of the effects of enhanced early-retirement benefits or "early-out windows" (Lumsdaine, Stock, and Wise, 1990). Because publicly available surveys on

29. The Retirement History Survey is employed by Rust (1988) and the National Longitudinal Survey by Berkovec and Stern (1988). Both data sources are criticized by Fields and Mitchell (1984) as being inadequate for the purpose of examining pension effects on retirement. This is because discontinuities in pension accrual profiles can be detected in the reported data, but the size of these discontinuities can only be crudely estimated.

30. A promising data set for such an analysis is the NLS Survey of Mature Women, which is being altered for use as a retirement survey by matching employer-provided pension data to files of pension-covered women and their husbands. The prospective Health and Retirement Survey (HRS) also holds promise in this regard.

the topic do not exist, this study uses data only from a single firm. Second, there is so far not enough information to compare data on actual pension incentives with evidence on what the workers themselves perceive about their pension plans. Such a comparative study would be valuable in comparing the biases from using self-reported versus actual pension formulas in the retirement context. To date, there is no objective evidence on the size of the biases that result when various types of self-reported information are used as a basis for estimating the retirement incentives in pension plans.[31]

Lack of data has also stood in the way of evaluating demand-side explanations for differences in pension incentives between one firm and the next. One motivation for designing pensions to promote early retirement posits that it becomes increasingly difficult to monitor workers as they age (Parsons, 1983). Another explanation is that firms encouraging early retirement utilize their pension formulas to "buy out" more expensive older employees. Empirical work on the topic is in its infancy, but suggests that the buy-out hypothesis may be a fruitful one to examine (Luzadis and Mitchell, 1989). Yet a different approach to understanding demand side differences in pension incentives postulates that some firms use defined benefit pension plans as a personnel tool to reduce older workers' compensation legally without violating age discrimination rules (Lazear, 1983; Hutchens, 1986a).[32] However, there remain some unanswered questions about a number of these hypotheses, especially those that suggest that pension provisions should be keyed to the attainment of particular ages (perhaps with the exception of some minimum service criteria). More than 40 percent of all workers in defined benefit plans have years of service rather than age as a key factor determining pension eligibility (Gustman and Steinmeier, 1989a).

Once again a data set which includes information about firms, their pension plans, and features of their work forces would go a long way toward promoting better understanding of the jointly determined pension and retirement outcomes. Such a data set would vastly facilitate testing of the demand side hypotheses about the motivation for pensions. Also, it would be possible to investigate the simultaneous interaction of demand and supply side relationships between pensions, compensation structure, and retirement practices.

31. The Survey of Consumer Finances provides self-reported plan descriptions together with employer descriptions of the plans, but the survey was meant for other purposes and is not well suited for analysis of retirement. Bernheim (1988) has conducted a similar study in the case of Social Security benefit structures.

32. Though recent regulations require pensions to credit for work after normal retirement age, many plans continue to embody real financial penalties for work after early retirement eligibility.

The Pension-Mobility Relationship

Several empirical studies have examined the relationship of pension coverage to turnover, quits, and layoffs. On the whole, these studies demonstrate that pensions not only affect mobility at older ages (retirement) but are associated with reduced turnover among younger employees as well.[33] Tenure has also been found to be positively related to pension coverage.[34]

It is generally assumed that the pension-mobility relation reflects the effect of a disincentive to move created by backloading of pension benefit formulas. Backloading means pension benefit accruals rise more than proportionately as retirement age approaches. However, there are a number of unanswered questions about the pension-mobility relation, which lead us to doubt the importance of backloading in reducing the cost of turnover by newly hired or prime age workers.

One explanation for the pension-mobility relationship is that some firms invest in workers by paying for substantial hiring and training costs. Hence these employers need to regulate turnover so as to guarantee a pay-back period that is long enough to warrant the investment in human capital. A negative pension-mobility link may be due to the efforts of the firm to reduce mobility incentives among those already employed. A related hypothesis focuses on the selection of workers who are least likely to leave by virtue of their own preferences. If some workers are likely to be "stayers" while others expect high turnover ("movers"), it will pay the firm to discriminate between these types of employees by sorting out those workers who, by preference, are movers. A bonus that is conditional on long-term attachment is worth less to a mover and will achieve the desired goal (Salop and Salop, 1976). Such a bonus system also improves productivity since search, hiring, and training costs are reduced. Without a deferred payment system, workers contemplating changing employers have little incentive to take into account the effects on the employer of their decision to move.

Some criticize this theory on the grounds that defined benefit pension plans are not particularly efficient ways to screen out likely quitters at the time of initial hire. This is because hiring and training costs typically occur at the beginning of the employment period, so employers would find most costly turnover close to the time of hire. However, defined benefit pension plans typically do not penalize short-time

33. See for instance Allen, Clark, and McDermed (1987); Bartel and Borjas (1977); McCormick and Hughes (1984); and Mitchell (1982 and 1983).
34. See for instance Wolf and Levy (1984) and Allen, Clark, and McDermed (1987).

employees the most. Instead, pension formulas are typically quite back-loaded—defined benefit plans impose large mobility costs on workers within ten years of qualifying for early retirement, but create much less of a turnover disincentive among newly hired employees (Gustman and Steinmeier, 1987, 1989a).

Another way in which pensions might reduce turnover is through their vesting provisions, which deter workers from leaving firms until they have worked long enough to be guaranteed an eventual retirement benefit (Schiller and Weiss, 1979). However, pension accruals are small enough at the time of vesting so that losses due to turnover during the first years of employment are likely to be slight (Kotlikoff and Wise, 1985, 1987b). Direct calculations of the effects of reducing vesting from ten to five years also suggest that recent changes in vesting rules, and related requirements for crediting work at young ages, are unlikely to affect turnover behavior substantially (Gustman and Steinmeier, 1989d).

Whether pension coverage is truly correlated with the difference between a worker's wage on his current job and on his next-best alternative is a fundamental question that still requires an answer. If there is a positive correlation, then estimating the effect of pension coverage on turnover will overstate the true effect of pension backloading in reducing turnover unless the gap is appropriately controlled for. Simply including a measure of the level of the wage on the pension-covered job, without controlling for alternative wages, will not eliminate this bias.

Empirical studies disagree on the actual extent to which pension backloading explains turnover. In some studies, backloading appears to explain much of the difference in turnover between those in pension- and non-pension-covered jobs (Allen, Clark, and McDermed, 1987). However, these estimates are not internally consistent, since they suggest that a dollar of benefits due to pension backloading has a much greater effect on turnover than does an extra dollar of wages (Gustman and Steinmeier, 1987). A recent study suggests that the lower turnover is explained by a wage premium which is also paid to workers on pension-covered jobs and not pension backloading (Gustman and Steinmeier, 1990). Another of that study's findings also casts doubt on the view that pensions strongly deter mobility. It turns out that workers covered by defined contribution plans are also less likely to change jobs, even though defined contribution plans are not back-loaded. This suggests that the apparent negative relationship between plan coverage and mobility may reflect the effects of omitted variable bias, with the pension measure taking the credit for the effects of an unmeasured wage premium.

At least as perplexing as the findings on backloading is evidence indicating that pensions reduce layoffs as much as they reduce quits, or maybe even more. Allen, Clark, and McDermed (1988) attribute this finding to the constraints that the implicit pension contract creates for the dismissal policies of the firm. Mitchell (1982) attributes the finding to a reduction in quits from the layoff status. Neither explanation has been tested directly.

Once again, firm-level data would prove invaluable in understanding whether pensions have been designed to affect mobility and whether such policies have been motivated by a desire to economize on hiring and training costs. Thus far, only limited data are available indicating the hiring and training costs of firms.[35] A data set obtained from firms which provided information on benefits, hiring and training, turnover rates of the covered work force, and wages would be enormously helpful.

Pensions and Work Incentives

Under a defined benefit plan, the pension accrual rate declines after early or normal retirement age. The reason is that, after qualifying for retirement, there is a cost to continued work that was not previously relevant (i.e., benefits are forgone) (Bulow, 1982). As noted above, productivity may fall below compensation with increasing frequency even though downward wage adjustments for workers at older ages are precluded by law. Therefore, the decline in the accrual rate may help to bring productivity into line with compensation.

Lazear (1979) has shown that, as part of a compensation scheme designed to increase productivity over the life cycle, it may pay for the firm and the worker to agree to make the wage profile steeper than the productivity profile. In that way the worker posts a bond which will be forfeited if he or she is terminated due to shirking. The proceeds from the consequent increase in worker productivity can then be shared, hence we call it the "productivity-enhancement" theory of pensions. At the end of such a contract, employment must be terminated, otherwise workers would like to extend the employment relation beyond the optimal time period. Lazear's analysis thus motivates mandatory retirement policies as devices adopted to overcome older workers' desire to continue to be paid above their productivity levels. An alternative to mandatory retirement is a defined pension benefit formula which

35. The EEOP survey, a survey of firms, was undertaken in connection with an experimental Labor Department program that was terminated before completion. These data emphasize hiring and training costs for newly hired low-wage workers.

generates benefit cuts for those working beyond normal retirement age; this brings compensation of older workers back into line with productivity. Lazear (1982) further argues that some pension plans' early retirement features provide severance pay that allows termination when a superior opportunity is available to the worker elsewhere.[36]

Direct tests of this productivity-enhancement theory are not currently available. In principle, it would be necessary to observe wage and productivity profiles for the same firm in the presence and absence of a pension in order to determine whether productivity is higher, or the wage profile is made steeper, when a pension is offered for the firm time. Simple comparisons of productivity or wage profiles between firms with and without pensions will not do. When a set of systematic differences between the firms motivates one to adopt a pension of a particular type and the other to choose not to be covered, pensions are a dimension of outcome, not an explanatory variable determined by considerations outside the problem. Along the same lines, it should also be recognized that deferred compensation is only one of a number of compensation policies available to firms. Thus far there are no surveys that would permit analysts to relate pension provisions to parameters reflecting the availability (and efficacy) of alternative supervision or compensation policies. Nor do we have any information on the differences among firms in the characteristic paths of worker productivity over the life cycle, or typical terms of attachment.

Though no direct tests of the productivity-enhancement theory have yet been formulated, indirect approaches exist to evaluate the empirical applicability of the model. One approach asks whether observed plan characteristics and accrual profiles are consistent with the model. A second approach uses the model to explain differences among pensions adopted by different firms, to see whether observed behavior coincides with the model's predictions about relationships between pensions, mandatory retirement, and other characteristics of firms'

36. There remain several unanswered questions about the productivity-enhancement hypothesis. It is not yet clear how this theory explains the importance of service-related criteria for retirement eligibility, and why it is not necessary to provide a strong work incentive for an individual hired at an early age who has qualified for retirement benefits, while a worker of the same age who joined the firm later may face a large cost to delayed retirement. Nor is it clear that the pattern of penalties which is directly created by pension backloading corresponds to the pattern which would be ideal to discourage shirking. The absolute value of the penalty rises, peaks typically after a decade or two of attachment, and then declines. In relative terms, the penalty rises as a fraction of the remaining wage until early or normal retirement age is reached. More generally, a given pension formula will create a contract that varies in its effect on workers hired at different ages, and with the inflation rate. These issues are not yet well addressed in current theory.

personnel and supervisory policies. Last, pension plans are examined over time to determine whether they changed in a manner coincident with observed changes in the economic environment or in regulatory policy, as predicted by the model. Each approach is described briefly.

Broadly speaking, many if not all observed plan characteristics, accrual profiles, and the association of pension coverage and mandatory retirement are consistent with the productivity-enhancement view of pensions. In accordance with predictions, benefit accruals often become negative after the firm's early retirement age (Lazear, 1982). It should be noted that it is important to distinguish between actuarial and economic incentives when evaluating incentives for early retirement (Ippolito, 1990). For instance, a retiree accepting an early pension may appear to benefit from an actuarial subsidy if he retires early, but because continued wage growth is forfeited on leaving, the worker also forfeits the right to future benefit improvements once he leaves. Hence an actuarial early retirement incentive may fail to provide an economic incentive to accept early retirement. Nevertheless, when economic pension incentives are computed which take this into account, some researchers still find evidence for economic early retirement incentives (Fields and Mitchell, 1984). Nevertheless, negative accrual rates after early retirement are certainly not universal in the defined benefit arena (Gustman and Steinmeier, 1989a). Whether the accrual profile turns negative upon qualification for early retirement, and the associated extent of backloading up to the point where the worker qualifies for early retirement, appear to depend on the generosity of special early retirement benefits (Kotlikoff and Wise, 1987c).

One might try to evaluate the productivity-enhancement theory and other behavioral pension models by using cross-sectional data to explain differences among pensions adopted by diverse firms. The evidence shows that cross-sectional studies often do reveal general patterns of association.[37] However, there is a problem with efforts to draw conclusions on the motivation for the pensions from cross-section profiles in that there is usually no information on what productivity, wages, and employment would have been in the absence of pension plans. This is a standard selection problem: it cannot be concluded that removing a pension would produce outcomes similar to those in a firm which never had a plan, and vice versa. Hence such findings cannot generally be used to distinguish among theories because of the inability to be certain that observable variables adequately adjust for differences among firms adopting different pension plans. An innovative

---

37. Kotlikoff and Smith (1983) analyze the relation between plan characteristics and a wide variety of firm and industry factors. A related study using the SCF appears in Gustman and Steinmeier (1986c).

approach posits that delayed payment contracts of the Lazear type will result in discrimination in hiring against older workers (Hutchens, 1986a). The evidence is consistent with this view, inasmuch as pensions and mandatory retirement rules appear to have been more common in firms that avoided hiring older workers. A later chapter finds supporting evidence that long-term contracts are more in evidence when firms have a difficult time supervising employee output (Hutchens, 1986b). Unfortunately the data sets used contain no information on individual worker productivity, precise measures of supervision technology, and changes in product demand; and perhaps as a consequence, empirical results are subject to alternative interpretations.[38]

Evidence contrary to the productivity-enhancement theory is offered by Crockett and Stern (1989), who review historical data on mandatory retirement provisions and find that relatively few workers were covered in the past, casting doubt on the notion of this type of long-term contract. These authors somewhat overstate their case, since they claim that all workers in a Lazear-type world would have been subject to mandatory retirement before it was prohibited, whether or not they had a pension. As Hutchens (1989) points out, whether a firm would adopt a long-term contract of this type depends on supervision costs and the economic prospects of the firm. Nevertheless, prior to recent reforms, half the labor force was not subject to mandatory retirement, which raises questions about the theory's generalizability. Better data would permit identification of cases when the theory applies and when it does not; researchers should be warned against applying this model uniformly.

Crockett and Stern also offer other evidence against Lazear's theory. They argue that pension programs should all include powerful early retirement incentives, but find this prediction to be inconsistent with the data. They also contend that the theory predicts that workers who are subject to mandatory retirement should be less likely to retire early than are those who are not, and again do not find this prediction empirically substantiated. It must be said, however, that this study does not fully explain observed differences among firms in accordance with the costs of supervision or other factors affecting the value of a long-

38. The limited power of cross-sectional tests when conducted with sparse data sets currently available is particularly striking when looking at union-nonunion pension plan differences. One-third of all workers covered by defined benefit plans were employed in union firms in 1983 (Gustman and Steinmeier, 1986c), where dismissal for cause in these firms is notoriously difficult (Medoff, 1979). Hence it would seem that unionized firms would not use pensions to deter shirking. Yet evidence in favor of the shirking hypothesis is drawn from a sample of union plans where the shirking hypothesis might appear to be least relevant (Luzadis and Mitchell, 1989).

term pension contract. Indeed, the contribution of this study is that it emphasizes the importance of having more detailed information about the firm for use in pension analysis, and highlights the fact that there is probably more than one explanation for pensions' role and function in the labor market. The tests provide a clue that the motivation described by Lazear does not apply uniformly across all firms, but as yet do not establish why plan provisions have been adopted in some firms but not in others, nor can we say with any precision how plan provisions help companies attain multiple goals.

A different way to explain cross-sectional differences among pension plans focuses directly on productivity consequences of pension choices. One study added a productivity index to an industry-level wage equation where a pension measure already appeared as a control (Allen and Clark, 1987). This productivity factor was found to have no significant impact on the estimated positive pension-wage tradeoff. That study also investigated the relationship between pensions and productivity in several descriptive specifications, concluding again that the relationship was not statistically significant. This is a puzzling conclusion, since it seems likely that profit-seeking firms would not offer costly pensions if they did not enhance productivity (assuming that pension benefits are not offset by equalizing wage differentials). However, it could also be argued that statistically insignificant findings might result because entry eventually competes away productivity and profit advantage, and not because pensions fail to improve productivity. Moreover, it is important to recognize once again that cross-section data do not provide observations on productivity before and after the pension is adopted, and there is no easy way to remove the effects of self-selection by firms and subsequent market adjustments. In general, no strong conclusions can be drawn, since at best the evidence is suggestive.

Last but not least, some researchers examine pension theory by evaluating whether pension plans changed over time in a manner coincident with observed changes in the economic environment or in regulatory policy, as predicted by the model. While this strategy comes closest to testing the theory, it has thus far been difficult to take into account all possible changes in other explanatory variables while dealing appropriately with unobservables. One example of this approach focuses on the sensitivity of pension incentives to inflation. Pension accrual profiles prove to be quite variable depending on the overall inflation rate (Kotlikoff and Wise, 1985, 1987b), which surprises observers expecting either that inflation would be neutralized by pension benefit formulas, or that inflation would be factored into the formulas so as to enhance productivity and deter mobility. So far, no longitudinal study systematically investigates the effects of inflation on pension plan provisions.[39] A different "natural experiment" occurred when mandatory retirement was abolished in the U.S. (the mandatory age was first extended to 70, and then abolished for the majority of all employees). If, as the model predicts, firms used pensions to offset the change in regulations, it would be expected that early retirement benefits would have increased when the mandatory retirement cap was lifted (Lazear, 1983). Evidence consistent with this hypothesis has been detected in large firms (Lazear, 1983) and union pension plans (Luzadis and Mitchell, 1989). However, as those authors recognize, the results do not rule out the possibility that other policies were responsible for the findings, since several other tax and regulatory changes occurred during the period under study.

In sum, pension researchers have not yet distinguished empirically between different theoretical models of the effects of pensions on productivity. This should be a high priority in future research, in order better to inform analysis of the consequences of adopting alternative pension policies. In our view, a fruitful approach is to use longitudinal data on firms offering pensions through time, with careful documentation on the plans themselves, the firms' characteristics, and information about the workers at the firms. Only then will it be possible to standardize for observable and unobservable firm characteristics. Testable implications should then be developed and examined, and careful econometric specification developed to isolate key structural parameters. In this way it will be possible to glean information about how regulatory changes interact with characteristics of specific firms and work forces.

Interdependence in Decisions Determining Pensions, Savings, Insurance, and Labor Market Outcomes

Although a review of the insurance and savings motivations for pensions is beyond the scope of this chapter, it is useful at least to mention within the present context the relations between labor market outcomes, pensions, and savings and insurance decisions.[40] This is because workers' demand for pensions, and firms' supply of pensions, are intimately related to the supply of and demand for insurance and non-pension savings.

39. Convincing explanations are also lacking for post-retirement pension adjustments documented by Allen, Clark, and Sumner (1986).

40. For recent reviews of the insurance and retirement savings literature, see Bodie (1989) and Hurd (1989).

If workers and firms had perfect foresight, they could design pension and earnings streams to compromise in an optimal fashion between their conflicting objectives. In such a hypothetical world, analysts could focus solely on pay and pension profiles to evaluate the way that labor markets work.

Information on older workers' consumption paths could provide a check on estimates of key parameters, such as the rate of time preference, estimates which have been obtained by observing retirement outcomes. However, as noted in the discussion of retirement behavior, retirees' consumption appears to decline with age, a path inconsistent with predictions from a simple life-cycle certainty model (Hurd, 1989; Robb and Burbidge, 1989). Of course in reality many different types of uncertainty plague both employees and employers, making work and savings behavior interdependent and more complex than would be the case in the hypothetical perfect-certainty world.

Pensions in a risky environment

One type of uncertainty shaping the structure of pensions is uncertainty about the length of life, though this insurance motivation is clearly not the sole rationale for pensions (Kotlikoff and Spivak, 1981). Pensions are also uniquely suitable as a vehicle for overcoming the effects of asymmetric information and adverse selection which would otherwise undermine the annuity market. If workers strongly value the annuity feature of the defined benefit plan, then the decision to provide pensions, and features of these plans, should reflect the basic labor market considerations relevant to pension and retirement policy, as well as the demand for annuities derived from the savings and insurance motivation. What this means is that the decisions relating pensions to the interesting labor market outcomes like retirement and job change are not easily separated from workers' and firms' decisions regarding savings and insurance. On the one hand this makes it very hard to model the workers' valuation of pensions, but on the other hand information on savings may be used to learn more about the relation of pensions to retirement. For example, Rust (1988, 1989) has used information on older people's joint labor supply and savings behavior to isolate tradeoffs between income and leisure in a dynamic context, as they adjust to unforeseen events such as changes in market opportunities.[41]

41. Empirical researchers face many pitfalls when incorporating information on savings and compensation into labor supply analyses, because (a) savings is measured very poorly in many data sets; (b) it is difficult to isolate changes in asset prices over time;

Another way that risk plays a role in the pension arena has to do with the risks presented by changes in the economic environment. For example, workers may use a defined benefit pension plan to insure each other against fluctuations in the economy, transferring benefits from well-off cohorts to those who experienced unusually low returns on invested pension assets (Ippolito, 1987). Another very important type of risk implicit in the pension promise has to do with the fact that workers do not actually know the real value of eventual benefits at retirement. For workers with defined contribution plans, pension assets fluctuate day by day as portfolio values change, and these fluctuations can dramatically alter benefit payouts. In the case of defined benefit plans, covered workers are also at risk (Green, 1985). Importantly, if a defined benefit plan terminates, current law guarantees nominal benefits (and only up to a cap); the worker is not guaranteed the full value of benefits indexed to wages until the worker's retirement date (Ippolito, 1989). What this implies is that terminated workers in a defined benefit plan bear inflation costs (having their benefits eroded between the termination and retirement dates), and also the loss of an option on benefits tied to pre-retirement wages that they would have accrued if the plan had not terminated (Ippolito, 1985c; Gustman and Steinmeier, 1989c). Termination and reversion patterns are being studied to determine whether worker and firm behaviors are responding predictably to pension reversions, in light of the theories outlined above. Because of the emergence of financial innovations affecting the incentives for pension plan termination, and the rise in pension overfunding due to the stock market boom, careful analysis is required to determine whether these have substantially changed the way firms and workers value pension promises.

More complete models are required which spell out the relation between pension uncertainty and the way pensions are valued, in order better to predict behavioral responses to pension policies. For example, requiring pensions to credit continued employment after the plan's normal retirement age raises the implicit price to the firm of providing a pension. These policies will have a smaller impact on demand for pensions if workers strongly value the insurance these plans provide, versus the pension of which the sole purpose is as a tool of personnel policy. Conversely, the form and function of pension risk may in turn

---

(c) many simplifying assumptions are required to estimate such models which may make the model fairly unrealistic; and (d) people save for a number of different reasons, and the relative importance of the different motivations for savings probably varies with income (Rust, 1988; Bernheim, 1987). Thus far analysts primarily interested in retirement, for instance, have not formulated models sufficiently well specified to explain all relevant savings motivations.

affect workers' labor supply decisions: for instance, a worker may postpone retirement in the event of adverse investment outcomes (Bodie and Samuelson, 1989). This area of research is as yet in its infancy.

Pensions and capital market imperfections

A few analysts have noted the importance of capital market imperfections and, in particular, liquidity constraints affecting older workers' decisions on when to retire (Blinder, 1981; Crawford and Lilien, 1981; Burtless and Moffitt, 1984 and 1985). This is important in the pension context because borrowers cannot generally secure a loan with their future labor income; nor can lenders legally attach pension (or Social Security) assets in the event of default. This produces differences between the rates at which people can lend and borrow money, in turn influencing the labor market behavior of people who would have preferred to reallocate consumption from the post-retirement to their pre-retirement period by borrowing.

Some affected individuals who would have wished to borrow may instead alter their retirement behavior so as to reallocate consumption from the period of retirement to the period of work. In other words, for some people, pensions or Social Security may concentrate too much income in the post-retirement period (Blinder, 1981).[42] For those individuals, the retirement and savings decisions become inextricably intertwined. The degree of interrelationship could vary by income: for instance, pensions are often designed to benefit highly paid executives, yet lower wage workers become covered because of tax law, which requires their coverage if the pension accruals are to be tax-exempt. On this notion, liquidity constraints could bind selectively for lower-income workers (a tendency reinforced by the progressive structure of Social Security benefits). Higher-wage workers, not on the margin of borrowing, may act as though capital market imperfections are irrelevant to their pension and labor market behavior.

Although no empirical researchers have examined this phenomenon in the pension arena, some contend that Social Security has played

42. Liquidity constraints may work in the opposite direction when workers desire insurance against disability and can use pension plans' early retirement provisions to provide this protection (Nalebuff and Zeckhauser, 1985; Lapp, 1985).

If capital markets impose binding liquidity constraints, savings, or at least the flow of marginal adjustments in savings, is in the opposite direction from that predicted by more traditional life-cycle explanations of savings. That is, despite the fact that earnings are realized prior to retirement, consumption is redistributed via pensions from the post- to the pre-retirement period.

a similar role. Specifically, as a consequence of the start-up phase of the Social Security system, some workers may have attained old age with unexpectedly high post-retirement incomes (Burtless, 1986). This in turn may have lowered other forms of savings including, presumably, pension saving. There are, however, important reasons to doubt that pensions caused too much income to be concentrated in the retirement period for the typical worker attaining retirement age in the 1980s. For one thing, pensions differ from Social Security in that they are compensation packages voluntarily arrived at (from the viewpoint of employee groups, if not for individual workers). In other words, workers who agreed to be voluntarily liquidity-constrained by a pension would have to be promised some other benefit to offset the cost of being over-pensioned. This seems logical even if pensions were a "self-control" mechanism used to force employees to save for their own retirement (Thaler and Shefrin, 1981); it is unlikely that resulting liquidity constraints would be highly distortionary.[43]

It should also be noted that current retirees with pensions were highly unionized during their working careers. The major effect of unions is to increase the probability of pension coverage. They do not appear to raise pension values, at least not among currently covered workers (Freeman, 1985; Gustman and Steinmeier, 1986c). It seems unlikely that unions would have overburdened their workers with pensions. Indeed, in industries such as construction, there historically was no explicit bargaining over pensions; rather, bargaining was over total compensation, and the union was free to allocate compensation between pensions and wages (Gustman and Segal, 1972). Hence there remains a question as to why unions in such a position would choose to over-pension their members.

In sum, analysts interested in studying pensions and labor market outcomes should recognize more clearly the interdependencies among retirement, savings, and insurance in order to avoid a distorted view of the behavior underlying pension choice. This suggests that future studies of the demand for and provisions of pension plans should attempt to incorporate information on both workers' and firms' finan-

---

43. On the assumption that the life-cycle model explains the pattern of consumption and savings over time, a direct examination of saving and dissaving provides ambiguous evidence about whether liquidity constraints are binding. On the one hand, there appears to be little direct savings for retirement (Venti and Wise, 1989b). This suggests a corner solution due to excess annuity income in retirement years. On the other hand, assets in the older population take the form of housing equity, and retirees do not tend to draw down their housing wealth even when it is possible to do so (that is, even in the case of those who move anyway; see Venti and Wise, 1989a). This suggests that there is little desire among retirees to shift consumption toward the present from the remaining retirement years or from bequests.

cial status, though the burden of obtaining such data will be formidable.

III. Pensions, Market Structure, and Labor Market Institutions

This section reviews available evidence on the impact of market structures and labor market institutions on pension outcomes. Four areas are investigated: the effects of imperfect information, the role of market structure, union effects, and regulatory constraints.

Imperfect Information

Because pensions are remarkably complex, modelers have begun to recognize that both workers and firms may be laboring under poor information and lack of understanding regarding what the pension plan does, and such imperfect information may lead to unexpected behaviors. For instance, workers who miscalculate may consume less optimally, or retire earlier or later, than they would wish if they had a better understanding of their pension rewards and risks. Also, pensions may be so complicated that it is not cost effective for firms to purchase all the information required for optimal decision making. [44] Bodie (1989) argues, for example, that even pension experts make mistakes, focusing inappropriately on the replacement rates at the age of retirement, rather than on the more economically relevant path of pension incentives over the full range of retirement possibilities. Worker descriptions of plans have been compared with actual plan formulas and show that employees are poorly informed as to the details of the pension formula, including plan type (Mitchell, 1988). These comparisons also suggest that although the median worker has reasonable expectations about when he or she will be eligible for early or normal retirement benefits and pension amounts, a sub-group of workers is highly overoptimistic (Gustman and Steinmeier, 1989a). Some analysts have also compared people's retirement intentions with realized behavior, but this exercise requires using particular statistical assumptions about how expectations are both formed and realized (Anderson, Burkhauser, and Quinn, 1986; Bernheim, 1989; Manski, 1989).

To date, only one nationally representative data set, the Survey of Consumer Finances (SCF), matches worker descriptions of pension

---

44. Lazear (1985a) treats the plans themselves as distortionary and discusses the nature of these distortions.

characteristics with plan descriptions provided by the employees' firms. Efforts are needed to collect more data of this kind which can be used to assess systematically how well workers and firms understand their pension plans' provisions, and the consequences of misinformation. Two target groups of workers should be mentioned: those approaching retirement for whom retirement benefit rules are most pertinent, and younger workers for whom accrual and eligibility rules are more important. The latter group is presumed to be able to adjust work effort and job-change behavior in view of pension accruals and perceived pension losses upon termination. In addition, it would be helpful to obtain some indication of how well informed benefits administrators and personnel officers are, insofar as these individuals are instrumental in designing and implementing pension incentives. A survey of worker and firm knowledge of pension incentives and their time paths would provide the kind of consumer information that can enhance market efficiency.

Market Structure Effects

There is a fundamental problem which will continue to plague all research on the supply of and demand for pensions. This arises because the economics profession remains uncertain as to the specific mechanisms generating wage and employment outcomes at the level of the firm. While new data are providing some new methods of approach, there remain questions about the rationales behind particular wage profiles and, perhaps more fundamentally, about whether market rents play a role in shaping the compensation structure.

One set of questions focuses on the relative importance of human capital and on-the-job training, incentive contracts, and the matching of workers to jobs. Research by Abraham and Farber (1988) questions whether observed positive wage/tenure relationships reflect true productivity increases with time worked or, instead, better matching of long-time workers' skills with their job requirements. Various methods have been proposed to purge the selection bias discussed by Abraham and Farber, including one by Topel (1987) who focuses on lateral job changes of more experienced workers. Related questions arise about the extent to which firms use layoffs to purge workers who are less well matched to their jobs. Recent evidence suggests that workers suffering job loss due to plant closings find better jobs than do those who are laid off from ongoing firms (Gibbons and Katz, 1989). A related question is whether employee compensation is tightly linked to the supply price of labor, or whether specific workers receive rents on their jobs. Early efforts to address this question (Segal, 1986) have been taken up more recently by Blanchflower, Oswald, and Garrett (1989), who suggest that workers' wages include rents reflecting their firms' economic condition.

It has been established empirically that large firms pay higher wages even after controlling for all available measures of worker quality (Brown and Medoff, 1989; Katz and Summers, 1989). Pension coverage is more common in large than in small firms; pension coverage is 76 percent in large firms, but only 22 percent in small firms (Andrews, 1985).[45] Efforts to explain this phenomenon have compared the wages of pension-covered workers with those of non-covered workers with similar measured characteristics, and arrive at the same conclusion: pensions are more common in large firms even after many other factors are held constant (Ippolito, 1986a; Mitchell and Pozzebon, 1987; Andrews, 1989).

Continuing uncertainty about the mechanisms determining compensation and employment will certainly spill over into the analysis of pensions. If labor markets, especially nonunion ones, are not fully competitive, future models of pension determination must begin to be modified to take these structural imperfections into account. If firms offering pensions are also paying higher salaries than pay levels their employees could obtain elsewhere, then a steeper wage profile may not be necessary to avoid shirking by workers in pension-covered jobs. Moreover, as can be seen by our emphasis on Lazear's productivity enhancement theory, discoveries about the compensation/employment mechanism, which would show that the human capital theory, the matching theory, or efficiency wage theories are of more or less importance than have previously been realized, will have implications for our understanding of the pension/wage tradeoff over the term of job attachment.

Union Effects

A great deal of empirical evidence shows that union workers are more likely to have pensions than are their nonunion counterparts, and that pension plan characteristics vary systematically with union status.[46] For instance, despite the recent decline in unionization, Gustman and Steinmeier (1986c) found that in 1983 unionization raised overall pension coverage of U.S. private sector workers by about eight per-

45. Although over 40 percent of all employees are attached to firms employing fewer than 100 workers (Oi, 1983; Oi and Raisian, 1985), 85 percent of pensions are held by workers in firms with more than 100 employees (Kotlikoff and Smith, 1983).

46. See Freeman (1985); Hatch et al. (1982); Kotlikoff and Smith (1983); and Leigh (1981).

centage points, or 15 percent above what coverage would have been in the absence of unions.

While this research has yet to move beyond the descriptive stage, it seems clear that it must do more than simply graft a union variable onto empirical equations. This is because the union and nonunion sectors may differ fundamentally in terms of their pension objectives. A rich set of possibilities has been suggested in the literature, but no unifying theme has yet emerged. For instance, Freeman's (1985) "voice" model suggests that unions give more weight to "median" older workers, as opposed to the nonunion work places where the marginal worker is favored. Hence pension rules would be expected to differ markedly in union versus nonunion plans; for example, underfunded pensions may help redistribute monopoly rents in favor of older union members (Weiss, 1985). When enhanced retirement benefits and age-related incentives are adopted to induce older members to retire, there is a quid pro quo for younger members. They move up the seniority queue and obtain greater job security. Others, notably Ippolito (1985b), contend that pension plan underfunding plays a key role in maintaining an efficient contract between unionized workers and their employers; in this case, pension underfunding provides the union with incentives to keep the firm in business. Unions also appear to have a differential effect on pension retirement incentives, tilting benefit rules so as to encourage earlier retirement (Fields and Mitchell, 1984; Gustman and Steinmeier, 1989a). However, among workers with pension plans, unionized employees do not appear to contribute more (Freeman, 1985), or have higher projected benefits (Gustman and Steinmeier, 1989a). On the other hand, reported benefits for currently retired union workers are higher than are the benefits received by currently retired nonunion workers (Allen and Clark, 1986).

Though many of the answers are as yet unknown, there are nevertheless some empirical implications from the conclusion that pension mechanisms differ in the union and nonunion environments. One should be suspicious of descriptive efforts which include dummy variables representing union coverage, while constraining all other coefficients in the estimating equation to be the same between the union and nonunion sectors. This caution will become more important as one proceeds from reduced form to structural analyses where the behavior, and thus the reactions to policy, may be very different between the two sectors.

Taxes, Social Insurance, and Regulatory Constraints

Tax policies, regulatory constraints, and provisions of related government programs (most importantly Social Security) affect the choice of pension coverage and plan provisions, and the associated price, quantity, and quality related outcomes resulting from the interactions of workers' and firms' decisions. While a detailed analysis of specific policies is beyond this chapter's purview, this section sketches in general terms how government regulation affects the environment in which workers and firms make pension decisions.[47]

Most analysts agree that tax policy has played a key role in motivating the growth of pensions in the United States since World War II. The progressive income tax structure and changes in tax provisions over time increased workers' effective tax rates, and analyses of substitutability between pensions and wages explicitly model the tax advantages of deferred compensation (Ippolito, 1985a; Woodbury, 1989). As noted earlier, this tax advantage was especially strong for management; until the recent tightening of discrimination rules and ceilings, it was possible to target large tax breaks on management while controlling pension costs for lower-paid workers.

Another important set of regulatory policies shaping the pension environment are laws affecting the way in which pension benefit accruals are permitted to change as workers age. For instance, regulations in the last two decades raised the mandatory retirement age and then, for most of the private sector, outlawed the practice of imposing mandatory retirement ages. Anti-discrimination rules and provisions of the tax code now require the crediting of pensions after normal retirement age, mitigating the fall in compensation upon qualifying for normal retirement. Benefit ceilings have been lowered. Changes in discrimination rules reduce discrepancies between benefits paid to high and low wage workers, and reduce the use of Social Security offsets and bridge payments meant to raise pension benefits until Social Security kicks in. With the scheduled smoothing of relatively sharp incentives to retire at age 65 created by the Social Security benefit structure, and with the abolition of mandatory retirement, pensions emerge as the fundamental, but constrained instrument for firms to affect retirement behavior. Projecting from the past stream of legislation, it would not be surprising to see further regulatory efforts to limit early retirement incentives. Other legislation under consideration would regulate coverage and the provision of post-retirement adjustments, and further regulate plan terminations. As is evident, a successful model of pensions must incorporate these effects of taxes, social insurance, and regulation.

---

47. Pension studies with a policy focus are too numerous to list here in their entirety, but include work by Anderson (1987), Andrews (1989); Clark, Gohmann, and McDermed (1988); Feldstein (1981, 1983); Fields and Mitchell (1987); Gustman and Steinmeier (1985b, 1986b); Ippolito (1986a, 1989); Lazear (1983, 1985b); Mitchell and Luzadis (1988b); Mitchell (1990); Munnell (1984); Summers (1983); and U.S. Congress (1987).

A general point to make is that mechanical (i.e., non-behavioral) approaches to examining pension policy must be inadequate. For instance, policy makers have from time to time proposed requiring all employers to offer pension coverage. A mechanical assessment of mandating pension coverage might assume, inappropriately, that firms without pensions would simply adopt them without changing other compensation and personnel policies. On the other hand, a more informed policy evaluation would take into account changes in other forms of pay and employment levels, as a result of the rule change. A different pension policy suggested on Capitol Hill would mandate actuarial neutrality for pension benefit formulas. Some ignore the likely effects of doing so, but a careful analysis of such a policy must recognize that firms would certainly react by altering benefit levels and other provisions, as well as the availability of plans. Analogously, there is evidence that when the government abolished mandatory retirement rules, firms did not simply do away with mandatory retirement provisions, but rather altered their pension benefit rules to mitigate this change in the structure of labor costs. To understand the effects of these and numerous other actual and potential pension policies, one must understand the underlying and interdependent behaviors of individual workers, the firms employing them, and other factors which become important at the market level.

IV. Conclusions

This paper has surveyed the literature analyzing the reasons for and consequences of pensions in the labor market. The available evidence suggests that pensions are part of a long-term employment relation.

On the labor supply side, we have described a number of behavioral models relating pension incentives to workers' mobility, retirement, consumption, and savings patterns. Many risks and benefits of various pension arrangements have been examined in the literature. However, we still have an incomplete picture of how workers value specific plan features including the provision of an annuity, uncertainties due to premature plan termination, imperfect inflation protection of benefits, and so on. To date, there is evidence consistent with many of the different worker-side rationales for pensions, but there is also evidence inconsistent with the theories as well.

On the labor demand side, several theories suggest that companies use pensions as a personnel tool to affect productivity. However, existing research does not yet identify which of the competing theories is most accurate, or point out the relative importance of complementary explanations. Empirical work has not yet identified many of the needed structural parameters. Thus there is no direct evidence of the value to the firm of using pension incentives to induce retirement, reduce mobility by cutting hiring and training costs, or identify "stayers." More remains to be learned about how pensions fit into an overall compensation structure which enhances work effort. While there is evidence consistent with many of these explanations, we have also noted findings inconsistent with the various firm-side motivations for offering plans and for structuring the plans in specific ways.[48]

In order for labor market analysis of pensions to advance, it is necessary to move beyond descriptive studies toward structural models which permit tests between pension theories. There is reason to worry that existing empirical estimates of the determinants of pension-related outcomes may be misspecified, because observed pension and related labor market outcomes are not yet fully understood. For example, models which estimate wage/pension tradeoffs could suffer from serious omitted variable bias, because they typically ignore the question of why firms offer pensions.

Structural pension models are also needed to inform pension policy in the next decade. If analysts are to judge whether observed or potential changes in pension regulation will be beneficial or detrimental, it is essential to develop a better understanding of how specific pension features are valued by both workers and firms. We must determine not only the broad outlines of behavior, but also the sizes of key parameters in equations reflecting choices made by the relevant economic agents. Because researchers have not yet formulated a comprehensive idea of what pensions do and why they exist, labor analysts are hampered in their ability to predict with any precision the likely effects of pension reforms of all kinds.

Structural estimation has heavy data requirements. For instance, developing and testing new models of pensions' effects on retirement, savings, and consumption in view of uncertainty cannot be carried out with available surveys. Existing longitudinal data bases do not include good enough pension information to press forward on this front. Research breakthroughs also await the development of information of recent cohorts, so as to determine whether behaviors of people who retired during the 1970s still hold for retirees in more recent years. This is especially important for studies on the effects of pensions on women's mobility and retirement patterns in the context of family

---

48. For example, Bodie (1989), in discussing the retirement insurance motivation for pensions, recognizes the potential importance of personnel policies, and Lazear (1985a), in discussing the incentive models of pensions, recognizes the importance of the retirement insurance motivation. But these motivations are not integrated in the context of a single analysis.

retirement decisions. The National Institute on Aging is seeking to meet some of these needs through their proposed Health and Retirement Survey; also promising in this regard is a current proposal to incorporate pensions into the National Longitudinal Survey of Mature Women.

In sum, we believe there is a pressing need for a nationally representative survey where the unit of observation is the firm, the establishment, or the pension plan. To understand the pension-wage and the pension-turnover/retirement relationship, more information is required on the processes determining compensation and employment. Combining information on employee characteristics, turnover and retirement patterns, company inputs and outputs, and the firm's overall financial characteristics would go a long way toward helping researchers distinguish among the leading explanations for why firms offer pensions.

V. Data Needs: Recommendations

There is a clear and pressing need for more and richer data sets on pensions, the firms offering the plans, and the workers covered. Poor or nonexistent data have seriously hampered researchers from developing the type of detailed understanding required for evaluating many pension regulations and predicting the effects of many proposed policies. Policy and research analysis would be best served by gaining access to information about workers, their pensions, and their firms. Specific data needs and priorities for future data collection efforts include the following:

- A nationally representative panel of pensions with ongoing information on changes in plan provisions would be useful for documenting changing pension incentives over time.
- A nationally representative data set, preferably longitudinal and centered around the firm, is needed. It should match information on employee characteristics with the employer-side data on the pension plans as well as other characteristics of firms, their inputs, and their financial structure. Pension plan descriptions would best be accompanied by information on the distribution of wages of covered workers, their numbers, and other characteristics. Such information is highly sensitive. Perhaps relevant data could be collected but saved, to be made available only after a suitable number of years.
- A nationally representative survey would be useful, which augmented the information described in the point above with time

series of turnover and retirement rates by pension-covered workers. Information on offers of pension benefit enhancements would also be valuable. A statistical base with information about the firms offering such plans, their pension plans, and characteristics of their labor markets could be used to test demand side hypotheses about the motivation for pensions, and to investigate the simultaneous demand and supply side relationships between pensions, compensation structure, and retirement.

- If the data described above were augmented by longitudinal information on each firm's employees, it would be possible to make more significant progress on the structure of supply and demand determining pensions. Two target groups of workers would be worth focusing on: older workers approaching retirement, and younger employees who may adjust their work effort or other behaviors in view of their pension accrual paths and perceived pension losses upon termination. It is important that information be gathered on the workers' activities once they leave the firm, to determine their alternative activities. It would also be helpful to obtain some indication of how well informed personnel officers are.

- Updated longitudinal information based on nationally representative surveys of individuals is being gathered to study retirement behavior. Crucially, plan descriptions from employers will be matched with information provided by individuals in the survey. To further analysis of retirement decisions, these data should provide more detailed information on workers' consumption and asset patterns over time. Efforts to determine covered workers' understanding of their pensions would improve behavioral analysis.

- Pension plan descriptions obtained from employers are complex and exceedingly expensive to code correctly. A centralized facility should be developed for coding employer plan descriptions in a standardized format, and for developing and maintaining appropriate pension software.

Such information is highly sensitive, and expensive to collect and archive. Nevertheless, updated information on plans that could be used to derive representative information on pension values, and the wages and characteristics of covered workers and their firms, would facilitate a great deal of future labor market analysis.

References

Abowd, John M. and Steven Manaster. 1982. "A General Model of Employment Contracting: An Application of Option Theory." Unpublished manuscript. University of Chicago, 1982.

Abraham, Katharine G. and Henry S. Farber. 1988. "Returns to Security in Union and Nonunion Jobs: A New Look at the Evidence." *Industrial and Labor Relations Review* 42, 1 (October 1988): 3–19.

Akerlof, George A. and Lawrence F. Katz. 1989. "Workers' Trust Funds and the Logic of Wage Profiles." *Quarterly Journal of Economics* 106 (August 1989): 525–36.

Allen, Steven G. and Robert L. Clark. 1986. "Unions, Pension Wealth and Age-Compensation Profiles." *Industrial and Labor Relations Review* 39 (July, 1986): 502–17.

———. 1987. "Pensions and Firm Performance." In Morris Kleiner, Richard Block, Myron Roomkin, and Sidney Salsburg, eds., *Human Resources and the Performance of the Firm.* Madison, WI: Industrial Relations Research Association, 1987. pp. 195–242.

Allen, Steven G., Robert L. Clark, and Ann A. McDermed. 1987. "Pensions and Lifetime Jobs: The New Industrial Feudalism Revisited." Final draft report for U.S. Department of Labor, contract no. J-9-M-5-0049, July 1987.

———. 1988. "Why Do Pensions Reduce Mobility?" NBER Working Paper No. 2509, February 1988.

Allen, Steven, Robert L. Clark, and Dan Sumner. 1986. "Post-Retirement Adjustments of Pension Benefits." *Journal of Human Resources* 21, 1 (Winter 1986): 118–27.

Anderson, John. 1987. "Effects of Mandatory Pensions on Firms, Workers and the Economy." In Dallas Salisbury, ed., *Government Mandating of Employee Benefits.* Washington, DC: Employee Benefit Research Institution, 1987.

Anderson, Katharyn H., Richard V. Burkhauser, and Joseph F. Quinn. 1986. "Do Retirement Dreams Come True? The Effects of Unanticipated Events on Retirement Plans." *Industrial and Labor Relations Review* 39 (July, 1986): 518–26.

Anderson, Katharyn H., Robert L. Clark, and Thomas Johnson. 1980. "Retirement in Dual Career Families." In Robert L. Clark, ed. *Retirement Policy and Further Population Aging.* Durham, NC: Duke University Press, 1980.

Andrews, Emily S. 1985. *The Changing Profile of Pensions in America.* Washington, DC: Employee Benefit Research Institute, 1985.

———. 1989. *Pension Policy and Small Employers: At What Price Coverage?* Washington, DC: Employee Benefit Research Institute, 1989.

Barnow, Burt S. and Ronald G. Ehrenberg. 1979. "The Costs of Defined Benefit Pension Plans and Firm Adjustments." *Quarterly Journal of Economics* 93 (November, 1979): 523–40.

Bartel, Ann P. and George J. Borjas. 1977. "Middle-Age Job Mobility: Its Determinants and Consequences." In S. Wolfbein, ed. *Men in Their Preretirement Years.* Philadelphia: Temple University Press, 1977.

Berkovec, James and Steven Stern. 1988. "Job Exit Behavior of Older Men." Unpublished manuscript, February 1988.

Bernheim, B. Douglas. 1987. "Dissaving After Retirement: Testing the Pure Life Cycle Hypothesis." In Zvi Bodie, John B. Shoven, and David A. Wise, eds., *Issues in Pension Economics.* Chicago: University of Chicago Press, 1987. pp. 237–74.

———. 1988. "Social Security Benefits: An Empirical Study of Expectations and Realizations." In E. Lazear and R. Ricardo-Campbell, eds., *Issues in Contemporary Retirement.* Stanford, CA: Hoover Institution, 1988. pp. 312–48.

———. 1989. "The Timing of Retirement: A Comparison of Expectations and

Realizations." In David A. Wise, ed., *The Economics of Aging*. Chicago: University of Chicago, 1989. pp. 335–55.

Blanchflower, David G., Andrew J. Oswald, and Mario D. Garrett. 1989. "Insider Power in Wage Determination." NBER Working Paper No. 3179, November 1989.

Blinder, Alan S. 1981. *Private Pensions and Public Pensions: Theory and Fact*. W. S. Woytinsky. Lecture No. 5. University of Michigan, Ann Arbor. December 1981.

Bodie, Zvi. 1989. "Pensions As Retirement Income Insurance." NBER Working Paper 2917, April 1989; *Journal of Economic Literature* (March 1990).

Bodie, Zvi and William Samuelson. 1989. "Labor Supply Flexibility and Portfolio Choice." NBER Working Paper No. 3043, July 1989.

Brown, Charles and James Medoff. 1989. "The Employer Size-Wage Effect." *Journal of Political Economy* 97 (October, 1989): 1027–59.

Brown, James N. and Harvey S. Rosen. 1982. "On the Estimation of Structural Hedonic Price Models." *Econometrica* 50 (1982): 765–68.

Bulow, Jeremy I. 1981. "Early Retirement Pension Benefits." NBER Working Paper 654, April 1981.

——. 1982. "What Are Corporate Pension Liabilities?" *Quarterly Journal of Economics* 97 (August 1982): 435–52.

Burkhauser, Richard V. 1979. "The Pension Acceptance Decision of Older Workers." *Journal of Human Resources* 14 (Winter 1979): 63–75.

Burtless, Gary. 1986. "Social Security, Unanticipated Benefit Increases and the Timing of Retirement." *Review of Economic Studies* 53 (October 1986): 781–805.

Burtless, Gary and Robert A. Moffitt. 1984. "The Effect of Social Security Benefits on the Labor Supply of the Aged." In H. Aaron and G. Burtless, eds., *Retirement and Economic Behavior*. Washington, DC: Brookings Institution, 1984. pp. 135–74.

——. 1985. "The Joint Choice of Retirement Age and Post Retirement Hours of Work." *Journal of Labor Economics* 3 (April 1985): 209–36.

Clark, Robert L. 1987a. "Employer Health Care Plans for Retirees." Faculty Working Papers, North Carolina State University, July 1987.

——. 1987b. "Increasing Use of Defined Contribution Pension Plans." Final report for U.S. Department of Labor. November 1987.

Clark, Robert L., Stephan F. Gohmann, and Ann A. McDermed. 1988. "Declining Use of Defined Benefit Pension Plans: Is Federal Regulation the Reason?" Unpublished manuscript.

Crawford, Vincent and David M. Lilien. 1981. "Social Security and the Retirement Decision." *Quarterly Journal of Economics* 46 (August 1981): 505–29.

Crockett, Petra and Steven Stern. 1989. "A Test of Lazear's Mandatory Retirement Model." Unpublished manuscript.

Dorsey, Stuart. 1987. "The Economic Functions of Private Pensions: An Empirical Analysis." *Journal of Labor Economics* 5, Part 2 (October 1987): 5171–89.

Ehrenberg, Ronald. 1980. "Retirement System Characteristics and Compensating Differentials in the Public Sector." *Industrial and Labor Relations Review* 33 (1980): 470–83.

Ehrenberg, Ronald G. and Robert S. Smith. 1987. *Modern Labor Economics*, 3rd ed. Glenview, IL: Scott, Foresman Company, 1987.

Ellwood, David. 1985. "Pensions and The Labor Market: A Starting Point." In

D. Wise, ed., *Pensions, Labor and Individual Choice*. National Bureau of Economic Research. Chicago: University of Chicago Press, 1985.

Feldstein, Martin. 1981. "Private Pensions and Inflation." *American Economic Review* (May 1981).

———. 1983. "Should Private Pensions Be Indexed?" In Zvi Bodie and John A. Shoeven, eds., *Financial Aspects of the U.S. Pension System*. National Bureau of Economic Research. Chicago: University of Chicago Press, 1983.

Fields, Gary S. and Olivia S. Mitchell. 1984. *Retirement, Pensions and Social Security*. Cambridge, MA: MIT Press, 1984.

———. 1987. "Restructuring Social Security: How Will Retirement Ages Respond?" In S. Sandell, ed., *The Problem Isn't Age: Work and Older Americans*. New York: Praeger, 1987. pp. 192–205.

Freeman, Richard B. 1985. "Unions, Pensions and Union Pension Funds." In David A. Wise, ed., *Pensions, Labor, and Individual Choice*. National Bureau of Economic Research. Chicago: University of Chicago Press, 1985.

Gibbons, Robert and Lawrence Katz. 1989. "Layoffs and Lemons." National Bureau of Economic Research Working Paper 2968, May 1989.

Gordon, Roger H. and Alan S. Blinder. 1980. "Market Wages, Reservation Wages and Retirement." *Journal of Public Economics* 14 (1980): 277–308.

Green, Jerry. 1985. "The Riskiness of Private Pensions." In David A. Wise, ed., *Pensions, Labor, and Individual Choice*. National Bureau of Economic Research. Chicago: University of Chicago Press, 1985. pp. 357–75.

Gustman, Alan L. and Martin Segal. 1972. "Wages, Fringes and the Interaction of Bargains in the Construction Industry." *Industrial and Labor Relations Review* 25 (January 1972): 179–85.

Gustman, Alan L. and Thomas L. Steinmeier. 1983. "Minimum Hours Constraints and Retirement Behavior." In *Contemporary Policy Issues*, a Supplement to *Economic Inquiry*, pp. 77–91.

———. 1984. "Partial Retirement and the Analysis of Retirement Behavior." *Industrial and Labor Relations Review* 37, 3 (April 1984): 403–15.

———. 1985a. "The Effects of Partial Retirement on Wage Profiles for Older Workers." *Industrial Relations* 24 (1985): 257–65.

———. 1985b. "The 1983 Social Security Reforms and Labor Supply Adjustments of Older Individuals in the Long Run." *Journal of Labor Economics* 3 (1985): 237–53.

———. 1986a. "A Structural Retirement Model." *Econometrica* (May 1986): 555–84.

———. 1986b. "A Disaggregated Structural Analysis of Retirement by Race, Difficulty of Work and Health." *Review of Economics and Statistics* LXVIII, 3 (August 1986): 509–13.

———. 1986c. "Pensions, Unions and Implicit Contracts." NBER Working Paper 2036. October 1986.

———. 1987. "Pensions, Efficiency Wages, and Job Mobility." NBER Working Paper 2426. November 1987.

———. 1989a. "An Analysis of Pension Benefit Formulas, Pension Wealth and Incentives from Pensions." In R. Ehrenberg, ed. *Research in Labor Economics* 10. Greenwich, CT: JAI Press, 1989. pp. 33–106.

———. 1989b. "Evaluating Pension Policies in a Model with Endogenous Contributions." NBER Working Paper 3085, August 1989.

———. 1989c. "The Stampede Toward Defined Contribution Pension Plans: Fact or Fiction?" NBER Working Paper 3086, August.

————. 1989d. "Changing Social Security Rules for Workers over 65: Proposed Policies and Their Effects." NBER Working Paper 3087. August 1989.

————. 1990. "Pension Portability and Labor Mobility." Unpublished manuscript, 1990.

Hanoch, Giora and Marjorie Honig. 1983. "Retirement, Wages and Labor Supply of the Elderly." *Journal of Labor Economics* 1 (April 1983): 131–51.

Hatch, Sarah et al. 1982. *Financial Retirement Incentives in Private Pension Plans.* Washington, DC: Urban Institute, 1982.

Holzer, Harry J., Lawrence F. Katz, and Alan B. Krueger. 1989. "Job Queues and Wages." Unpublished manuscript.

Honig, Marjorie. 1985. "Partial Retirement Among Women." *Journal of Human Resources* (Fall 1985): 613–21.

Hurd, Michael D. 1988. "The Joint Retirement Decision of Husbands and Wives." NBER Working Paper 2803, December 1988.

————. 1989. "Issues and Results From Research on the Elderly. III: Consumption and Savings." NBER Working Paper 3018, June 1989.

Hutchens, Robert. 1986a. "Delayed Payment Contracts and a Firm's Propensity to Hire Older Workers." *Journal of Labor Economics* 4 (1986): 439–57.

————. 1986b. "An Empirical Test of Lazear's Theory of Delayed Payment Contracts." Unpublished manuscript.

————. 1989. "Seniority, Wages, and Productivity: A Turbulent Decade." *Journal of Economic Perspectives* 3, 4 (Fall 1989): 49–64.

Ippolito, Richard A. 1985a. "Income Tax Policy and Lifetime Labor Supply." *Journal of Public Economics* 26 (April 1985): 327–47.

————. 1985b. "The Labor Contract and True Economic Pension Liabilities." *American Economic Review* 75 (December 1985): 1031–43.

————. 1985c. "The Economic Function of Underfunded Pension Plans." *The Journal of Law and Economics* 28. (October 1985): 611–51.

————. 1986a. *Pensions, Economics and Public Policy.* Pension Research Council. Homewood, IL: Dow Jones-Irwin, 1986.

————. 1986b. "Pension Terminations for Reversion." *Compensation and Benefits Management.* 2, 4 (Summer 1986): 261–72.

————. 1987. "The Implicit Pension Contract: Developments and New Directions." *Journal of Human Resources* (Summer 1987): 441–64.

————. 1989. *The Economics of Pension Insurance.* Pension Research Council. Homewood, IL: Dow Jones-Irwin, 1989.

————. 1990. "Toward Explaining Earlier Retirement After 1970." Unpublished manuscript. Revised 1990.

Ippolito, Richard A. and Walter W. Kolodrubetz, eds. 1986. *Handbook of Pension Statistics.* Chicago: Commerce Clearing House, 1986.

Katz, Lawrence F. and Lawrence H. Summers. 1989. "Industry Rents: Evidence and Implications." *Brookings Papers On Economic Activities.* (1989): 209–75.

Kotlikoff, Laurence J. and Daniel E. Smith. 1983. *Pensions in the American Economy.* Chicago: The University of Chicago Press. 1983.

Kotlikoff, Laurence J. and Avia Spivak. 1981. "The Family as an Incomplete Annuities Market." *Journal of Political Economy* 89, 2 (1981): 372–91.

Kotlikoff, Laurence J. and David A. Wise. 1985. "Labor Compensation and the Structure of Private Pension Plans: Evidence for Contractual versus Spot Labor Markets." In David Wise, ed., *Pensions, Labor, and Individual Choice,* 55–85. Chicago: University of Chicago Press, 1985.

————. 1987a. "Employee Retirement and a Firm's Pension Plan." NBER Working Paper 2323, July 1987.

————. 1987b. "The Incentive Effects of Private Pension Plans." In Z. Bodie, J. Shoven, and D. Wise, eds., *Issues in Pension Economics*. Chicago: University of Chicago Press, 1987. pp. 283–336.

————. 1987c. "Pension Backloading, Wage Taxes, and Work Disincentives." NBER Working Paper 2463, December 1987.

————. 1989. *The Wage Carrot and the Pension Stick*. Kalamazoo, MI: W. E. Upjohn Institute for Employment Research, 1989.

Krueger, Alan and Lawrence Summers. 1988. "Efficiency Wages and the Inter-Industry Wage Structure." *Econometrica* 56 (March 1988): 259–94.

Lapp, John S. 1985. "Mandatory Retirement as a Clause in an Employment Insurance Contract." *Economic Inquiry* (January 1985): 69–92.

Lazear, Edward P. 1979. "Why Is There Mandatory Retirement?" *Journal of Political Economy* 87 (December 1979): 1261–84.

————. 1982. "Severance Pay, Pensions, and Efficient Mobility." NBER Working Paper 854, February 1982.

————. 1983. "Pensions as Severance Pay." In Z. Bodie and J. Shoven, eds., *Financial Aspects of the United States Pension System*. National Bureau of Economic Research. Chicago: University of Chicago Press, 1983. pp. 57–85.

————. 1985a. "Incentive Effects Of Pensions." In David Wise, ed., *Pensions, Labor, and Individual Choice*. National Bureau of Economic Research. Chicago: University of Chicago Press, 1985. pp. 357–75.

————. 1985b. "Social Security and Pensions." In R. Ehrenberg, ed. *Research In Labor Economics* 7. Greenwich, CT: JAI Press, 1985. pp. 1–30.

————. 1987. "Retirement From the Labor Force." In O. Ashenfelter and R. Layard, eds., *Handbook Of Labor Economics* 1. New York: Elsevier, 1987. pp. 305–55.

Lazear, Edward P. and Robert L. Moore. 1988. "Pensions and Mobility." In Z. Bodie, J. Shoven, and D. Wise, eds., *Pensions In The U.S. Economy*. National Bureau of Economic Research. Chicago: University of Chicago Press, 1988. pp. 163–88.

Leigh, Duane. 1981. "The Effect of Unionism on Workers' Valuation of Future Pension Benefits." *Industrial and Labor Relation Review* 34 (July 1981): 510–21.

Leonard, Herman B. 1987. "Promise Them Anything: The Incentive Structures of Local Public Pension Plans." In D. Wise, ed., *Public Sector Payrolls*. National Bureau of Economic Research. Chicago: University of Chicago Press, 1987.

Lumsdaine, Robin, James Stock, and David Wise. 1990. "Three Models of Retirement: Computational Complexity versus Predictive Validity." Paper delivered at the NBER Conference on the Economics of Aging, April 1990.

Luzadis, Rebecca A. and Olivia S. Mitchell. 1987. "A Multinomial Logit Model of Pension Outcomes." Department of Labor Economics, Cornell University. October 1987.

————. 1989. "Explaining Pension Dynamics." NBER Working Paper No. 3084, August 1989.

Manski, Charles F. 1989. "The Use of Intentions Data to Predict Behavior: A Best-Case Analysis." Unpublished manuscript.

McCormick, Barry and Gordon Hughes. 1984. "The Influence of Pensions on Job Mobility." *Journal of Public Economics* (February/March 1984): 183–206.

McGill, Dan M. 1984. *Fundamentals of Private Pensions*. 5th ed. Homewood, IL: Richard D. Irwin, Inc., 1984.

Medoff, James. 1979. "Layoffs and Alternatives Under Trade Unionism." *American Economic Review* 69 (June 1979): 380–95.

Mitchell, Olivia. 1982. "Fringe Benefits and Labor Mobility." *Journal of Human Resources* (Spring 1982): 286–98.

———. 1983. "Fringe Benefits and the Cost of Changing Jobs." *Industrial and Labor Relations Review* (October 1983): 70–78.

———. 1988. "Worker Knowledge of Pension Provisions." *Journal of Labor Economics* (January 1988): 212–39.

———. 1990. "The Effects of Mandating Benefits Packages." In R. Ehrenberg, ed. *Research in Labor Economics: Labor Economics and Public Policy* 11. Greenwich, CT: JAI Press, 1990.

Mitchell, Olivia S. and Emily Andrews. 1981. "Scale Economies in Private Multi-Employer Pension Systems." *Industrial and Labor Relations Review* 34 (July 1981): 522–30.

Mitchell, Olivia S. and Gary S. Fields. 1982. "The Effects of Pensions and Earnings on Retirement: A Review Essay." In R. Ehrenberg, ed., *Research In Labor Economics* 5. Greenwich, CT: JAI Press, 1982. pp. 115–56.

Mitchell, Olivia S. and Rebecca A. Luzadis. 1988a. "Changes In Pension Incentives Through Time." *Industrial and Labor Relations Review* 42, 1 (October 1988): 100–108.

———. 1988b. "Pension Responses to Changes in Social Security." Final report to the Social Security Administration, Grant No. 10-P-98289, Priority area SSA86-003, submitted December 1988.

Mitchell, Olivia S. and S. Pozzebon. 1987. "Wages, Pensions and the Wage-Pension Tradeoff." Department of Labor Economics Working Paper, Cornell University. Revised August 1987.

Mitchell, Olivia S. and Robert S. Smith. 1989. "Public Sector Pensions: Benefits, Funding and Unionization." Cornell University, Department of Labor Economics, November 1989.

Montgomery, Edward, Kathryn Shaw, and Mary Ellen Benedict. 1989. "Pensions and Wages: An Hedonic Price Theory Approach." Unpublished manuscript.

Munnell, Alicia H. 1982. *The Economics of Private Pensions.* Studies in Social Economics. Washington, DC: The Brookings Institution, 1982.

———. 1984. "ERISA—The First Decade: Was the Legislation Consistent with Other National Goals?" *New England Economic Review* (November/December 1984).

Nalebuff, Barry and Richard J. Zeckhauser. 1985. "Pensions and the Retirement Decision." In D. Wise, ed. *Pensions, Labor, and Individual Choice.* National Bureau of Economic Research. Chicago: University of Chicago Press, 1985. pp. 283–316.

Oi, Walter. 1983. "The Durability of Worker-Firm Attachments." Unpublished manuscript.

Oi, Walter and John Raisian. 1985. "Impact of Firm Size on Wages and Work." Unpublished manuscript.

Parsons, Donald O. 1983. "The Industrial Demand for Older Workers." Unpublished manuscript.

———. 1988. "Aging and the Employment Contract." Unpublished manuscript.

Pontiff, Jeffrey, Andrei Shleifer, and Michael Weisbach. 1989. "Revisions of Excess Pension Assets After Takeovers." London School of Economics. LSE Financial Markets Group Discussion Paper 68, November 1989.

Pozzebon, Silvana and Olivia S. Mitchell. 1989. "Married Women's Retirement Behavior." *Journal of Population Economics* 2, 1 (1989): 301–53.

Quinn, Joseph F., Richard V. Burkhauser, and Daniel A. Myers. 1990. *Passing the Torch: The Influence of Economic Incentives on Work and Retirement.* New York: Basic Books, 1990.

Rappaport, Anna M. 1988. *Managing Postretirement Medical Benefits.* Prentice Hall Personnel Management Series. Englewood Cliffs, NJ: Prentice-Hall, 1988.

———. 1989. "Postemployment Benefits." *Compensation and Benefits Management* 5, 4 (Autumn 1989).

Robb, A. L. and J. B. Burbidge. 1989. "Consumption, Income and Retirement." *Canadian Journal of Economics* 22 (August 1989): 522–42.

Rust, John. 1988. "Behavior of Male Workers at the End of the Life-Cycle: An Empirical Analysis of States and Controls." Unpublished manuscript.

———. 1989. "A Dynamic Programming Model of Retirement Behavior." In D. Wise, ed. *The Economics of Aging.* Chicago: University of Chicago Press, 1989. pp. 359–98.

Salop, Joanne and Steven Salop. 1976. "Self Selection and Turnover in the Labor Market." *Quarterly Journal of Economics* 90 (1976): 619–27.

Schiller, Bradley and Randall D. Weiss. 1979. "The Impact of Private Pensions on Firm Attachment." *Review of Economics and Statistics* (August 1979): 369–80.

Segal, Martin. 1986. "Post-Institutionalism in Labor Economics: The Forties and Fifties Revisited." *Industrial and Labor Relations Review* 39 (April 1986): 388–403.

Smith, Robert S. and Ronald G. Ehrenberg. 1983. "Estimating Wage-Fringe Tradeoffs: Some Data Problems." In J. Triplett, ed. *The Measurement of Labor Cost.* National Bureau of Economic Research. Chicago: University of Chicago Press, 1983. pp. 347–67.

Stock, James H. and David A. Wise. 1988a. "The Pension Inducement to Retire: An Option Value Analysis." Unpublished manuscript.

———. 1988b. "Pensions, the Option Value of Work, and Retirement." NBER Working Paper 2686, August 1988.

Summers, Lawrence H. 1983. "Observations on the Indexation of Old Age Pensions." In Z. Bodie and J. Shoven, eds. *Financial Aspects of the US Pension System.* National Bureau of Economic Research. Chicago: University of Chicago Press, 1983.

Thaler, Richard and H. M. Shefrin. 1981. "Pensions, Savings and Temptation." Graduate School of Business and Public Administration Working Paper 81-26. Cornell University, November 1981.

Topel, Robert. 1987. "Wages Rise with Seniority." Unpublished manuscript. University of Chicago, November 1987.

Turner, John A. and Daniel J. Beller. 1989. *Trends in Pensions, 1988.* Washington, DC: U.S. Government Printing Office, 1989.

U.S. Chamber of Commerce. 1989. *Employee Benefits.* Washington, DC: U.S. Chamber Research Center, 1989.

U.S. Congress. 1987. Congressional Budget Office. *Tax Policy for Pensions and Other Retirement Savings.* Washington, DC: U.S. Government Printing Office, 1987.

Venti, Steven F. and David A. Wise. 1989a. "But They Don't Want to Reduce Housing Equity." NBER Working Paper 2859, February 1989.

———. 1989b. "Aging and the Income Value of Housing Wealth." Unpublished manuscript, revised September 1989.

Weiss, Yoram. 1985. "The Effect of Labor Unions on Investment in Training: A Dynamic Model." *Journal of Political Economy* 93 (October 1985): 994–1007.

Wolf, Douglas A. and Frank Levy. 1984. "Pension Coverage, Pension Vesting, and the Distribution of Job Tenure." In H. J. Aaron and G. Burtless, eds., *Retirement and Economic Behavior.* Washington, DC: The Brookings Institution, 1984. pp. 23–60.

Woodbury, Stephen. 1989. "Current Economic Issues in Employee Benefits." In *Investing in People: A Strategy to Address America's Workforce Crisis.* Commission on Workforce Quality and Labor Market Efficiency Background Papers. Washington, DC: U.S. Department of Labor, September 1989.

———. 1983. "Substitution Between Wage and NonWage Benefits." *American Economic Review* 73 (March 1983): 166–82.

ents by Anna M. Rappaport

Alan Gustman and Olivia Mitchell survey the literature and research on this topic and present requirements for a data base. As they point out, this is an extremely complex topic, and they point to many of the complexities. This topic can be viewed as a mosaic, including many colors and many different shapes and patterns. My perspective and view of the mosaic is that of an actuary and a consultant working with plan sponsors to design and manage plans. I have tried here to point out some of the concerns that I believe practitioners may have in dealing with the issues discussed in the chapter. Traditionally, the academic approach to pension issues, built from economic theory, has been foreign to many working in the field, so that the theoretical economists and practitioners have seen issues in different ways. I hope that these comments will help to point out some differences and to bring the viewpoints closer together.

My comments will be organized as follows:

(1) Definition of the retirement package and retirement.
(2) Some practical concerns about building a linked data base and reservations about its usefulness.
(3) Observations about plan sponsors and employees.
(4) Union issues and pensions.
(5) Observations about the 1980s that may create difficulty with historical comparisons.
(6) Anticipated issues of the 1990s.
(7) Recommendations.

Definition of the Retirement Package and Retirement

Pension research generally deals with pension plans. Where employers offer combinations of defined benefit and defined contribution plans to the same employees, it is unclear whether the combination is dealt with, or whether the research focuses on a single plan only.

The retirement package today for many employees consists of three components:

(1) A pension plan.
(2) A savings program.
(3) A retiree medical benefit.

A generous retiree medical benefit for an individual retiring at age 55 could easily have a present value of $50,000 for an unmarried retiree and, for a spouse five years younger, an additional $70,000. In a few cases, employees also get long-term care benefits. For an early retiree with relatively minimal service at early retirement, it is not uncommon for the retiree medical benefit to be worth more than the pension plan. These benefits are generally unfunded, and typically do not vest prior to retirement (nor do they specifically vest at retirement, even though it is quite unusual to discontinue benefits to retired employees).

Another problem that arises in connection with retirement and retiree benefits research is the definition of retirement. Many individuals have entitlement to retirement-related benefits from a variety of sources, including Social Security, multiple employers, military retirement, and personal savings and assets. Within a family, each spouse may have access to different sources of retirement benefits. It is possible to collect benefits from one employer and to earn income by working for another or through self-employment; people frequently collect military pensions and have other employment. Some people collect pensions and continue to work (usually, but not always, on a limited basis) for the same employer. Some people retire and go to work full-time for another employer. This raises the question: What is retirement? The response is probably quite different depending on one's perspective. One way of dealing with this issue is to recast the question, and ask not "What is retirement?" but rather "What are the conditions for benefit eligibility?" This issue may become much more important in the decades ahead as relatively more of the population will be in what is today's retirement age range.

Mitchell and Gustman discuss the relationship of benefits to the retirement decision. The availability, coverage, and cost of retiree medical benefits is also a factor, particularly for early retirements. Employers not offering the coverage have, on a number of occasions, cited the lack of retiree medical benefits as a deterrent to early retirement.

It is my feeling that research on the retirement package, and on employer and employee response to benefit plans, needs to focus on the integrated package. This is a critical point with regard to the structure of the data base because, for some retirees, the medical benefits are worth more than the pension benefits. In their paper, Mitchell and Gustman also discuss and agree with this point. This issue creates additional complexity for any data bank, and creates issues in interpretation of existing research.

I also suggest that the issue of the definition of retirement deserves further consideration. I am not sure whether that is an issue that affects the data base, but I suspect it is, because the data base would probably be considerably more useful if it is able to relate to benefits from multiple employers and sources. This creates substantial additional complexity in the creation of a data base and raises additional questions about the very feasibility of a comprehensive data base.

Some Practical Issues

The proposed data bank focuses on the desirability of linking information about firms with information about their pension benefits, and with information about employees and retirees. The recommendation states:

A nationally representative data set, preferably longitudinal and centered around the firm, is needed. It should match information on employee characteristics with employer-side data on the pension plans as well as other characteristics of firms, their inputs, and financial structure. Pension plan descriptions would best be accompanied by information on the distribution of wages of covered workers, their numbers, and other characteristics. Such information is highly sensitive.

The paper recognizes that this is an ambitious task, but I fear that it may be so ambitious as to be out of reach at a reasonable cost. I will describe a situation (based on real life experience) that serves to illustrate some of the difficulties.

Firm "X" has been in business for many years. It is engaged in various types of manufacture and construction and has, at all times over the last fifteen years, had fewer than 20,000 employees. It offers pension and other retirement benefits to a large number of employees through:

A salaried employees' pension plan covering employees in all divisions;
Several hourly employee pension plans, some covering negotiated groups and some covering other groups; within the company-sponsored plans are more than 30 benefit levels (for some companies, the number is more than 100);
A large number of multi-employer pension plans, where coverage is

sometimes for short periods, and where some plans cover very few people;

Some supplemental benefits covering certain highly paid employees in non-qualified plans;

Company matching contributions to a savings program with 401(k) features offered to some groups of the employees;

Limited continuation of medical coverage to some groups of employees; cost sharing varies depending on the group and circumstances at termination; the definition of who is eligible for medical continuation does not fit the specific definition of eligibility for certain pension plans.

Determining pension benefits for current and former employees of "X" is complicated, and there is no single source where benefits for all employees can be determined because:

The company has no records of the benefit formulas under the multi-employer plans; primarily, it has contribution information. This is unlikely to change; the company has been unable to secure other information from some of the multi-employer plans when it attempted to do so.

Employees have transferred between hourly and salaried status and vice versa. Some employees have done so more than once. This is a function of the way employment is structured in periods of growing and declining business, and is not true in many other types of businesses. Transfers are common in many businesses, but multiple transfers in both directions are unusual. The consequence of these transfers is that individual records and plans must be understood to calculate benefits.

"X" has shut down and phased out some operations, so that an inventory of former employees cannot be viewed as the former employees of an operation comparable to today's operation. Some of the plans also calculated benefits differently for phase-outs than for retirements from ongoing businesses.

"X" has purchased annuities for some benefits earned as a result of employment with "X," so that the benefits provided under the company's plans represent only a part of the benefit earned as a result of employment with "X."

"X" has acquired other businesses in the past. In some cases, employees of acquired businesses have benefits determined on the basis of the plans in effect in the other businesses before acquisition.

Adjustments in hourly plan benefit levels are made a number of times each year to different parts of the benefit schedule. These are often tied to labor negotiations. It is not uncommon for a specific group to have a benefit stated as $15.00 per month per year of service in the current year, $16.00 in the following year, and $17.00 beginning in two years. Effective dates of change are often tied to labor contracts, not calendar years, and usually not more than two advance changes are negotiated.

Company "X" and its actuary can determine pension benefits from the defined benefit plans that it sponsors. Neither has enough information to determine the benefits under the multi-employer plans without a major data collection effort. However, such determination is a very time-consuming process requiring knowledge of the plans built up over years. Company "X" and its defined contribution recordkeeper can determine existing balances and contribution levels in the savings program. Neither has attempted to determine on a widespread basis the amount of retirement income the savings program is expected to generate. However, the company did consider the savings program contributions as part of the retirement package in its last round of plan design changes in the pension plans. Company "X" and its actuary have been through a major research project on the retiree medical, and can now match who has retiree medical coverage with the pension records.

The description of Company "X" over time is also fluid. It went through a period of acquisitions, when several companies were added. It went through a number of changes, including sales of companies and shutdowns, as well as a total change of ownership. As these changes evolved, it experienced considerable downsizing in its corporate staff, and attempts to build a unified, company-wide payroll system were abandoned.

A story similar to this could be constructed about a large number of industrial corporations in America. The implications for collection and utilization of a data base are as follows:

For each firm, a method of tracking major changes in the firm would be needed.

It is difficult to define what a firm is. It is very common for a firm to be sold, and then for several pieces to be sold off, some of which become independent, at least for a time.

Each firm is likely to have not a single retirement program, but many pension plans, a savings program, and some differing retiree medical plans.

Multi-employer plan benefits will have to be treated differently.

Custom programming will probably be needed to estimate benefits for each firm.

There is an added area of complexity with regard to linking benefit and employee information. Payroll data typically are matched with pension data only for pay-related pension plans, so that neither the firm's pension records nor the actuarial records have pay for employees with flat dollar plans in a pension-related data base. In addition, many firms have two or more sets of payroll data, with executive pay being handled through a confidential payroll, so that this information is not in the normal pension and payroll data base. In addition, for employees who receive part of their pay through an incentive or variable pay system, there may be special problems collecting pay data.

Many companies have worked over the last decade to build human resource and pension data bases, or have explored the feasibility of doing so. The most common source of descriptions for employee benefits would be summary plan descriptions, which are benefit descriptions given to employees and required by law. Generally, it is possible to learn a great deal about the operations of benefit plans through the summary plan descriptions. If one wanted to understand a company's retirement benefits, it would be logical to request summary plan descriptions. However, some of the difficulties in working with summary plan descriptions that may be encountered are as follows:

(1) The summary plan descriptions (SPDs) are not up-to-date. This is particularly likely at present because many organizations have not finalized their compliance with the Tax Reform Act of 1986 since they are waiting for key portions of the regulations.
(2) For profit-sharing plans, the plan descriptions do not give an indication of the amount contributed but rather merely state that the plan is discretionary.
(3) There are often no separate SPDs for retiree medical plans, but rather a few paragraphs in an active employee medical plan indicating that benefits are continued to retirees. Neither the eligibility for benefits nor the retiree contributions are shown in some SPDs, so that it is not possible to determine the company-provided benefit.

It is suggested that, in order to test whether difficulties of coping with firm, plan, and employee data would be insurmountable and whether the data could be obtained at all, it would be logical to select a few large firms for intensive interviewing to determine:

An understanding of firm history and the complexities of such history.

An understanding of the retirement benefit plan structure of the firm and the history of the structure.

An understanding of the existing records that would enable the firm to contribute to a data base, if it wished to do so.

An understanding of the circumstances under which firms would support an effort, and what resources they could commit to such support.

Public sources yield some of this information on firm history and plans, but the data available are quite limited compared to what is actually needed if benefits are to be calculated. It is possible to determine what can be found from public sources by interviewing those involved in the acquisition process. Generally, individuals or firms involved in unfriendly acquisitions are willing to invest considerable money to acquire any data publicly available, and they are aware of the limitations of such data.

Another set of practical difficulties arises in trying to work with and compare benefits provided in different types of plans. In defined contribution plans, the plan may offer a discretionary contribution or offer a formula for the contribution. The contribution may be a match of an employee's savings. It is necessary to project both current account balances and future contributions and make an investment return assumption in order to estimate a benefit comparable to a benefit under a defined benefit plan. Such projections are extremely sensitive to the assumptions made. In defined benefit plans, there are four basic formula types: final average pay plans, career average pay plans, flat dollar plans, and account-based plans. Final average plans have increases for preretirement changes in wage levels built into the formula directly. Career average pay plans and flat dollar plans have no such changes built into the formula, but have an implicit expectation that benefits will be kept up-to-date through benefit increases.

One cannot generalize about account-based plans. If benefits under these various plans are compared without any projection of future benefit changes, it is somewhat unfair and not predictive of what will happen at retirement. It is also not possible to project what changes plan sponsors must make. It is, therefore, very difficult if not impossible to fairly compare benefits for future retirees across many different plan types. One way to avoid these difficulties is to compare benefits for current retirees or for someone currently at retirement age assuming a uniform pay and service history. A different but parallel set of issues exists for retiree health plans. It is not known at any time what the benefits will be worth in the future, and estimating the value of benefits under different plans is quite complex and somewhat speculative, particularly since many plan sponsors are likely to change their benefits.

To summarize my practical concerns, I do not disagree that from a theoretical point of view, a data base linking firms, plans, and current and former employees would be very helpful. However, I have real concerns about whether such a data base could actually be constructed and maintained, and whether reasonably accurate benefit calculations could be done on a broad enough sample. These concerns are based on experience over a period of years working with individual employers to help them manage their own benefits. I have the additional concern that individuals with benefit entitlement from one firm may have additional benefit entitlement from another firm and/or from self-employment and the military, so that understanding individuals' benefits goes beyond the single firm. Additional practical concerns relate to estimating benefits under different types of plans so that they can be validly compared.

What Plan Sponsors and Employees Know and Consider

Gustman and Mitchell survey the research on what plan sponsors and employees know and its relationship to policy. The models are based on certain theories about behavior. For example, in the discussion about a spot market, the comment "Data on wages and pension accruals would be predicted to show that, for workers of a given productivity level, in any given year, higher pension accruals are offset by lower wages." It is my impression that many plan sponsors do not have information on pension accruals by individual for a given year. Those that do generally do not have them connected to the information used to establish wages. Setting wages is usually done in a way that does not directly tie to length of service or other variables that affect pension accruals. I suggest that some research on the wage development process (by interviewing employers) would indicate that the spot theory is not consistent with employer operations in light of the way pension and wage systems are administered and the connections between them.

As a practitioner, I have a view on what plan sponsors know and what they consider when they decide to adopt or change a plan. I believe that some researchers do not understand those issues and that it would be very helpful to researchers to gain more insight into plan sponsor concerns, and I would suggest that research with both plan sponsors and their advisors on how decisions are made and what information is considered would be very interesting. (This would not require a large data base.)

I will also share some observations based on my practice with larger and medium-sized employers:

The drivers of plan design decisions are custom and tradition, human resource objectives (including employee need and responding to labor relations issues), public policy, and tax considerations. Community practice is often very important. Cost is a major constraint.

Decision making is usually based on a tradeoff between financial constraints and a desire to meet employee needs.

Understanding how plans operate and are financed over time is complex. Information for decision-making nearly always includes:

Effect on current cash contributions and current charge to the profit and loss statement.

Some benefit illustrations showing the effect of change on retirement benefits, often at various retirement ages.

Analysis of links to objectives and business needs.

In some situations, projections of cost, and more extensive benefit illustrations are also prepared. There is a trade-off between use of a lot of information and the difficulty of digesting it and the cost of producing it, and working with relatively little information. In many cases, decision-makers do not want long and complex reports.

In some cases, the pension plan is looked at alone, and in others, the total retirement package or total benefit package is the focus. In some situations, it is the total compensation package that is reviewed.

I am unaware of any situation where lifetime earnings or career earnings have ever been considered in a real situation.

In firms where avoidance of financial risk is the driving force, defined contribution plans usually are used. Such firms avoid retiree medical plans.

In firms where employee need is a major consideration, where career employment and rewarding long service are goals, and where there is reasonably long-term stability, traditional defined benefit plans are usually adopted, often in combination with a matched savings program. Such firms typically offer and pay at least part of the cost for retiree medical. When constraints require benefits below what is seen as theoretically adequate, often a great deal of agonizing occurs over the decision.

When spending for retirement requires less spending elsewhere, there is no common or general source of what is to be traded.

With a well-funded pension plan, benefit improvements are often

funded through existing assets or by gradually reducing funding
   levels.
Legal requirements have driven many of the plan changes of the last
   few years.
Existing benefit structures are often the product of history and not of
   applying logic to current business conditions and needs; companies
   looking at current needs and finding that something else makes
   sense may try to move over a period of years. Change is often very
   difficult.
Pension design decisions are usually regarded as reasonably long-term
   decisions. They are expected to be permanent but with the potential for further change, and in some cases decisions are made with
   planned further change. This can be very difficult in environments
   where companies are concerned about takeovers and change in
   ownership.

Employers often feel a strong sense of obligation to employees, in a
long-term and a short-term sense. I have the sense that policy makers
often do not understand the motivation of the typical major employer
in offering benefits. Research and policy input on this issue from non-
employer-directed sources would be interesting and probably quite
helpful.

These observations are personal, and not supported by data. It
would be desirable to develop a more systematic understanding of
these issues over time.

I also have some impressions based on interaction with clients and
other consultants about employee knowledge. It would be very interesting to confirm some of these. I believe that what employees know
has implications for which models are reasonable and which are not. In
the Overview of Theoretical and Empirical Issues, the paper sets forth
some of the underlying framework for research and theory. It states:
"Our review of the role of pensions in the labor market is organized
within a supply and demand framework, where references to the supply side should be understood as pertaining to workers supplying their
labor, and references to demand pertaining to firms' demand for workers. Specifically, on the supply side, as workers evaluate different wage
offers, non-wage benefit offerings, and job attributes when deciding
which job to accept, they determine the rate at which they are willing to
trade off pensions for wages." I am troubled by this, because I do not
believe that workers have adequate information at the time of choosing
jobs to evaluate pensions. Most people will know whether there is a
pension plan; very few, if any, will have detailed information about how
to calculate benefits, and if they had it, they would not have enough

expertise to do the calculation. What a sample of people know at the time of hire and how they decide which jobs to take could be determined through some focus groups with different types of employees.

It is my sense that many individuals go through three phases with regard to knowledge of defined benefit retirement plans (and retiree medical). In the first phase, which probably lasts through their late 30s for many people, individuals know virtually nothing about their retirement plans, except to be aware that they have benefits. The presence of the benefit is important but its amount is unclear, as is how it is calculated. It seems highly unlikely to me that workers consider expected amounts of pensions in job decisions in their 20s and early 30s. In the middle phase, employees understand a little more about their plans, but it is doubtful whether most could accurately estimate benefits. Even if they could produce a dollar-of-income amount, it is unlikely that they would know what that amount was worth or the impact of inflation. In the third phase, employees become much more knowledgeable about their benefits. This generally occurs when they start personal retirement planning. In such cases, workers are likely to know about benefit eligibility and they may well know about expected benefit amount, often because they have received a benefit estimate. Even in this case, they are unlikely to understand the impact of inflation well, even though they may be quite worried about it.

The situation with regard to understanding of defined contribution plans is quite different. Employees seem to be well aware of amounts contributed to these plans, and many employees are well aware of their account balances. This is true regardless of age. However, employees are likely to understand neither the retirement income equivalent of a particular balance nor the implication of spending now versus leaving the money for retirement. The reaction to changes in defined contribution plans frequently indicate that employees are very aware of these plans and of their account balances. Employees are also much more likely to be aware of the level of their contributions to defined contribution plans at time of hire than they are of defined benefit plan formulas.

There are some other important issues with regard to employee understanding and defined contribution plans. Where investment choices are offered, it very often happens that about 90 percent of the investments go into a guaranteed principal, fixed-income investment vehicle. Where money is in equities (or company stock), and its value declines, there is often dissatisfaction. It appears that employee understanding of investment issues is not very good.

The paper points out that the research indicates that pensions have a strong influence over retirement decisions. Discussions with clients would support this. Continued medical coverage also has such an influence. Experience with early retirement windows confirms the influence of pensions on retirement decisions. When employees are offered additional benefits to retire within a limited period, many will accept the offer.

Research on what information employees have and how they use it should be helpful in determining whether the models based on long-term decision making about pensions reflect individual behavior. On a single-firm level (or for several firms), it should be possible to determine what individuals know about their benefits. Firms might be happy to support such research. Many do work on benefits knowledge for their own businesses. Some of the current research and theory is troubling to me personally because the models seem to be based on assumptions about more knowledge on the part of individuals than I find reasonable.

It should also be pointed out that a number of groups have done extensive research on what individuals know in areas related to financial decision making, purchase of insurance, and/or retirement. These groups include the American Council of Life Insurance and the American Association of Retired Persons. Their research staffs may have valuable insights on what individuals might be expected to know.

Union Issues and Pensions

In their discussion of union effects, the authors point out that unionization has raised pension coverage over what it would have been in the absence of unions. Unions have certainly been important in the growth of the entire private pension movement in the United States. Their effect may well go beyond what is easily measured in research. Some of the questions that might be considered include:

What are the effects of unions on benefits for non-unionized employees in the same firm?

Are comparisons of benefit levels with non-union employees difficult because union plans tend to be flat dollar plans whereas non-union employees are offered coverage in pay-related plans? (The flat dollar plans are improved frequently, whereas the pay-related plans automatically factor in the effect of inflation.)

What are the effects of unions on benefits in a firm that is non-unionized but in an industry where other firms are unionized?

How do unions affect the overall competitiveness of the firm and its ability to manufacture in the United States versus elsewhere?

How does one properly account for multi-employer plans in comparisons?

The questions serve to reinforce some of the subtleties that need to be considered in structuring a data base for pension research. Much insight could be developed from analysis of the data, but it may not tell the story well unless appropriate understanding also goes into the structure of the data base and framing of the questions.

Observations About the 1980s That May Increase the Complexity of Research

From a practitioner's viewpoint, the 1980s were a period of changing environment. These changes affected the way many plans were structured and affected the decisions that plan sponsors were making about their plans. Some of the interesting events of the 1980s are discussed here.

Buyouts and changes in corporate ownership. During the 1980s a big increase occurred in the number of corporate buyouts, some of them unfriendly. Prior to the 1980s, it was generally believed by practitioners that it was not possible to terminate a defined benefit plan, remove the surplus, and then start a similar plan. However, early in the 1980s, the IRS, PBGC, and DOL issued a joint statement permitting such a transaction and permitting the spinoff-termination. Under either transaction, benefits earned to date are vested and annuities are purchased. The plan sponsor recovers the surplus, but benefits then continue to accrue under the old formula. Many plans were well funded, and pension surplus became a material factor in financing many leveraged buyouts. Companies that had not been concerned about buyouts became concerned that buyouts could be a factor for them.

Business restructuring. While many companies were experiencing changes in ownership, those that were not were often involved in restructuring their operations. Many companies reduced the size of their work forces and moved to a more mean and lean organization. Plant shutdowns were commonplace. Early retirement windows were often a part of the restructuring process. In other cases, they followed changes in ownership. In situations involving restructuring, it is quite possible that employees viewed early retirement windows as an offer they effectively had to take. It was probably the best basis on which they could phase out.

There is considerable focus on the effect of pensions on employees' decisions about termination of employment. During the 1980s a considerable amount of involuntary termination of employment occurred, often of longer-service employees. Some of this affected only individuals, but often it was groups of people. In such situations, early retirement is often viewed by the employer as a way to reduce the number of people not eligible for retirement who must be terminated. Early retirement windows are common in this setting. In a company experiencing restructuring or downsizing, voluntary termination and retirement may be difficult to separate from involuntary termination.

Change in accounting rules. Until the mid-1980s, most plan sponsors accounted for pension benefits so that cash pension contributions were equal to the amount charged as an expense in the profit and loss statement. They had considerable funding flexibility. In late 1985, the Financial Accounting Standards Board released new accounting rules for pension plans. Starting in 1987 (in most cases), it was no longer possible to expense and fund the same amounts. Under these rules a uniform actuarial method for determining pension expense and new assumptions guidelines applied. For many plan sponsors, this meant a substantial reduction in pension expense and more volatility. The effect of the new rules differed greatly by company, but many companies had "pension income," as they were in effect taking amounts previously recognized as pension cost back into income. The new rules also permitted recognition of a substantial one-time gain whenever benefits were settled or curtailed, so that a few plan sponsors were making decisions about pension management based on the implications for their profit and loss statements.

Under "pension valuation in both spot and long-term contexts," the paper presents a discussion about calculation of pension liabilities and the balance sheet. This discussion needs to be expanded and clarified. It states, "For many years, corporate balance sheets specifically highlighted the spot market accrued liability, delegating projected liability to a footnote. In recent years, however, there has been increasing emphasis on funding for projected liabilities." Accounting practice follows the rules promulgated by the accounting authorities, now the Financial Accounting Standards Board (FASB). Prior to the release of the Statement Number 87, the footnotes of plan sponsors showed the accrued benefit obligation only, which is the amount the paper indicates as analogous to the spot liability. After the effective date of Statement 87, the projected benefit obligation is shown in the footnote. Neither amount is shown on the balance sheet (or was before) except that the full projected benefit obligation is put on the balance sheet where a change has occurred in company ownership, and an amount equal to the excess of minimum liability (based on the accrued benefit obligation) is put on the balance sheet if pension plan assets are less than certain amounts.

The statement is made that in recent years more emphasis has been placed on funding for projected liabilities. As indicated below, it has been my experience that cash contribution levels have generally declined compared to historical levels (except in cases of underfunding, where the legal requirements have become more stringent). All the changes in accounting and pension contributions must be interpreted in the light of changing requirements and the changed business environment.

Trends in pension funding. The changed accounting rules did not change funding requirements. Accounting rules do not define funding requirements. However, federal legislation (OBRA 1987) did change the requirements for many. OBRA 1987 reduced flexibility in funding and prohibited tax-deductible contributions for many employers who could previously make them. It also increased minimum funding requirements for poorly funded plans.

The traditional wisdom of many conservative plan sponsors had been that funding conservatively was a good idea. Such funding offered a margin of extra protection to participants and a way to help finance plan improvements and increased benefits for retirees. The takeover situation of the 1980s changed that thinking, because now a well-funded plan could help make a company a takeover target. The accounting rule change also encouraged lower funding because, in many cases, the new pension expense charges were considerably lower than traditional pension contribution levels.

Also during the 1980s, equities earned good returns and well-funded plans increased their surpluses. The net effect of the takeover situation, the new accounting rules, the investment returns, and other factors was to encourage much lower levels of pension funding. Many plan sponsors changed their actuarial assumptions and the method used to determine costs in order to reduce funding. Many made no contributions to plans for several years during the 1980s. The accepted "wisdom" about funding has changed and is considerably less conservative than it was a decade ago.

Legislation. The 1980s were a period of unprecedented employee benefit legislation, particularly pension legislation. Regulations were not available as laws became effective. The decade started with the Economic Recovery Tax Act, and continued with TEFRA, DEFRA, REA, the Tax Reform Act of 1986, and several budget reconciliation acts. For many plan sponsors, virtually all of their energy and time for benefit planning and innovation was occupied with trying to comply with the many new requirements. The constant change created a sense of instability on the part of plan sponsors and their advisors alike.

Many medium-sized and smaller employers gave up on their
benefit plans. Some of the major changes during the decade include

Introduction of top-heavy rules.
Reduction of the maximum benefit limits from tax-qualified plans, in
   three different pieces of legislation.
Change in integration rules to permit much less integration of quali-
   fied plans.
Sweeping new approach to nondiscrimination rules.
Reduced limits and tighter tests for 401(k) plans.
Mandated five-year (or equivalent) vesting.
Expansion of benefit requirements for spouses.
Requirements for spouse consent if benefits not paid as joint and
   survivor benefits.
New, more stringent coverage rules.
New distribution rules.
Overhaul of plan termination rules and introduction of excise taxes on
   reversions.
Introduction of excise taxes on large distributions.
Introduction of excise taxes on early distributions.
Less favorable taxation of lump-sum benefit payments.
Withdrawal of right to establish 401(k) plans from not-for-profit em-
   ployers.
Less flexibility in funding.
Implementation of user fees for government filings, and increased
   penalties for noncompliance.
Requirements for continued pension accruals after normal retirement
   age.
Requirement for distribution of benefits after age 70.5 even if the
   employee is still working.

   Several of the most important changes are in effect today; but with
major portions of the regulations missing, plan sponsors are unclear
on what some of these changes mean. Special regulations have been
issued to permit some "interim approaches to compliance" until final
regulations are known.
   The effect of the legislation has been to make it more difficult to
provide benefits to highly compensated employees and to require a
different balance between benefits for the highly compensated and the
non-highly compensated. The combined effect of the large amount of
legislation has also been to cause the entire community working with

plans to feel as if it is under siege. The speed and magnitude of change have created a sense of continuing uncertainty and instability.

An understanding of the legislative events of the 1980s is important in interpreting time-linked data from that period.

Early retirement windows. During the 1980s, a large number of employers implemented special early retirement programs. Some had several programs. Their reasons varied. The frequency and prevalence of these programs may have changed the normal retirement decision process for many individuals.

The recognition of retiree medical benefits as an important corporate matter. Until well into the 1980s, few corporate managers recognized that retiree medical coverage was costly and that it would be very important to their companies. Companies continued retirees in their health plans and often did not separately look at the costs of their benefits. Companies believed that they had the right to change the benefits. A number of discontinuities during the 1980s changed perceptions about retiree medical benefits and a number of lawsuits challenged the right of employers to modify benefits even if the plan documents reserved the right to do so. The most recent decisions tend to follow the documents, and the legal basis for these decisions is often contract law. However, the accepted understanding of what an employer can do, and what has been promised, is less clear than a decade ago, and these benefits are viewed as more risky. During the 1980s, the Financial Accounting Standards Board announced that it would apply rules similar to pension accounting rules to these benefits, and it released an exposure draft defining new rules in February 1989. The traditional method of cost recognition is pay-as-you-go, so that costs are deferred until after retirement. This pending change in rules has forced plan sponsors to focus on the cost and value of these benefits. LTV attempted to cancel its retiree medical benefits when it went into Chapter 11, thereby producing a lot of attention in Washington and the press. At this point, these benefits are recognized as important and costly. The traditional approach to defining benefit adequacy can also be seen as one that assumed that medical benefits would continue. Today this is much less certain.

The Major Issues of the 1990s

It seems very likely that if a comprehensive data base is to be developed, it will take several years to get it up and running, with many preliminary steps and investigations. It is important in the interim, and as the data base is designed, to be sure that the major issues of the 1990s can be addressed. I have tried to define here what seem to me to be some of these key issues.

Retiree medical coverage. This will continue to be a major issue for employers. Employers will be deciding whether to continue their plans and how to modify and manage them. Many will not continue their benefits in present form. At the same time, Congress will have a number of legislative proposals before it and will have to act on them. Increasingly, it will be recognized that this is a pension benefit in a different form.

Shortages of workers. A number of observers have predicted shortages of some kinds of workers during the 1990s. Recent discussions with a major national U.S. employer indicated that one of their key human resource issues at present is finding the right people, and that lack of qualified people is a major concern. Many employers have found that the entry-level people entering the work force do not have needed skills. Special problems exist in health care with nurses. (This is not a pension and retirement issue, but is related.) One solution, at least theoretically possible for dealing with this issue, is later or phased retirement. Observers disagree about how much serious merit this solution has. This issue also relates to the pension issues, in that the structure of hiring packages and incentives is likely to change.

Demographic changes. As the baby boom is aging, the age distribution of the population is shifting. By 2020, the proportion of the population aged 65 and over will have increased markedly, with many questions about the implications of these demographic issues for retirement and for the benefit systems supporting retirement. Some of the issues include the definition of retirement, the age at which individuals get benefits, and the conditions under which they get benefits.

Career employment. Traditional defined benefit plans work best for those with long-term employment with a single employer. Employers today differ in their view of whether career employment will be a thing of the past or an important part of the employment picture of the future. The investment that employers have in individual employees is great and the cost of replacing them is great, so that employers may value long-term employees even more in the future. Opposing this view is one that with technological change employees will not be able to meet employer needs over long periods of time.

Education of the individual with regard to savings. Many observers feel that the individual will need to take more responsibility for financial security in old age. This is particularly true for the individual who has many different jobs over a working lifetime. Few people understand the importance of saving early and the implications of long-term saving. Research on this issue would be a natural adjunct to research on what people know and understand about retirement plans.

Public policy. An unprecedented number of changes have been made in pension and retirement-related law over the last decade. Some of the areas of change are listed above. Public policy questions remain un-answered, and retirement-related issues are likely to continue on the legislative agenda for the next decade. A fairly widespread concern has been expressed that integrated retirement policy is needed, rather than fragmented change tied to each tax bill that comes along. Some of the specific issues likely to be on the agenda are:

Plan termination and reversions (bills have been introduced already).
Maximum benefits in tax-preferred plans.
Nondiscrimination rules—as the changes in the 1986 law are imple-mented, some of these changes may be found unworkable.
Portability, and the extent to which inflation protection continues after termination, if any.
Lump-sum payments and whether they should be permitted, and if so, whether they should be discouraged.
Role of the goverment versus the employer.
Medicare changes.
Retirement-age-related issues.

Allocation of resources for retirement and the elderly versus resources for education and other needs. At a public, employer, and individual level, the issue of allocation of resources to the elderly versus allocation of resources to other groups is likely to be a significant issue. A review of the budget cuts and fiscal changes of the last decade indicates that the elderly participated much less in the budget cuts than other groups. Education and maintenance of skills is a critical issue for Americans today.

Defined benefit versus defined contribution. This has also been an issue for the last decade. It can be restated in many ways and these plans can be shaped in different ways. Public policy may well "push" employers in one direction or the other. Underlying the plan-type issue are often the issues of how risk is distributed between employer and employee, and how benefits are earned early and late in a career.

World competitiveness and business restructuring. The role of benefits in overall competitiveness and the structure of business will continue to be important. Retiree medical (and all medical benefits) may get par-ticular attention here.

This list of some of the issues of the 1990s serves to illustrate that public policy makers and employers alike will be dealing with major issues in the management of retirement benefits. Often, during the 1980s, it seemed that some of the public policy changes were made without sound information about the implications of changes proposed and implemented. Better research, if it could improve the understanding of the implications of changes, is very important.

Recommendations

Pension and retirement related issues will continue to be of major importance to the public, plan sponsors, and individuals. Improving the research base, if the information could assist in public policy building and if it could assist plan sponsors, would be valuable. The authors of the paper have recommended building a linked data base tying together information on firms, retirement benefits, and individuals covered by the plans, to provide a better basis for research. They would also like to see data looking at behaviors over time.

I view this as an ideal, but one that is not necessarily feasible in the real world. The recommendations here are designed to help assess feasibility and to help deal with some of the shorter real-term issues.

1. Through focus groups, interviews, and/or questionnaire-structured research, develop a better understanding of the range of what individuals know about retirement and retirement plans at different stages in their life cycles and how they incorporate this information into decisions about employment acceptance, employment termination, and retirement.
   Use this information to be sure that the data base fits well, but also to test models and theories and their underlying assumptions.
2. Through focus groups, interviews, and/or questionnaire-structured research, develop an understanding of the range of how employers make decisions about the retirement benefits they will offer, how they structure compensation programs, and how pensions and other elements of the compensation program relate.
   Use this information to be sure that the data base fits well, but also to test models and theories and their underlying assumptions.

Steps 1 and 2 are desirable regardless whether a linked data base is ever developed. The following steps are suggested to help determine whether a linked data base is feasible.

3. Investigate issues relating to the definition of the firm, and how the structure of firms changes over time. Also investigate how

widespread changes in firm structure are over time. Determine how issues of the evolving firm could be handled in a firm-linked data base. Services providing data to investors provide substantial amounts of data about firms over time, and have probably investigated many issues relating to firm data bases.

4. Explore with a sample of firms their retirement benefit structure, history, and employee data base situation to determine how a research data base could be structured to handle such data. Find out if up-to-date plan descriptions of the entire retirement package are available. Also, begin exploring whether firms would be willing to provide data to such a data base and what they would charge to do so. Once data are collected, they also must be updated to be useful. Find out how firms would work to provide data for updating.

5. The earnings histories maintained by Social Security are probably the best potential for linking one individual to many firms. Explore the issue of how it might be possible to create data for individuals spanning multiple programs.

6. At the conclusion of the preliminary steps, it would be necessary to determine whether it is feasible to build a linked data base at all and, if so, to attempt some design. Any design should be developed on the basis that it would first be implemented on a pilot basis.

At this point, it should be possible to determine whether a linked data base is feasible. However, if it is not, the outstanding issues of the 1990s do not go away. Ideally, work should be progressing on these issues at the same time that work is proceeding to determine if a data base can be built.

Comments by John A. Turner

Alan Gustman and Olivia Mitchell have done an excellent job of reviewing the literature on pensions and labor market behavior. This literature has focused predominantly on defined benefit plans, and that focus is reflected in their chapter. Defined benefit plans have traditionally been the predominant plan in the United States and indeed in all other countries with well-developed private pension systems (Dailey and Turner, 1989: 22).

The continued predominance of defined benefit plans is now in question. Between 1975 and 1986, the percentage of the work force covered by a defined benefit plan fell from 39 percent to 32 percent. Over that same twelve-year period, however, the percentage of the work force covered by a defined contribution plan increased from 14 percent to 30 percent (Turner and Beller, 1989: 359). The scattered available evidence suggests that both these trends have continued through 1990, so that more participants are now probably in defined contribution plans than in defined benefit plans.

Economic research has not adequately addressed issues raised by the dramatic increase in defined contribution plans. These comments on the Gustman and Mitchell chapter will focus on labor market research issues concerning defined contribution plans, and will, thus, extend the scope of the Gustman and Mitchell chapter and provide an agenda for possible future research and data collection. The comments follow the outline of section two of that chapter, "Modeling the Role and Function of Pensions in the Labor Market." That section is divided into five subsections.

The first subsection deals with the nature of the pension promise. This subsection addresses whether pensions are part of a short-term spot contract or an implicit long-term contract between firms and workers. This issue is important when attempting to measure the wage-pension tradeoff, and the wage-pension tradeoff is of great importance in determining who ultimately bears the cost of pension reform. When workers pay for increased pension benefits with reduced wages, then all attempts by reformers to increase the lifetime wealth of workers by improving their pension benefits are doomed to fail. While economists generally hold the view that workers pay for pension reform, the wage-pension tradeoff has proven to be extraordinarily difficult to estimate.

The problems of measuring the value of accrued pensions for purposes of estimating that relationship would be solved if a study were done using data on defined contribution plans, since such plans clearly are valued on a spot market basis. While such a study could not answer all interesting questions related to the wage-pension tradeoff, such as whether workers give up less in wages for defined benefit plans because of the potential for portability losses (or more because of the lower investment risk the worker bears), a study using data on defined contribution plans may help establish that there is a wage-pension tradeoff. That basic fact has not been established with studies that use data on defined benefit plans.

The second subsection deals with pensions and retirement. A potentially important issue concerning the effect of defined benefit plans on retirement has not been addressed in any study. A very strong negative relationship exists between lifetime income and mortality risk (Duleep, 1986), as well as a strong positive relationship between lifetime income and the level of pension wealth. Mortality risk plays a potentially important role in the retirement decision because it affects the workers' valuations of pension wealth and of the wealth effect of the adjustment of benefits with postponed retirement. Workers with low mortality risk will tend to postpone retirement in comparison to workers with high mortality risk. An adjustment of future pension benefits that is actuarially fair for the entire population will favor late retirement for workers with low mortality risk, because an increase in future benefits is worth more for them since they expect to receive it for more years. The relationship between mortality risk and lifetime income effect biases estimates of both pension wealth and pension wealth increments with postponed retirement. It potentially biases estimates of the effects of these variables on retirement age, but the empirical importance of these biases has not been examined. This problem is not present when calculating defined contribution pension wealth, since defined contribution pension wealth is simply the value of the assets in the individual's account.

The third subsection deals with the pension-mobility relationship. Simple cross-tabulations show a very strong correlation between being a participant in a pension plan and having relatively long job tenure, with the effect being stronger for defined benefit plans than defined contribution plans. This correlation and several studies reviewed by Gustman and Mitchell suggest that participation in a defined benefit pension plan decreases job mobility.

The plausibility of this finding, at least as it is interpreted that pensions play a major role in reducing job mobility, is subject to question. Defined benefit pension accrual generally is only a small part of a worker's compensation. For workers covered by a pension plan, pension contributions averaged less than 5 percent of compensation in 1988 (Turner and Beller, 1989: 433). While this figure probably understates the percentage which pension accrual is of total compensation, because favorable investment markets had reduced pension contributions in that year, it may overstate accrual in defined benefit plans since it includes contributions to defined contribution plans. Taking into account both supplementary defined contribution plans and Social Security, defined benefit plans are generally only a small part of the pension benefits that a worker will receive. As indicated in the chapter in this volume by Andrews and Hurd, in 1986 only 2 percent of elderly households received more than 50 percent of their income from private pensions.

To the extent that defined benefit plans are used to reduce job mobility, they are presumably part of an overall compensation policy that aims at such a reduction. It is unreasonable to expect that the firm's entire effort to reduce job mobility would be focused on less than 5 percent of its compensation package. The negative estimated effects of pensions on job mobility may be overstated because pensions may be picking up the effects of omitted aspects of compensation. That may also account for the longer tenure of workers with only defined contribution plans in comparison to workers without any plan. Defined contribution plans are not expected to have any effect on tenure, but empirical research on pensions and labor market behavior has often lumped the two plan types together in one pension variable. In the section on pensions and work incentives, Gustman and Mitchell discuss incentive effects of defined benefit plans, but do not discuss incentive effects of defined contribution plans. Profit sharing and Employee Stock Ownership Plans may have incentive effects, especially on workers in small firms, which may arise because the workers have a direct stake in the profitability of the firm. Conte and Svejnar (1990) and Kruse (1991) have done research in this area. Kruse (1992) is also working on the related area of whether profit-sharing plans reduce fluctuations in employment. Since compensation through profit-sharing plans declines when a firm's profit declines, less need exists to adjust the firm's aggregate compensation by laying off workers.

The last subsection is on the interdependence in decisions determining pensions, savings, insurance, and labor market outcomes. Gustman and Mitchell discuss the possibility that workers are liquidity constrained because they cannot borrow against their pension benefits.

Such a liquidity constraint could cause an interdependence between the pension, savings, insurance, and labor market decisions of workers causing, for example, workers to save more for retirement and to retire earlier than they would if they were not so constrained. While it is nearly always the case that workers cannot borrow against their defined benefit plans, that is not true for defined contribution plans. In 1986, 44 percent of all 401(k) plan participants were in plans that permitted participants to borrow against their accounts. Only 12 percent of the participants in plans that allowed loans took them, suggesting that in plans where loans are not permitted, liquidity constraints may affect a minority of participants (U.S. General Accounting Office, 1988: 40).

Gustman and Mitchell indicate that a problem with defined contribution plans is that pension assets may fluctuate day by day as portfolio values change, and these fluctuations can dramatically alter benefit payments. This argument does not consider that workers with participant-directed accounts have the option of shifting the risk of their money purchase defined contribution plans to an insurance company. In 1988, plans holding about 95 percent of the total assets in 401(k) plans had the option of participant-directed accounts (U.S. General Accounting Office, 1988: 34). For 401(k) plans, purchases of Guaranteed Investment Contracts (GICs) have been popular. In 1988, 31 percent of the assets invested in 401(k) plans were in GICs (U.S. General Accounting Office, 1988: 36). These contracts guarantee the investment returns to the worker for a fixed period of time. This eliminates the investment risk to the worker over that time period (barring default), but the worker still has a reinvestment risk.

The discussion of policy issues in this book is intended to highlight the data needed to address those issues. A specific point and a general point that need to be considered when constructing a data wish list will conclude these comments. First, the specific point—this comment has stressed the need for distinguishing between defined benefit and defined contribution plans and directing research attention toward defined contribution plans. To do this requires data obtained from employers, because employees frequently are unable to provide accurate information on whether they belong to a defined benefit or defined contribution plan. Second, referring back to the wage-pension tradeoff discussed earlier, another wage-pension tradeoff is of importance to researchers—the tradeoff between the wages of researchers and the cost of collecting pension data. Since contract research and pension data collection are frequently supported out of the same governmental agency's budget, an increase in funding for data collection causes a decrease in funding for contract research. At least in the short run, the tradeoff is one for one.

References

Conte, Michael and Jan Svejnar. 1990. "The Performance Effects of Employee Ownership Plans." In Alan S. Blinder, ed., *Paying for Productivity: A Look at the Evidence,* Washington, DC: Brookings Institution, 1990.

Dailey, Lorna M. and John A. Turner. 1989. "U.S. Pensions in World Perspective." In John A. Turner and Daniel J. Beller, eds. *Trends in Pensions.* Washington, DC: U.S. Government Printing Office, 1989.

Duleep, Harriet O. 1986. "Measuring the Effect of Income on Adult Mortality Using Longitudinal Administrative Record Data." *Journal of Human Resources* 21 (Spring 1986): 238–51.

Kruse, Douglas. 1991. "Profit Sharing and Employment Variability: Microeconomic Evidence on the Weitzman Theory." *Industrial and Labor Relations Review* 44, 3 (April 1991): 437–53.

———. 1992. "Profit Sharing and Productivity: Microeconomic Evidence from the United States." *Economic Journal* (January 1992).

Turner, John A. and Daniel J. Beller., eds. 1989. *Trends in Pensions.* Washington, DC: U.S. Government Printing Office, 1989.

U.S. General Accounting Office. 1988. "401(k) Plans: Incidence, Provisions, and Benefits." March 1988.

Chapter 3
What Is the Impact of Pensions on Saving?

Alicia H. Munnell and Frederick O. Yohn

The enormous growth in both Social Security and private pension plans has stimulated much interest in the impact of these retirement programs on individual saving behavior and the level of national saving. The first issue is the extent to which employees covered by pension plans reduce their own direct saving in response to expected retirement benefits; the response of individuals to guaranteed retirement income will determine, to a large extent, their well-being in retirement. For a nation concerned about saving and capital formation, the second issue is the impact of collectivized retirement saving plans on the national saving rate. This impact will depend not only on individual responses to promised pension benefits, but also on the extent to which firms undertake direct saving and, if they do not, the extent to which shareholders recognize and compensate for unfunded pension liabilities. The effect of pensions on national saving also requires determining the degree to which increased saving induced by favorable tax provisions exceeds the loss of government revenues.

This chapter will lay out the questions that need to be answered in order to determine the impact of private pension plans on saving, highlight those aspects of pensions that may complicate the analysis, summarize the results of empirical research in this area, and finally make recommendations for improvements in the data.

I. Pensions and Life-Cycle Saving

Many people who favor increased reliance on private rather than public provision of retirement benefits rest a large portion of their case on the rapid increase in private pension fund assets. Indeed, the growth has been extraordinary, from $5 billion at the end of 1945 to over $1.7

trillion by the end of 1989.[1] Proponents of private plans imply that the buildup of pension reserves represents a net increase in saving for the economy. Economic theory suggests, however, that it may simply reflect a shift in the form of saving. The life-cycle model predicts that, in an ideal world characterized by perfect labor and capital markets, no taxes and no uncertainty, people would simply substitute the increase in their expected pension benefits for their own saving.[2] As will become evident, the level of assets in pension funds tells little about either the well-being of individuals or the impact of private plans on aggregate saving.

A simple model may help clarify the issues. Suppose the population consists of individuals who expect to live exactly T years. People begin work at birth, earn E dollars of compensation per year while at work, and retire at age R. This leaves workers $T - R$ years in retirement, during which time they earn no wages. Ignoring interest, an individual's lifetime income is

$$(1) \qquad\qquad Y = RE \quad,$$

or the product of years at work and earnings per year.

Workers wishing to avoid starvation during their retirement will save during their working years.[3] According to the life-cycle model, they will save and dissave exactly enough so their annual consumption, C, is identical in each year of their life, including periods of work and retirement:

$$(2) \qquad\qquad C = \frac{RE}{T} \quad.$$

This consumption pattern implies that annual savings while at work will be

$$(3) \qquad\qquad S = E - \frac{RE}{T} = \frac{T - R}{T} E \quad.$$

---

1. In focusing on the distinction between the public pay-as-you-go Social Security program and privately funded pensions, the discussion omits any mention of plans sponsored by state and local governments. These public plans look very much like those in the private sector and are fairly well funded, with assets in excess of $600 billion at the end of 1989.

2. The life-cycle theory has come under criticism in recent years, primarily because of the alleged importance of intergenerational transfers as a saving motive and the apparent lack of asset decumulation on the part of the elderly. Despite the furor, this model provides the most useful framework for analyzing the impact of pensions on saving. For a brief description of the controversy, see Kotlikoff (1988) and Modigliani (1988).

3. The following discussion assumes no saving for bequests.

Assume that people live exactly 50 years and typically retire when they reach age 40 (that is, T = 50 and R = 40). If they earn $10,000 a year at work, in the absence of a pension plan, they will save on their own $2,000 a year while working in order to maintain a constant consumption level of $8,000 throughout their lives.

Now suppose the employer provides a compensation package that consists of cash wages, W, and a pension promise, P; that is,

(4)
$$E = W + P \quad .$$

In this case, an individual's annual saving, S, will consist of the promised future benefit from his employer, P, and other saving (OS) done on his own,

(5)
$$S = P + OS \quad .$$

The first step in sorting out the effect of the introduction of the pension plan on saving is to determine whether individuals reduce their own saving, OS, in response to the promised pension benefit. In order to isolate the relationship between pension and non-pension saving, equation 5 can be rewritten in terms of other saving,

(6)
$$OS = S - P = \frac{T - R}{T} E - P = \frac{T - R}{T} (W + P) - P$$
$$= \frac{T - R}{T} W - \frac{R}{T} P \quad .$$

Individuals committed to life-cycle saving will fully offset their own saving to account for employer-provided pension promises. Using the numerical assumptions identified above, people receiving pension promises of $2,000 will save nothing on their own. Similarly, persons receiving $9,000 in wages and $1,000 in pension promises will save $1,000 in order to bring their total up to the $2,000 required to maintain a constant level of consumption. (Note that fully offsetting behavior does not imply a coefficient of −1 on the pension variable.)

What happens in this simple example if people for some reason do not reduce their saving to offset fully promised pension benefits? Say, for example, the employer provides a $2,000 pension, and the employee reduces his own saving by only $1,000. In this case, the employee's consumption during his worklife falls from $8,000 to $7,000, and consumption during retirement rises from $8,000 to $12,000. Thus, the response of the employee to promised pension benefits has significant implications for the well-being of the individual and, in a growing economy, for the amount of aggregate national saving.

At the risk of some overstatement, one could argue that it is irrelevant whether the employer funds or does not fund the plan. Suppose that employers were required only to recognize the cost of pension promises as they accrue, which would be similar to the proposals currently under consideration for post-retirement health benefits. In this situation, the employer's income statement would show compensation expenses of $10,000, $8,000 in wages and $2,000 in increased promises of future pension benefits. After paying wages to the employee, the employer ends up with $2,000 in cash, which can be added to balance sheet assets offsetting the increase in accrued pension liability.

The employer can then do one of three things with this money: make a contribution to its pension fund, invest the money in the firm, or pay it out as dividends. In this simple model, none of these transactions should have any impact on aggregate saving. The first option will involve debiting corporate assets by $2,000 and crediting the pension fund with the same amount; the pension fund will hold the money until the employee retires, at which time it will pay it out in benefits. Under the second option the firm can either hold the $2,000 in its vault and pay out the benefits when the employee retires or it can use the money to buy a machine and sell the machine when benefits need to be paid. Again, neither of these transactions would affect saving.

The trickier issue is the effect on aggregate saving if the firm pays out the entire $2,000 in dividends. The immediate impact would be a $2,000 increase in the income of shareholders. Without any futher adjustments, this would lead to a $1,600 increase in their consumption and would lower national saving. But, assuming the pension payment was an inescapable commitment, shareholders would also experience a $2,000 decline in the net worth of their firm as a result of the creation of a $2,000 unfunded pension liability. Assuming perfect knowledge about the firm's future commitments, shareholders would not increase their consumption, but rather would increase their direct saving by $2,000 to offset the failure of the firm to save for future pension expenditures. Through this mechanism, even paying out the recognized cost of future pension liabilities in dividends does not alter the conclusion that pensions need have no effect on national saving.

To summarize. Aggregate saving will be unchanged by the introduction of pension plans if (1) employees and employers correctly perceive the increase in future income encompassed by pension promises and reduce wages by an equivalent amount, (2) employees reduce their direct personal saving by the increased value of future pension benefits, and (3) the firm transfers to the pension fund or some other firm investment an amount equal to the pension promise. Alternatively, if the firm chooses not to fund, the "no-effect" conclusion can still hold if the shareholders recognize that the dividend payments they receive are offset by the decline in the value of the net worth of the firm due to the increase in unfunded pension liabilities.[4]

Gauging the impact of pensions in the real world requires assessing the extent to which the behavior of markets and of individuals conforms to the predictions of this simple model. This means answering three questions. First, by how much do employees receiving part of their compensation in pension promises reduce their other saving? Second, to what extent do employers carry out the direct saving by investing either in a pension fund or in their company assets? And third, to the extent that the company fails to invest, do shareholders alter their direct saving to compensate for the increase in unfunded liability?

II. How Does the Real World Differ from the Simple Model?

Before looking at the existing evidence about the impact of pensions on saving, it is useful to consider ways in which the real world and pensions differ from the simple notions described above. Obvious factors omitted from the discussion so far are taxes, interest rates, inflation, and uncertainty. Even expanding the model to include these factors would be insufficient, however, because pensions themselves have some unique attributes that make analyzing their impact on saving particularly difficult.

Uncertainty About Benefits

Pensions are extremely complicated; in the past this complexity has made it difficult for employees to have a realistic assessment of the value of future pension benefits. Insofar as employees are unaware of or underestimate future retirement benefits, they will not reduce their own saving to offset their share of pension asset accumulation. On the other hand, an inflationary environment makes it difficult for people

---

4. No comparable mechanism is available in the case of pension plans sponsored by state and local governments. As a result, any shortfall or funding is likely to lead to lower national saving.

who change jobs frequently and others to have an accurate assessment of unindexed pension benefits, and workers could just as easily over-estimate future real pension benefits. Thus, uncertainty about pension provisions could induce employees to reduce other saving by either more or less than the increase in their promised future benefits.

Illiquidity of Pension Promises

The neutrality of pensions in the simplified life-cycle model hinges on the ability of workers for whom pension saving exceeds their desired level of saving to borrow at market rates against excessive future bene-fits. Imperfect capital markets, however, often prevent people from borrowing freely, thereby forcing them to save more than they other-wise would. Such forced saving is most likely to occur among lower-paid workers, who have little saving to reduce in order to offset exces-sive pension accumulation. Because these lower-paid workers cannot borrow against future benefits, they end up saving more than they would have on their own. In this case pension plans may increase national saving and capital accumulation.

Even those workers whose desired levels of saving equal pension levels may not wish to do all their saving through pension plans. Since the illiquidity of a future pension benefit reduces the substitutability of pensions for other private saving, people may reduce their own saving by less than one dollar for each dollar of increase in promised future benefits, and so contribute to a net increase in aggregate saving.

Induced Retirement

The retirement provisions accompanying private plans also may have stimulated aggregate saving. The introduction of pension plans has allowed many workers to retire earlier than they otherwise would. This early retirement would be expected to increase saving, since people who retire early are forced to save at a higher rate over a shorter working life in order to finance a longer period of retirement. Even if each individual were a perfect life-cycle saver with zero net saving over his lifetime, with a growing population aggregate saving would in-crease because the number of savers would outnumber the dissavers. Similarly, if incomes were rising, the amount saved by workers would exceed that dissaved by retirees. Since historically both the population and real per capita income have tended to increase each year, the trend toward earlier retirement that has accompanied the growth of private pension plans would be expected to have increased the rate of saving in the economy.

Pensions as Annuities

Because pensions are usually paid in the form of annuities—guaranteed benefit payments for the remainder of the employee's life—total saving may be less than if each worker saved for his own retirement. Without pension annuities, most people would be forced to accumulate sufficient assets to finance an extended retirement. By pooling risks, gearing retirement saving to the average life expectancy, and offering annuities, pension plans reduce the total saving required to ensure workers a continuous stream of benefits during their retirements.

Favorable Tax Provisions

Compensation in the form of deferred pension benefits is treated favorably under the U.S. personal income tax. By allowing the deferral of taxes on promised pension benefits until after retirement, compensation in the form of pension contributions offers three advantages over compensation in the form of wages. First, the full dollar of contribution without any reduction for income tax is available for investment during the employee's working years—in contrast to the situation in which a dollar is paid in wages and the employee has only the after-tax dollar to invest. Second, no tax is currently paid on the investment income from accumulated assets, whereas interest earned by the employee on ordinary saving is subject to tax as income accrues. Finally, when benefits are distributed in retirement, they are likely to be taxed at a lower marginal rate than if they had been taxed as they accrued.[5] As a result, those workers who receive a portion of their compensation in promised pension benefits pay less tax over their lifetime than those who receive all their compensation in wages.

These tax advantages, in effect, raise the net return on saving through deferred pension arrangements. Although higher returns create both an income effect that encourages greater consumption, and a substitution effect that encourages greater saving, the most common finding among studies on the effect of interest rates on saving seems to be that the substitution effect somewhat outweighs the income effect, leading to a small net increase in saving.[6] Hence, the favorable tax provisions associated with pensions would be expected to increase national saving. This intuitive conclusion, however, may not

5. This phenomenon was considerably more important before the Tax Reform Act of 1986, which significantly reduced the progressivity of the rate schedule.
6. The best-known study finding significant positive interest rate effects is Boskin (1978).

necessarily be correct. Two factors are particularly relevant in determining the outcome—the extent to which the higher rate of return enters into people's saving decisions and the extent to which the tax advantages simply result in less saving by the government.

Workers for whom pension saving is inframarginal—that is, their desired levels of saving exceed that provided by Social Security and private plans—will experience no change in the rate of return on saving at the margin. For them the favorable tax provisions for pension saving induce an income effect but no offsetting substitution effect, so they will reduce their current saving. On the other hand, employees who want to save less than their Social Security and pension will receive an increased return at the margin and, assuming the substitution effect dominates, will increase their saving. In other words, favorable tax provisions for pension plans will lead to a net increase in saving when pension levels exceed the amount of saving workers would have done on their own and will lead to a reduction in saving when pension levels are less than workers' desired level of saving.

In the United States, pension contributions and benefits tend to be small. According to data from the 1986 Current Population Survey, the median annual private pension benefit received by married couples and single individuals aged 62 to 64 was only $4,930; moreover, only 20 percent of these beneficiaries received an annual payment in excess of $10,000 (Grad, 1988: table 33, p. 72). Hence, it is highly likely that desired saving exceeds pension saving for most middle and high income people, and they experience no change in the rate of return at the margin. Thus, the favorable tax provisions probably have had little effect on aggregate saving.

At the same time, the tax-deferred status of supplementary pension benefits causes a loss to the Treasury of significant revenues; this loss is equivalent to a reduction in government saving or an increase in government dissaving. Although the precise amount of forgone revenues is subject to considerable controversy, the total is undoubtedly large. For example, the U.S. Office of Management and Budget (OMB) estimates that the revenue loss for 1991 (on a cash basis and hence not directly relevant for the current discussion) will be roughly $47 billion (U.S. OMB 1990, table C-1, p. A-73). On balance, then, the favorable tax provisions accorded compensation in the form of deferred pension benefits may not encourage individuals to save more and almost certainly cause the government to save less, resulting in lower national saving than if individuals saved on their own.

In short, a variety of complicating factors make it impossible to determine a priori the effect of pensions on saving. The illiquidity of pension promises and uncertainty about the value of future benefits raise a question as to whether individuals reduce their other saving dollar for dollar in response to promised future benefits. On the other hand, even if individuals do undertake fully offsetting behavior, the link between pensions and retirement behavior may increase aggregate saving in a growing economy and, in a world of uncertain lifetimes, the fact that pensions are paid as annuities may reduce national saving. Finally, the introduction of taxes and particularly favorable tax provisions for compensation in the form of deferred pension benefits further complicates the analysis; does the higher net rate of return for pension saving cause employees to increase their total saving? And to the extent that increased saving occurs, does it compensate fully for the loss in government revenues from the favorable provisions?

III. What Evidence Do We Have to Date?

The addition of taxes means that four, rather than three, questions need to be answered in order to determine the effect of pensions on saving. First, to what extent do employees reduce their own direct saving in response to promised pension benefits? Second, to what extent do employers carry out the direct saving by investing either in a pension fund or in their company assets? Third, to the extent that companies fail to invest, do equity prices decline to reflect the increase in unfunded liability and do shareholders alter their direct saving to compensate? Finally, do the favorable tax provisions stimulate enough additional private saving to compensate for the reduction in government saving? This section describes the work that has been done to date addressing each of these questions.

To What Extent Do Individuals Reduce Their Own Saving?

Most of the empirical work on the issue of pensions and saving has been geared toward determining whether employees reduce their direct saving in response to an increase in promised future benefits. The total number of studies, however, are relatively few and almost none incorporate all the desired data.

Despite the widespread acceptance of the life-cycle theory, the view that individuals might reduce their saving in anticipation of pension benefits is relatively new. Until quite recently, most experts argued that participation in any pension plan encouraged people to save more than they would otherwise. The authors of a 1968 Brookings study on Social Security commented, "The available evidence suggests that, over the long run, individuals covered by government and industrial pension plans tend to save more than those who are not covered"

(Pechman, Aaron, and Taussig, 1968: 186). This view, which was based in part on the historical stability of the savings rate, was buttressed by the results of two cross-sectional studies on the relation between private pension coverage and saving behavior.

In a 1965 study, Phillip Cagan analyzed the savings response of over 15,000 members of the Consumers Union in 1958–59 and found that those covered by private pension plans saved more than those not covered. Cagan's explanation of the surprising results was that pension coverage calls attention to retirement needs and prospects and thereby fosters a "recognition effect" that counteracts individuals' disinclination to plan for the future.

A study reported by George Katona (1965), based on personal interviews conducted by the Survey Research Center of the University of Michigan with representative samples of all U.S. families in 1962–63, also concluded that membership in pension plans stimulates voluntary saving. Katona added a second explanation for his results, hypothesizing a "goal feasibility" effect, wherein people intensify their saving efforts the closer they get to their retirement goal. Katona's results must be interpreted cautiously, however, since he focused on a very narrow concept of saving—namely, changes in financial assets. Since the self-employed and farmers, who accounted for 25 percent of the nonmember sample compared to 4 percent of members, would typically save through investment in their own businesses, this narrow definition of saving biases the results.

As part of a larger study, Munnell (1974) re-analyzed a subsample of Cagan's Consumers Union survey and found results that contradicted Cagan's earlier conclusions. Separate equations explaining total non-pension saving as a function of income, wealth, a variety of socio-economic variables, and pension coverage were estimated for three age groups (30–39, 40–54, and 55–64). The pension variable consistently entered with a negative sign, and the size and significance of the coefficient increased with the age of the group.[7] The main reason for the difference between these results and those found by Cagan was the ability to use regression analysis to standardize simultaneously for a large number of other characteristics such as education, family size, income, age, and other factors, and thereby isolate the impact of pensions.

A second study by Munnell (1976) examined the relationship between private pension coverage and saving using a sample of men in

7. Additional equations were estimated replacing the simple pension coverage variable with values for expected annual pension benefits; again the pension variables entered with negative signs.

their pre-retirement years over the period 1966–71, based on a series of surveys conducted by the U.S. Department of Labor. A major advantage of the Labor Department data was the inclusion of information on expected retirement age. The surprising results in the Cagan and Katona studies may have been, in part, due to the phenomenon mentioned earlier—namely, pension coverage is usually accompanied by earlier retirement; covered employees may simply have increased their saving in anticipation of earlier withdrawal from the labor force. A fully specified life-cycle model can make allowances for differences in expected retirement age between those covered and those not covered by pension plans. The results of the 1976 Munnell study showed that coverage by private pension plans discourages saving in other forms, at least for the older men included in that survey, for whom retirement is the primary saving motivation.

Precise estimates of the substitution effect were impossible, however, since the value of the increase in the promised pension benefits was not available. A rough estimate was made on the assumption that the increase in the present discounted value of future benefits was proportional to income for those covered by a private plan. This reduction was then compared to pension plan contributions. The implicit, and clearly imprecise, assumption was that the increase in pension contributions approximates the increase in pension promises for a given year. Using these assumptions and extrapolating the behavior of the sample to the entire population, Munnell concluded that employees reduce their direct saving by 62 cents for every dollar of increased pension promises. (In retrospect, the precision is somewhat embarrassing in light of the herculean assumptions.)

Several studies have focused on the relationship between stocks of pension and non-pension wealth instead of examining annual saving flows; the results have been mixed. For example, Blinder, Gordon, and Wise (1981) examined the pattern of asset-holding by age for a sample of 4,130 white men from the 1969, 1971, 1973, and 1975 waves of the Longitudinal Retirement History Survey. Despite good asset and income data and a careful application of the theory, they were not able either to find support for the life-cycle model or to discern any tradeoff between pension wealth and other assets.

Diamond and Hausman (1980), on the other hand, using data from the Labor Department Survey of Mature Men, did find results consistent with the life-cycle theory and identified substantial substitution between individual asset accumulation and pension benefits provided through organized savings programs. Their results indicated that family wealth was decreased by $5.84 for each dollar of annual pension benefits a family expected to receive after retirement. To use these results as a basis for calculating the actual offset between the increase in pension promises and individual direct saving requires information about the cost of an equivalent annuity. At an assumed interest rate of 10 percent, however, a rough estimate might be that individuals reduce their own saving by 58 cents for each dollar increase in future promised pension benefits.

Avery, Elliehausen, and Gustafson (1986) examined the relationship between non-pension net worth and pension wealth using the 1983 Survey of Consumer Finances, which includes detailed earnings, asset, and pension information for 3,800 families. They found that for a subsample of families headed by a married person age 50 or older each dollar of pension wealth reduced non-pension net worth by 66 cents. For families with unmarried heads, however, the regression results indicated only modest substitution (22 cents reduction in net worth for each dollar increase in pension wealth) and the coefficient was only marginally statistically different from zero.

The hypothesis that individuals reduce their own saving in anticipation of promised pension benefits also found support from studies that explored the relationship between private wealth accumulation and Social Security benefits. With data from the Federal Reserve Board's 1963 Survey of Financial Characteristics of Consumers, Feldstein and Pellechio (1979) related household net worth to various measures of income and each household's net Social Security wealth. For employed males between 55 and 64, they found a strong substitution effect of Social Security wealth for private wealth. Diamond and Hausman (1980) found that for each dollar of annual Social Security benefits people reduced their saving in other forms by roughly 69 cents. On the other hand, Blinder, Gordon, and Wise (1981) found somewhat less substitution of Social Security for private wealth among their sample of men from the Retirement History Survey. Their estimates indicated that one dollar of Social Security wealth displaced approximately 39 cents of other assets, but their results were not statistically significant. Finally, Kotlikoff (1979) determined that individuals reduced their other saving by 67 cents for each dollar of combined employer-employee payroll tax contributions.

In short, the bulk of the evidence to date provides some support for the prediction of the simple life-cycle saving model that individuals reduce their own saving in anticipation of benefits provided through public and private pension plans. However, with the exception of the Avery, Elliehausen, and Gustafson analysis based on the 1983 Survey of Consumer Finances, none of the studies employed good measures of anticipated pension benefits. Moreover, most of the studies focused on the behavior of older men for whom retirement was the primary saving motive; little progress has been made in terms of assessing the impact of pensions on the saving of the entire population. All that can reasonably be said is that some offsetting behavior occurs and that it is less than dollar-for-dollar.

To What Extent Do Employers Carry Out Direct Saving?

Almost no progress has been made toward answering this question. The problems are twofold. First, assessing the extent to which firms are saving in advance for future pension commitments requires some measure of the annual increase in firms' pension promises or liabilities; although considerable progress has been made in the area of pension accounting, the improved measures have only recently been put in place. Second, even with accurate measures of pension liabilities, the answer to the question of whether firms are saving directly cannot be found by simply looking at the change in the pension fund accumulations; the relevant focus of analysis is the entire company and the amount by which both the pension fund and the general treasury combined have increased their saving.

Pension accounting. The number required in order to determine the impact of pensions on national saving is the present discounted value of pension promises provided by all employers. Not that long ago the only pension information provided by companies was an income-statement item indicating the amount that the company actually transferred to the pension fund. A 1956 pronouncement by the American Institute of Accountants argued that accounting for pension costs be done on an accrual basis and that past service costs be amortized over some reasonable period. This pronouncement, however, had little effect since the accrual concept was applied only to vested benefits and, at that time, few plans had vesting provisions.

With the growth of pensions and the confusion created by the use of numerous divergent methods of accounting, the Accounting Principles Board commissioned a comprehensive study which formed the basis for APB Opinion 8, issued in 1966. The opinion officially endorsed and prescribed the accrual basis of accounting; thereafter, firms were required to reflect on their books a pension charge equal to the normal cost of the plan, interest on any unfunded actuarial liability, and, if indicated, an amortization payment for unfunded vesting benefits. Companies also reported the value of unfunded accrued vested benefits in a footnote to their financial statements.

The enactment of ERISA, combined with certain perceived deficiencies in Opinion 8, rekindled interest in accounting for pension costs. Critics charged that pension cost was not comparably measured company to company and often not even from period to period for the same company. In 1980 the Financial Accounting Standards Board issued statements 35, *Accounting and Reporting by Defined Benefit Pension Plans,* and 36, *Disclosure of Plan Information,* as interim measures to improve the reporting and disclosure of pension information until a major study of pension accounting could be completed. These statements required sponsors to disclose more information about the funding status of pension plans; specifically, they had to show the actuarial present value of all accumulated plan benefits and the market value of plan assets available to pay those benefits. With regard to pension expense, the statement required sponsors to report any changes in actuarial cost methods, actuarial assumptions, or plan provisions that affected the comparability of data from one period to the next. However, employers were free to use any of six actuarial cost methods sanctioned by the Internal Revenue Service for allocating pension cost to each period.

The most recent product from the FASB pension accounting project is Statement 87, *Employers' Accounting for Pensions,* issued in December 1985. This statement requires that net periodic pension costs recognize three separate components: service cost, interest cost (interest on the projected benefit obligation), and actual return on plan assets. The service cost component represents the increase in promised benefits earned during the period and is conceptually the same for an unfunded plan, a plan with minimum funding, and a fully funded plan. Moreover, Statement 87 requires that all plan sponsors use the projected unit credit method for allocating the cost of benefit accruals to each year of service. In addition to establishing uniformity, this means that the service cost for final pay and career average plans will be based on future compensation levels. In addition to identifying separately the three components of net periodic pension costs, the sponsor must also disclose the projected benefit obligation, the accumulated benefit obligation, the vested benefit obligation, and the market value of plan assets. These provisions of Statement 87 became effective in 1987. (Additional provisions requiring the inclusion of a measure of unfunded liability on the balance sheet became effective in 1989.)

For the first time, therefore, all companies will be providing meaningful and comparable data in a relatively accessible form on the increase in promised benefits. This information will not only offer an opportunity to define properly employee compensation and thereby saving, but also, for the issue under discussion, provide a measure against which to judge whether the firm undertakes direct saving to fund future benefit payments.

The relevance of pension funding. Even with perfect data, simply comparing the cost of new pension promises with the amount of money expensed for pension funds cannot provide a meaningful answer to this step in determining the impact of pensions on aggregate saving. The problem here is analogous to that which has arisen at the federal level in the attempt partially to prefund the Social Security system. Just as it is misleading to assume that saving occurs because assets are building up in the Social Security trust funds, it is equally misleading to conclude that firms are saving simply because they are making large contributions to their pension funds.

In both cases, it is important to explore the activities of the other parts of the entity. With regard to Social Security, this requires ascertaining the extent to which the saving in the Social Security trust funds may be offset by a reduction in saving or an increase in dissaving in the non-Social Security part of the budget. Similarly, when assessing the extent to which the firm is saving, it is important to look at the company as a whole to ensure that increases in pension assets are not offset by decreases in other assets or increases in liabilities. In terms of the earlier example, no saving will occur at the firm level if the company simultaneously makes a $2,000 contribution to the pension fund and uses $2,000 of existing cash to pay *additional* dividends.

The difficulty in assessing the behavior of both the federal government and the firm is comparing what actually occurred against a counter-factual situation. That is, it is necessary to know how much saving or dissaving would have occurred in the absence of the buildup in the Social Security trust funds and how large dividend payments would have been in the absence of the surplus created by the $2,000 deduction for pension expense. In short, progress in answering this second step in resolving the pension-saving puzzle may be difficult.

Do Shareholders Alter Their Direct Saving?

Since shareholders have no precise way of knowing whether firms have increased their unfunded liabilities, getting a definitive answer to this question is difficult. Nevertheless, on the assumption, presumably, that the firm does not take offsetting action in the non-pension area, a series of studies have examined the relationship between unfunded liabilities and share prices; a reduction in prices is the necessary trigger for individuals to adjust their own saving behavior to compensate for the failure to save at the firm level.

To determine whether common stock values reflect pension obligations, investigators have adopted a model proposed by Modigliani and

Miller (1958), which yields an equation that expresses the market value of a firm's common stock as a function of several financial variables. To this traditional equation subsequent researchers have added a variable for the firm's unfunded pension obligations.

The first empirical analysis of the effect of a firm's unfunded vested pension benefits on its share price was performed by Oldfield (1977). He found that for 166 manufacturing firms in 1974 the coefficient on unfunded vested benefits was negative, was significantly different from zero, and hovered around −1.5. His estimates indicated that each dollar of unfunded vested liability reduced share prices by $1.50, which implied that, according to the stock market, the unfunded liability for vested benefits somewhat understated the firm's true unfunded pension obligations. Nearly identical results were reported by Feldstein and Seligman (1981), who estimated a similar equation using inflation-adjusted financial data from 1976 and 1977. A 1982 study by Feldstein and Morck yielded similar results. Gersovitz (1982) estimated an equation like Oldfield's, but allowed for a separate estimation of the coefficient for unfunded vested benefits in excess of the amount insured by the Pension Benefit Guaranty Corporation (PBGC). His results indicated that equity values appear unaffected by the portion of unfunded vested benefits above 30 percent of the firm's net worth. With this more elaborate specification, however, the coefficient on unfunded vested benefits became even more negative (−2.3). A recent study by Bulow, Morck, and Summers (1987), based on a broader data set and a combination of cross-section and time series analysis, further confirmed the earlier results that the stock market valuation of firms reasonably accurately reflects the status of their pension funding.

Shareholders apparently view a shortfall of pension assets relative to pension liabilities as a reason to lower the price that they are willing to pay for a company's stock. This may be a reasonable response even though theoretically it should not matter whether a firm saves in the pension fund or in the non-pension portion of the company. Given the pressure and tax advantages to funding, those firms that do not put aside adequate assets in the pension fund are probably not saving elsewhere.

The question still remains about the response of shareholders to the drop in the value of their equity holdings as a result of the increase in the firm's unfunded pension liability. That is, do they increase their direct saving to compensate for the firm's failure to save? No empirical information exists with regard to this link in the chain of questions that need to be answered in order to determine the effect of pensions on aggregate saving.

Does Increased Saving Compensate for Government Revenue Loss?

As long as income, as opposed to compensation, is the basis for personal taxation in the United States, the favorable treatment tax accorded compensation paid in the form of deferred pension benefits results in a revenue loss. This loss has a direct impact on national saving, since government saving—the difference between government receipts and outlays—is a major component. The loss is large; as noted earlier, the tax expenditure associated with employer-sponsored pension plans for 1991 is estimated to be $46 billion.

The tax expenditure estimates currently published by the Treasury and the OMB are not really the appropriate numbers to consider, however, when assessing the impact of the favorable tax provisions on saving. These numbers, which are computed on a cash-flow basis, are designed to measure how much higher federal revenues would be in a given year if a particular subsidy had not been enacted. This approach is consistent with the expenditure side of the federal budget and is meaningful for permanent deductions and exclusions, but does not properly account for tax concessions in those cases where tax payments are deferred. Its limitations for qualified pension plans are seen clearly by considering a situation in which (1) annual contributions to private plans and pension fund earnings exactly equal benefit payments during the year, and (2) workers face the same marginal tax rate in retirement as they do during their working years. Under these assumptions, the revenue loss as calculated by the Treasury and OMB would be zero. Yet individuals who receive part of their compensation in deferred pension benefits would continue to enjoy the advantages of deferral and pay less tax over their lifetimes than employees who receive all their compensation in cash wages. The deferral is equivalent to an interest-free loan from the Treasury and reduces the present value of taxes to be collected.

A direct estimate of the annual revenue loss resulting from deferral would be the difference between (1) the present discounted value of the revenue from the current taxation of pension fund contributions and earnings under defined contribution plans and accrued pension benefits under defined benefit plans, and (2) the present discounted value of the taxes collected when benefits are taxed in retirement. Such a calculation requires assumptions about the average age of covered workers, the typical retirement age, life expectancy at retirement, the appropriate interest rate, and the marginal tax rates for workers and retirees. Very crude estimates prepared by Munnell (1984) showed that, depending on the assumptions, the difference in 1984 between the present values of the two revenue streams ranged from $45 billion to $62 billion. (The Treasury tax expenditure estimate calculated at that time on a cash basis for fiscal 1984 was $50 billion.) Annual present value numbers are needed in order to have a good understanding of the revenue loss associated with the favorable tax provisions.

Once the revenue loss is established, the next step is pinning down the response of individuals to changes in the rate of return to saving created by the favorable provisions. Although economists agree on the direction of the response to higher returns, they have not reached a consensus on the magnitude of this response. An average of extreme estimates (Boskin 1978 and Howrey and Hymans 1978) would indicate that a 10 percent increase in returns (say from 7 percent to 7.7 percent) would increase the private saving rate by 2 percent (say from 9.8 percent to 10.0 percent). At today's levels such a change is equal to roughly $15 billion. If the relative size of the revenue loss and the increased saving persists upon closer scrutiny, the favorable tax provisions may well contribute to lower national saving. Much work remains to be done on this issue.

Summary

This review of the evidence on the impact of pensions on saving highlights how little is known beyond the fact that individuals tend to reduce their own saving in response to anticipated pension benefits, and the offset tends to be less than dollar-for-dollar. The lack of good information about the value of expected pension benefits—at least until the advent of the 1983 and 1986 Surveys of Consumer Finances—has made it impossible to put a precise number on the size of the offset.

The individual response is only the first step in determining the impact of pensions on national saving. For this, it is necessary to know whether the reduction in individual saving is matched by direct saving by the company and, if not, whether shareholders increase their own saving. Finally, the question of the extent to which the tax expenditure for pensions acts as an effective stimulus for saving needs to be resolved. In short, we know less about the impact of pensions on saving than we think; much more empirical research is required. In the past, the research has been driven by the available data; the next section will discuss the data needed to answer the questions.

IV. How Do the Data We Have Compare to the Data We Need?

Given the advances in the collection of pension data and the inclusion of retirement expectations at the survey level, this section will focus primarily on the treatment of pensions in the national accounts. In accounting for pension transactions in the national accounts, three major considerations emerge from the preceding discussion about the potential impact of pensions on saving. The first is the need to distinguish between defined benefit plans and defined contribution plans. The second issue is the need to use consistent, accrual-based accounting for the measurement of pension wealth. The current-period increment in this wealth outstanding is the relevant component of national saving rather than the flow of benefit payments from these plans or the employer contributions and investment income inflows to these plans. Finally, the accounting of the current and capital accounts must be integrated.

Distinction Between Plan Types

Currently, no separate information is provided for defined benefit and defined contribution plans in either the National Income and Product Accounts (NIPA) or their capital account counterpart, the Flow-of-Funds Accounts (FOF). Several important differences between these plans argue for their separate treatment in the national accounts. The most significant distinction is the residual liability of defined benefit plan sponsors with respect to investment risk. By definition, defined contribution plans entail no such liability for the employer.

Differentiation between types of plans is particularly important in the NIPA accounts. Whereas the increment to pension wealth for defined contribution plans can be measured by employer and employee contributions, plus investment income earned on plan assets, this is not the case for defined benefit plans. For a variety of reasons, employer contributions under defined benefit plans may differ significantly from the pension rights accrued in a given year. Beginning in 1980, for example, employers significantly slowed their contributions to defined benefit plans, as substantial capital gains on pension fund assets raised funding ratios. Since benefit accruals did not slow, this phenomenon caused NIPA-measured personal income and saving to understate the increment to individuals' pension wealth. Without the boom in the stock market and the strong bond market, contributions to private pension plans in 1986 would have been nearly $30 billion higher than reported (Munnell and Ernsberger 1987). Adding this amount in personal income and saving raises the 1986 saving rate from 4.3 to 5.3 percent. Accrual-based accounting for defined benefit plans in the NIPA would avoid such distortions.

Under current Flow-of-Funds accounting, differentiation of plan types is less necessary, since the accounts refer only to the assets funding each plan type. The separate treatment of defined contribution plans, however, would help to sharpen the differences between these two broad classes of employer-sponsored plans. From the Flow-of-Funds capital account perspective, moreover, the separate treatment of defined contribution plans would reinforce the similarities between these employer-sponsored plans and "individual-sponsored" plans such as the familiar IRA and Keogh arrangements.

Accounting for Pension Benefits

The foundation for a meaningful representation of pensions in the National Income and Product and Flow-of-Funds Accounts is consistent accrual-based accounting for pension claims. Under such an approach, benefit accruals would represent the pension component of personal income and, in turn, personal saving.

As noted earlier, for defined contribution plans the pension-related component of personal income is simply the sum of employers' contributions and the investment income of the assets currently funding these plans. Individual-sponsored retirement arrangements, including IRA-Keogh arrangements, can be treated in a parallel fashion. For private employer-sponsored defined contribution plans, the accounting approach outlined above is consistent with the treatment implicitly accorded these plans in the NIPA. That is, the National Income and Product Accounts currently recognize as personal income the employer contributions to and investment income from *all* private-sector pension plans, including both defined benefit and defined contribution arrangements. Investment income earned by IRA-Keogh type plans in effect is also included in personal income since the NIPA add an estimate of income earned on these tax-deferred accounts to tax-basis personal income reported by the IRS.

For defined benefit (DB) plans, the current NIPA treatment diverges markedly from the accrual-based pension wealth approach, since employers' residual liability for provision of defined benefits serves as a wedge between the cash basis contributions plus investment income flow and the accrual of these plans' benefit obligations. On an accrual basis, the personal income arising from DB pension-covered employment in the current period is the present discounted value accrual of individuals' pension claims against defined benefit plans. As illustrated above, financial markets-induced variations in plans' funding levels can cause this accrual measure of pension saving for DB plans to diverge quite widely from the employer contributions plus investment income measure currently used in the NIPA.

The switch to an explicit benefit liabilities measure of households' pension wealth would also remove much of the pronounced fluctuations in pension wealth currently reported in the Flow-of-Funds Accounts. For example, less than 30 percent of the $190 billion decline in pension wealth currently reported in the FOF to have occurred as a result of the October 1987 stock market plunge would remain after conversion to accrual-based benefit claims accounting.

Integrated Treatment of the Current and Capital Accounts

From a capital account perspective, accrual-based pension accounting represents not only households' defined benefit pension wealth but also the pension sector's DB pension liability. This pension wealth liability claim measure provides a much more meaningful accounting linkage between households and the pension sector than does the funded assets measure of pension wealth currently used in the Flow-of-Funds Accounts. Moreover, this liability measure when combined with an estimate of the assets funding defined benefit plans effectively links DB pension plans' capital position to the sponsoring business sectors by showing an explicit unfunded liability of the business sector.[8]

This approach to accounting for defined benefit pensions clarifies the relationship between these plans' capital account and their more familiar current account. Since only benefit accruals are relevant in these plans' net saving, sponsors' asset funding decisions are clearly seen as a purely capital account transaction, albeit one with a significant impact on business taxes due to the deductibility of qualified pension contributions as a business expense.

This approach contrasts with the FOF's current use of pension funds' assets as a proxy for pension wealth since employer contributions are linked only to tax-basis current account reporting of qualified pension contributions. Under the current NIPA-FOF scheme, moreover, the employer contributions that are not qualified for deduction as a business expense under IRS maximum funding limitations would not be captured in NIPA employer contributions data, producing a potentially sizable discrepancy in the FOF's sources and uses of funds balance for the household sector.

---

8. This unfunded pension liability measure, of course, has some serious shortcomings for the analysis of pension policy. If summed across the population of all defined benefit plans, overfunding of some plans will tend to mask the more serious underfunding of other plans, implicitly assuming that overfunded pension monies still are the asset of sponsoring firms. One partial solution is to show separate under- and overfunding positions with the overfunded amount treated as residual net worth of the pension sector. Largely separate pension asset and liability calculations entail a further, potentially serious, complication of ignoring the efficiencies that can be obtained by asset-liability immunization strategies.

Explicit recognition of DB plan overfunding in the Flow-of-Funds Accounts would greatly help to clarify the treatment of pension asset reversions in the NIPA-FOF. At present, reversion funds are completely excluded from NIPA measures of business income under the assumption that these pension-derived receipts are entirely attributable to capital gains on the assets funding the plans. Given current FOF procedures, however, these reversion inflows to the corporate sector are captured as a use of funds without a corresponding source of funds.

In addition to providing an accounting framework for the late 1980s' pension asset reversion experience, DB plans' proposed capital account treatment would help to clarify the distinction between the plan sponsor, the plan trustee, and the Pension Benefits Guaranty Corporation (PBGC). While the sponsoring corporation bears the investment risk and residual liability for provision of defined benefits for ongoing plans, it is important to adopt a capital account structure in which the PBGC can be integrated.

Current Flow-of-Funds treatment fails to incorporate the PBGC's capital account and makes no provision for transfer of plan assets when default by a sponsor occurs. Accurate benefit liability and plan asset estimates are especially important in these cases. Since PBGC-insured benefits typically fall short of total plan benefits, a decline in households' pension wealth must be recognized when default occurs. The proposed measure of the PBGC's capital account, together with a measure of the DB pension sector's aggregate underfunding, would be very useful in putting this federal pension insurance operation in perspective.

Summary

The current treatment of pensions in the national accounts deviates substantially from the conceptual idea, and much of the analysis of pensions and pension policy has been distorted by the lack of appropriate data. Early studies relating measured private saving to pension saving (the increase in the book value of pension fund reserves) were based on notions of income, saving, and pension activity that differ greatly from those implied by the theory. The intense interest in pension fund assets as an indication of the contribution of pensions to national saving is another example where the mere availability of the data has driven the analysis.

The significant improvements in pension accounting and reporting create a wonderful opportunity to improve the data on pensions included in the national accounts. Careful analysis will be needed to determine the precise measure of pension accruals that should be adopted, but moving away from exclusive reliance on cash concepts should greatly enhance our ability to understand the role of pensions in the workings of the economy.

V. Conclusion

It is difficult to carry out economic analysis based primarily on accrual concepts in a world where activity is reported on a cash basis. Particularly in the pension area, the personal income and saving statistics produced by the National Income and Product Accounts differ substantially from the concepts used in most economic analyses. In the corporate sector, cash accounting tends to distort the measurement of pension commitments and thereby corporate profits. Accounts based on cash also fail to recognize the relationship between the federal government and the household and business sectors created by the Pension Benefit Guaranty Corporation insurance. Finally, tax expenditure estimates based solely on a cash flow analysis do not provide an accurate measure of the benefits of the tax-favored treatment of pensions.

The time is right for improving the data on pensions. Great strides have been made in the area of cross-sectional surveys of individuals; these improvements should permit better estimates of the extent to which employees reduce their other saving in response to guaranteed pension benefits. Comparable improvements are needed at the macro level; revising our national accounts to make use of available data should be given high priority.

References

Accounting Principles Board. 1966. *Accounting for the Cost of Pension Plans.* APB Opinion 8. New York: American Institute of Certified Public Accountants, 1966.

American Institute of Accountants, Committee on Accounting Procedure. 1956. "Accounting for Costs of Pension Plans." *Accounting Research Bulletin* 47 (September 1956).

Ando, Albert and Franco Modigliani. 1963. "The Life-Cycle Hypothesis of Saving: Aggregate Implications and Tests." *American Economic Review* 53 (March 1963): 55–64.

Avery, Robert B., Gregory E. Elliehausen, and Thomas A. Gustafson. 1986. "Pensions and Social Security in Household Portfolios: Evidence from the 1983 Survey of Consumer Finances." In F. Gerard Adams and Susan M. Wachter, eds., *Savings and Capital Formation: The Policy Options,* Lexington, MA: D. C. Heath and Company, 1986. pp. 127–60.

Blinder, Alan S. 1982. "Private Pensions and Public Pensions: Theory and Fact." NBER Working Paper No. 902, June. Cambridge, MA: National Bureau of Economic Research, 1982.

Blinder, Alan S., Roger Gordon, and David E. Wise. 1981. *An Empirical Study of the Effects of Pensions on the Saving and Labor Supply Decisions of Older Men.* Princeton, NJ: Mathtech, Inc., 1981.

Boskin, Michael J. 1978. "Taxation, Saving, and the Rate of Interest." *Journal of Political Economy* 86 (April 1978), part 2: S3–S27.

Bradford, David. 1989. "Saving: How Is It Defined and What Should Be Included?" Paper presented at American Council for Capital Formation symposium. Saving: The Challenge for the U.S. Economy, October 12, 1989, Washington, DC.

Bulow, Jeremy I., Randall Morck, and Lawrence Summers. 1987. "How Does the Market Value Unfunded Pension Liabilities?" In NBER Project Report, Zvi Bodie, John B. Shoven and David A. Wise, eds., *Issues in Pension Economics,* Chicago: University of Chicago Press, 1987. pp. 81–104.

Cagan, Phillip. 1965. "The Effect of Pension Plans on Aggregate Saving: Evidence from a Sample Survey." National Bureau of Economic Research, Occasional Paper 95. New York: Columbia University Press. 1965.

Diamond, Peter A. and Jerry A. Hausman. 1980. "Individual Savings Behavior." Paper prepared for the National Commission on Social Security, September 1980.

Feldstein, Martin S. 1978. "Do Private Pensions Increase National Saving?" *Journal of Public Economics,* 10 (December 1978): 277–93.

Feldstein, Martin S. and Randall Morck. 1982. "Pension Funding Decisions, Interest Rate Assumptions, and Share Prices." NBER Working Paper No. 938, July 1982. Also Chapter 7 in Zvi Bodie and John A. Shoven, eds., *Financial Aspects of the U.S. Pension System.* Chicago: University of Chicago Press, 1987.

Feldstein, Martin S. and Anthony J. Pellechio. 1979. "Social Security and Household Wealth Accumulation: New Microeconometric Evidence." *Review of Economics and Statistics* 61 (August 1979): 361–68.

Feldstein, Martin S. and Stephanie Seligman. 1981. "Pension Funding, Share Prices and National Saving." *Journal of Finance* 36 (September 1981): 801–24.

Financial Accounting Standards Board of the Financial Accounting Foundation. 1980, 1985. *Statement of Financial Accounting Standards No. 35: Accounting and Reporting by Defined Pension Benefit Plans* (1980). *No. 36: Disclosure of Plan Information* (1980). *No. 87: Employers' Accounting for Pensions.* (1985). Financial Accounting Series No. 012. Stamford, CT: Financial Accounting Foundation.

Gersovitz, Mark. 1982. "Economic Consequences of Unfunded Vested Benefits." *Journal of Public Economics* 19 (November 1982): 171–86.

Grad, Susan. 1988. *Income of the Population 55 or Older, 1986.* SSA Publication No. 13–11871. Washington, DC: Social Security Administration, June 1988.

Hemming, Richard and Russell Harvey. 1983. "Occupational Pension Scheme Membership and Retirement Saving." *Economic Journal* 93 (March 1983): 128–44.

Howrey, Philip E. and Saul H. Hymans. 1978. "The Measurement and Determination of Loanable Funds Saving." *Brookings Papers on Economic Activity* 3 (1978): 655–85.

Hubbard, R. Glenn. 1985. "Personal Taxation, Pension Wealth, and Portfolio Composition." *Review of Economics and Statistics* 67 (February 1985): 53–60.

———. 1986. "Pension Wealth and Individual Saving." *Journal of Money, Credit and Banking* 18 (May 1986): 167–78.

Katona, George. 1965. *Private Pensions and Individual Saving*. Ann Arbor, MI: Survey Research Center, Institute for Social Policy, University of Michigan, 1965.

Kotlikoff, Laurence J. 1979. "Testing the Theory of Social Security and Life-Cycle Accumulation." *American Economic Review* 69 (June 1979): 396–410.

———. 1988. "Intergenerational Transfers and Savings." *Journal of Economic Perspectives* 2, 2 (Spring 1988): 41–58.

Modigliani, Franco. 1988. "The Role of Intergenerational Transfers and Life Cycle Saving in the Accumulation of Wealth." *Journal of Economic Perspectives* 2, 2 (Spring 1988): 15–40.

Modigliani, Franco and Merton H. Miller. 1958. "The Cost of Capital, Corporation Finance, and the Theory of Investment." *American Economic Review* 48 (June 1958): 261–97.

———. 1963. "Corporate Income Taxes and the Cost of Capital: A Correction." *American Economic Review* 53 (June 1963): 433–43.

Munnell, Alicia H. 1974. *The Effect of Social Security on Personal Saving*. Cambridge, MA: Ballinger, 1974.

———. 1976. "Private Pensions and Saving: New Evidence." *Journal of Political Economy* 84 (October 1976): 1013–32.

———. 1982. *The Economics of Private Pensions*. Studies in Social Economics. Washington, DC: Brookings Institution, 1982.

———. 1984. "A Note on the Controversy over Tax Expenditure Estimates for Pension Plans." Unpublished manuscript.

Munnell, Alicia H. with Nicole Ernsberger. 1987. "Pension Contributions and the Stock Market." *New England Economic Review* (November/December 1987): 3–14.

Oldfield, George S. 1977. "Financial Aspects of the Private Pension System." *Journal of Money, Credit and Banking* 9 (February 1977): 48–54.

Pechman, Joseph A., Henry J. Aaron, and Michael K. Taussig. 1968. *Social Security: Perspectives for Reform*. Washington, DC: The Brookings Institution, 1968.

Pitelis, Christos N. 1985. "The Effects of Life Assurance and Pension Funds on Other Saving: The Postwar U.K. Experience." *Bulletin of Economic Research* 37 (September 1985): 214–29.

Schultze, Charles L. 1989. "Response to 'Saving: How Is It Defined and What Should Be Included?'" Paper presented at American Council for Capital Formation Symposium, Saving: The Challenge for the U.S. Economy, October 12, 1989, Washington, DC.

U.S. Office of Management and Budget. 1990. *Budget of the United States Government, Fiscal Year 1991*. Washington, DC: U.S. Government Printing Office.

Comments by Robert B. Avery

Alicia Munnell and Frederick Yohn have written an excellent summary of the existing evidence relating pensions to savings. They carefully enumerate why the issue is interesting and lay out a simple framework in which to view the problem. They qualify their presentation, however, with a detailed list of reasons as to why the "real world" may deviate from their simple framework. They present an exhaustive and critical survey of the existing empirical evidence, both micro and macro. Finally, they conclude with a discussion about how the existing data, particularly those in the national accounts, compare with data we need.

Since my co-discussant, Robert Parker, has a clear advantage in evaluating macro data and the national accounts, my comments focus on issues relating to the use of individual household data. I shall not repeat Munnell and Yohn's excellent summary of existing work, but rather shall highlight gaps in our knowledge and summarize the major methodological tasks confronting researchers working in this area.

In order to conduct an empirical analysis of the relationship between pensions and savings behavior at the individual household level, it is necessary to measure both variables. This presents a formidable task. To measure household savings properly requires an evaluation of household wealth at two points in time. This involves either a panel data set or a faith, not shared by many survey professionals, that households can accurately recall their wealth and/or can report accurate information on wealth changes. Unfortunately, good panel data on household wealth are extremely rare; consequently many researchers have resorted to alternative methods of analysis utilizing cross-sectional data on wealth. With cross-sectional data, saving is not actually measured, but rather inferred from differences in wealth between households after controlling for exogenous factors. Wealth is viewed as the accumulation of a savings flow. This procedure requires assumptions about the stability of the wealth function and is subject to significant cohort problems.

Several good panel surveys have collected household wealth data.

These include the Retirement History Survey (RHS), the Survey of Income and Program Participation (SIPP), and the recent Surveys of Consumer Finances (SCF). However, even with these surveys, which purport to include saving measures, the use of these measures is fraught with difficulty.

In measuring saving, the ideal sampling element would be dollars of saving, not households. To the extent that they differ, implications drawn from a household-based frame will not apply directly to an aggregate concept of national personal saving. The dollar-based and household-based frames differ in two important ways. First, the household-based frame may miss saving and dissaving associated with new household formation. Second, the frames can differ because of analytic uncertainties about the treatment of household structural change, particularly in the case of marriage, separation, divorce, or death.

The seriousness of the issue of household structural change can be seen from the following statistics drawn from my work with Arthur Kennickell utilizing the 1983 and 1986 SCFs (see Avery and Kennickell, 1990). During the three-year interval between the surveys, 27 percent of sample households experienced a change in marital status and/or had an adult relative move into or out of the household. Moreover, households experiencing a structural change were not an inconsequential group in terms of wealth holdings or saving: 21 percent of total household wealth in the 1986 sample was held by households that had experienced a change in household structure since 1983; such households had a similar share (19 percent) of the total saving of net savers over the three years. They had an even larger share (31 percent) of the dissaving of those households losing wealth over the three-year period. To put the latter figure in perspective, the dissaving of households undergoing a change in status was more than 20 percent of the total U.S. gross private saving over the three-year period.

Theoretical economists have made little headway in developing frameworks for modeling saving and wealth in the presence of changes in household composition. The empirical evidence that has been developed is not much better. Because of definitional problems, samples are often pruned to drop all non-intact families. However, if one assumes that transitions are known by households, but unknown to the econometrician, the use of intact samples may still create bias; if one assumes that transitions are stochastic and generate dead-weight costs, the use of purely intact samples almost surely induces sample selection bias.

Another problem with saving data is the fact that both saving and wealth are very narrowly held. Over one-quarter of U.S. household wealth is held by the top 0.5 percent of households. Saving is equally concentrated. Over 40 percent of the net real savings reported in the

1986 SCF was done by the top 0.5 percent of 1986 wealthholders. In a random sample, even one as large as SIPP, this would represent only 60 households. If the entire distribution of saving is to be represented, proper sampling of the upper tail of the wealth distribution is crucial. Yet with the exception of the SCF, this has not been done in any national survey.

A final concern with the use of micro saving data is the problem of measurement. Wealth data are difficult to collect and typically fraught with problems of missing information. Unless procedures are developed that explicitly take account of the data in other periods to impute panel wealth data, extraneous measurement error will be introduced into the calculation of saving. This will make saving appear much noisier than it is.

As detailed by Munnell and Yohn, good individual pension data are even more difficult to obtain. There is little agreement regarding the appropriate way to quantify the "quality" of an individual's pension, particularly defined benefit plans. Even if there were agreement on this issue, evidence suggests strongly that survey respondents would have difficulty providing the information. For example, in the 1983 SCF respondents were asked about their expectations for Social Security income. Over 80 percent of the sample refused to give an answer. Similarly, over 50 percent of all respondents were unwilling even to venture a guess as to their expected benefits from company pension plans.

There is a clear need to determine what pension information households have and how to turn such information, particularly with defined benefit plans, into quantifiable measures of pension quality. At best such calculations will require assumptions about retirement dates, future contributions, discount rates, and investment performance. An alternative approach is to solicit information directly from employers. However, this method is expensive and requires respondents to report their employer's name, a request that makes many survey organizations uncomfortable. Moreover, this approach would only work with defined benefit plans. Even if successful, the use of employer data raises the interesting question of which is the most relevant in a behavioral equation for saving, the *true worth* of a pension or the respondent's *perception* of the value of their pension. Clearly much methodological work needs to be done to address these questions.

Although the tone of my discussion has been discouraging, I see several hopeful signs on the horizon. The 1989 SCF comes as close as any survey to addressing a number of the problems raised in this discussion. About one-half of its respondents will have been interviewed as part of the 1983 and 1986 SCFs, thus providing multiple measurements on wealth; it has a high-income supplement drawn from tax files; it contains measures of the division of wealth in divorce; it has a pension module and an extensive list of wealth questions. The hope is that it will also include a pension survey of employers as did the 1983 SCF. Another positive sign is the potential for a new Retirement History Survey. Properly executed, such a long-run panel of both wealth and pension data should offer great potential for addressing the kinds of questions raised by Munnell and Yohn.

Reference

Avery, Robert B. and Arthur B. Kennickell. "Household Saving in the U.S.," 1990. "Measurement of Household Saving in the U.S. Obtained from First-Differencing Wealth Estimates." Presented at the 21st General Conference of the International Association for Research in Income and Wealth. Lahnstein, Germany, August 20–26, 1989, revised February 1990. *Review of Income and Wealth* (1991).

Comments by Robert P. Parker

The paper by Munnell and Yohn reviews several important definitional issues associated with the relationship between pensions and
household saving and suggests changes in the measurement of pensions in the U.S. National Income and Product Accounts (NIPA).

Given that a major concern of the Bureau of Economic Analysis
(BEA) is to see that these accounts provide information that facilitates
research and analysis of these types of relationships, my comments will
first focus on the authors' three proposals for changing the NIPA.
Then, I will identify several other definitional issues relating to the
NIPA measure of personal saving that should be considered in studying the effects of pensions on saving.

Three Proposals for Changing NIPA

The authors make the following three proposals for changes in the
measurement of pension-related transactions in the NIPA:

- ". . . distinguish between defined benefit plans and defined contribution plans";
- ". . . use consistent, accrual-based accounting for the measurement
  of pension wealth"; and
- integrate ". . . the accounting of the current and capital accounts."

The first proposal would not redefine any NIPA components and
would enhance the analysis of various aspects of pension plans. A lack
of adequate source data might prevent introducing such detail; tabulations of data from Form 5500 could provide the necessary information.

The second proposal would value the pension part of personal
income and saving as benefit accruals. This approach, however, would
require a redefinition not only of personal income and saving but also
of national income and business saving. In national income, as pres-
ently defined, contributions by employers to both defined contribution

and defined benefit pension plans reflect the current cost of providing pension benefits; these costs, the cash contributions, are deducted from business incomes—mainly corporate profits—and are included in employee compensation. These contributions also are included in personal income along with the interest, dividends, and rental income earned on the assets of the pension plans.

The authors propose that contributions to defined benefit plans be restated from the cash funding to an accrual accounting basis, the latter reflecting the present discounted value of accrued pension benefits. The difference between the two measures would affect NIPA employee compensation and the business income components by the same amount, but with opposite signs. In personal income, other labor income (OLI)—the component that includes pension contributions—would be affected in the same way as employee compensation. However, because the calculation of an accrual measure reflects such factors as benefit payments and the difference between projected and actual returns on plan assets including capital gains and losses, it is unclear how the other components of personal income would be affected by the authors' proposal. These considerations are important because benefit payments and capital gains and losses do not enter the present measure of personal income.

From a national income accountant's perspective, there are several problems with the accrual approach. First, the nonwage part of employee compensation is defined as the labor cost to employers, not the value to the employee. Second, the accrual approach would result in business incomes that reflect contingent liabilities; the NIPA do not recognize such liabilities, which include additions to bad debt reserves and write-offs in anticipation of restructurings. (In this respect, NIPA business incomes are defined more like those reported for income tax returns than for financial statements.) Another important effect of the accrual approach would be to count unfunded liabilities as personal rather than as business saving, even though business has access to and control over these funds. Finally, two measurement issues are associated with the use of accrual accounting for pensions. The accrual-based data are not available for all businesses. Where they are available, they are subject to revisions to the underlying actuarial assumptions. For example, changes in projected retirement patterns or interest rates could create a large prior service cost element to the accrual value. A complete accrual approach would require incorporating the change into this value for all periods affected by the revised projection. In view of all of these problems, I would not support the adoption of this proposal.

The third proposal, in my view, has the greatest potential to provide substantially more useful data. An integrated set of current and capital accounts would show both the cash and the accrual-based contributions without changing the present NIPA income measures. These accounts also would serve as the core of what national income accountants call a satellite account. Such accounts cut across the usual sectors—persons, business, government, and foreign; incorporate additional types of information not found in the regular accounts; and are designed for the analysis of specific areas of economic activity. (BEA already has such an account for pollution, abatement, and control expenditures, and is considering similar accounts for research and development, pensions, and natural resources.)

The balance sheet for a pension satellite account would provide detail on the different types of pension funds, the types of investments of the funds, and other identifiable forms of retirement savings—for example, IRAs and thrift savings plans. The balance sheet also would feature revaluation accounts, which capture the impact on household wealth of changing asset values. The integrated current account would show different measures of income and saving—for example, measures reflecting capital gains and losses and the treatment as investment of consumer purchases of durable goods other than dwellings. In addition, to enhance the research value of this satellite account, it could include a microdata base that would provide comparable information on the income and wealth of individuals, their occupations, and demographic characteristics such as age, race, and sex. Such a file for income can be developed by matching various existing survey and administrative record files, as was demonstrated for 1972 by BEA as part of its now defunct income-size work. (This file is described in an article by Daniel Radner, "Distribution for Family Income: Improved Estimates" in the July 1982 issue of the *Social Security Administration Bulletin*.)

Other Definitional Issues

As indicated in my opening remarks, analysts should consider other definitional issues underlying the NIPA measure of personal saving in studying the impact of pensions. The life-cycle theory looks primarily at income in terms of wages and salaries. This restrictive approach appears to assume that personal saving does not relate to other forms of income, an assumption that seems no more valid than assuming that personal taxes relate only to wages, because most people with more than one income source withhold only from wages. Consequently, I do not think it is sufficient to recommend adjusting the NIPA to account for the contributions to pension plans on an accrual basis without looking at other definitional issues to determine whether the proposed measures of income and saving are compatible with the life-cycle model. Here are four examples of definitions that should be considered.

(1) The NIPA personal sector is defined to include nonprofit institutions serving individuals. For example, personal income includes investment income earned by private universities, the donations universities receive from businesses, and payments to universities by governments for research. Personal outlay, which is subtracted in calculating personal saving, includes the operating expenses of universities. Thus, the present measure of personal saving includes the difference between universities' non-operating income and operating expenses. Because it is unlikely that pensions affect this part of saving, one should consider removing the saving of nonprofits before studying these effects.

(2) The NIPA define homeownership as a business in which purchases of houses by owner-occupants are treated as investment, and rental payments are imputed to the owner based on equivalent market rates. The difference between these payments (which are included in outlays) and homeownership expenses (such as mortgage interest, depreciation, property taxes, and maintenance and repair) is included in the "rental income of persons" component of personal income. Therefore, the present measure of personal saving is reduced by the difference between the imputed rental payment and rental income. (The problem with this treatment of homeownership in studying pensions and saving is referred to in the Andrews-Hurd chapter.)

(3) As indicated above, purchases of homes are treated in the NIPA as investment; purchases of other consumer durable goods, such as motor vehicles, are not treated as investment as they are in the flow of funds accounts. If such purchases are defined as investment, personal outlays would be reduced by expenditures for new vehicles and increased by a measure, such as depreciation, that serves as a proxy for the flow of services generated by the use of the vehicle. Thus, changing the NIPA to conform to the flow of funds treatment usually results in higher personal saving.

(4) Farm income of unincorporated farmers is included in personal income. These entrepreneurs are seldom covered by pension plans. Most likely, their saving is the hoped-for appreciation of their farmland. The omission of such capital gains from NIPA saving represents another potential distortion to the pension-saving relationship.

I note that the authors did mention one important definitional issue—the classification of state and local pension plans. They suggested that these plans should be defined as private rather than public plans. This view reflects the fact that these plans "behave" like private pension plans in that their funds are invested primarily in private securities. The funds associated with federal government pension plans, on the other hand, are invested in federal securities—a system that many consider tantamount to having these pension plans unfunded. Reclassifying the state and local plans would increase personal saving by transferring the savings associated with these plans from the government sector to the personal sector. (For those interested in this subject, I recommend a paper by Thomas M. Holloway, "Present NIPA Saving Measures: Their Characteristics and Limitations," in the 1989 NBER Studies in Income and Wealth volume 52, edited by Robert E. Lipsey and Helen Stone Tice, entitled *The Measurement of Saving, Investment, and Wealth.*)

Conclusion

I have not discussed improving source data, which is the main topic of this volume, for three reasons. First, I wanted to stress the notion that our most important concern is to develop a sound accounting framework for pensions. Second, a discussion of source data issues would require an article more comprehensive than these comments. Third, the subject of source data is dealt with elsewhere in this volume.

In conclusion, I want to express agreement with the authors' statement that this is a "wonderful opportunity to improve the data on pensions included in the national accounts." BEA is in the process of organizing information about the data that are available. This information will enable us to identify gaps and inconsistencies and to begin the development of a comprehensive set of pension data. At the same time, we are planning to develop the framework for a satellite account for pensions. This volume will be very helpful to us in these efforts.

Chapter 4
Pension Fund Finance

Zvi Bodie and Leslie E. Papke

Introduction

From a finance perspective, pension plans are intermediaries—repositories of household savings invested in the capital markets. This essay describes the goals and financial policies of pension plans and their impact on the financial system. While the essay focuses on plans sponsored by private firms in the U.S., most of the observations apply equally to plans sponsored by labor unions or by governments both in the U.S. and abroad.

The manifest function of a pension plan is to replace an employee's preretirement earnings when combined with Social Security retirement benefits and private savings (Bodie, 1990a). Employers, however, also use pension plans as a device to attract, retain, and motivate employees, and eventually to encourage them to retire.

The government affects the pension system in a number of important ways. It provides a "floor" of retirement income through the Social Security system, encourages the private provision of pensions through tax incentives, establishes rules regarding eligibility and benefit security, and provides pension insurance.

Once the income replacement goal of a pension plan has been set, there are two basic financial issues that must be addressed:

1. The funding decision—how much to set aside during the employee's working years to provide future retirement benefits.
2. The investment decision—how to invest the funds that are set aside.

The authors' research was supported by Department of Labor Contract J-9-P-8-0097.

The way these decisions are made depends critically on the type of plan.

Defined Contribution and Defined Benefit Plans

Pension plans are classified into two types: defined contribution and defined benefit. As the names suggest, in a defined contribution plan a formula determines contributions (e.g., 15 percent of annual wages), whereas in a defined benefit plan a formula defines benefits (e.g., 1 percent of final pay per year of service).

In a defined contribution plan, each employee has an account into which the employer (and usually the employee) make regular contributions. Contributions from both parties are tax deductible, and investment income accrues tax free. At retirement, the employee receives a benefit whose size depends on the accumulated value of the funds in the retirement account.

In a defined contribution plan much of the task of achieving the income replacement goal falls on the employees. Often they must choose both the level of contributions and the way the defined contribution account is to be invested. In principle, contributions may be invested in any security, although in practice most plans limit investment options to bond, stock, and money market funds. The employee bears all the investment risk, and the firm has no formal obligation beyond making its periodic contribution.

In a defined benefit plan, the employee's pension benefit is determined by a formula that takes into account years of service for the employer and, in most cases, wages or salary. The plan sponsor or an insurance company hired by the sponsor guarantees the benefits and thus absorbs the investment risk. In the U.S., the Pension Benefit Guaranty Corporation (PBGC), an agency of the federal government, backs the sponsor's guarantee of pension benefits up to specified limits.

Each of the two plan types has both advantages and disadvantages (Bodie, Marcus, and Merton, 1988). For example, while defined benefit plans seem to offer employees more complete retirement income insurance, they do present problems for employees who switch jobs during their working careers, especially if benefits are not automatically protected against inflation.

Vested employees retain the pension benefits earned when they stop working for the employer sponsoring the pension plan. In the U.S., full vesting usually occurs after five years of employment, but employees who have accrued benefits under one employer's defined benefit plan usually cannot transfer those accruals to another employer, even if they are vested.

Very few private sponsors in the U.S. offer pension benefits that are explicitly indexed for inflation. Instead, benefits are often tied to an employee's pay in the final years of employment. Some observers see this practice as implicit indexation, since pay generally keeps pace with inflation. But unlike Social Security benefits, whose starting value is adjusted to a general index of wages, private pension benefits even in final-pay formula plans are "indexed" only to the extent that (1) the employee continues to work for the same employer, (2) the employee's own wage or salary keeps pace with the general index, (3) the employer continues to maintain the same plan, and (4) increments in pension benefits are not offset by decreases in other components of the compensation package (Bulow, 1982).

This lack of automatic indexation gives rise to a portability problem. Workers who change jobs receive lower pension benefits at retirement than otherwise identical workers who stay with the same employer, even if the employers have defined benefit plans with the same final-pay benefit formula and the employee is vested. In contrast to the U.S., in the U.K. a law passed in 1988 requires pension sponsors to index accrued pension benefits for inflation to the age of retirement, subject to a 5 percent per year cap. Thus even a terminated employee has at least partial indexation for general inflation up to retirement age.

After retirement, full cost-of-living adjustment of private pension benefits is rare in both the U.S. and the U.K. In continental Europe, however, such adjustments are more common (Clark, 1990). Many sponsors in the U.S. have voluntarily given ad hoc benefit increases to plan participants in the past (Clark, Allen, and Summer, 1983). Some observers interpret these increases as evidence of implicit cost-of-living indexation (e.g., Ippolito, 1986). Since the sponsor is under no obligation to provide such increases, however, they are more like a voluntary profit-sharing arrangement than a cost-of-living allowance (COLA).

As measured both by number of plan participants and total assets, the defined benefit form dominates both in the U.S. and abroad, although the trend in the U.S. since the mid-1970s is for sponsors to choose the defined contribution form when starting new plans. But the two plan types are not mutually exclusive. Many sponsors adopt defined benefit plans as their primary plan, in which participation is mandatory, and supplement them with voluntary defined contribution plans.

Funding

With defined benefit plans, there is an important distinction between the pension *plan* and the pension *fund*. The plan is the contractual arrangement setting out the rights and obligations of all parties; the fund is a separate pool of assets set aside to provide collateral for the promised benefits. In defined contribution plans, by definition the value of the benefits equals that of the assets, so the plan is always exactly fully funded. But in defined benefit plans, there is a continuum of possibilities. There may be no separate fund, in which case the plan is said to be unfunded. When there is a separate fund with assets worth less than the present value of the promised benefits, the plan is underfunded. And if the plan's assets have a market value that exceeds the present value of the plan's liabilities, it is overfunded.

In the U.S., the federal government requires private-sector plan sponsors to fund their defined benefit plans either by insuring them through an insurance company or by making contributions to a special pension trust. There are no such requirements, however, for pension plans sponsored by state and local governments. In Germany and Japan, even private-sector firms are not legally required to fund their pension liabilities, and many do not.

Many critics of unfunded pension systems have argued that lack of funding reduces national saving. But funding per se does not affect saving, if saving is measured properly. The mistaken belief that an accrued benefit is not part of personal saving unless funded stems from the way benefits under defined benefit plans are treated in the U.S. national accounts, where unfunded benefits are ignored (Munnell and Yohn, this volume). From an economic point of view, however, a defined benefit pension entitlement is part of labor compensation when it is earned, and its present value is therefore part of personal saving whether or not it is funded.

In the U.S. there are two main reasons why firms fund their defined benefit pension plans: minimum standards imposed by law and tax incentives. The purpose of the funding standards is to help secure the promised pension benefits against the risk of default by the sponsor and to discourage abuse of the insurance provided by the government. The tax incentives are designed to encourage employers to offer pension plans to their employees.

Black (1980) and Tepper (1981) have shown that the tax advantage to pension funding stems from the ability of the sponsor to earn the pre-tax rate of return on pension investments after taxes. To exploit this legal tax shelter fully, it is necessary to invest in assets with the highest spread between pre-tax and after-tax rates of return for a given risk level. In the U.S., this means investing in fixed-income securities issued by non-tax-exempt entities—mostly corporate bonds and mortgages. This tax advantage also creates an incentive for plan sponsors to overfund their pension plans and, therefore, creates the need for the government to set limits on contributions. Sponsors are allowed to make additional tax-qualified contributions as long as pension assets are less than 150 percent of the current liability.[1]

Additionally, funding provides the sponsoring corporation with financial "slack" that can be used in case of possible financial difficulties the firm may face in the future.[2] Because the law still allows plan sponsors facing financial distress to draw upon excess pension assets by reducing funding or, in the extreme case, voluntary plan termination, the pension fund may serve as a tax-sheltered corporate contingency fund.

Pension Investment Strategies

The special tax status of pension funds creates the same incentive for both defined contribution and defined benefit plans to tilt their asset mix towards assets with the largest spread between pre-tax and after-tax rates of return. In a defined contribution plan, because the participant bears all of the investment risk, the optimal asset mix also depends on the risk tolerance of the participant.

In defined benefit plans, optimal investment policy may be different because the sponsor absorbs the investment risk. If, as usually assumed, the sponsor has full claim to the fund surplus, then to maximize the tax advantages for the sponsor, the fund should be invested in fixed-income securities issued by non-tax-exempt entities—mostly corporate bonds and mortgages, as discussed above.

If the sponsor has to share some of the upside potential of the pension assets with plan participants, there is further incentive to invest in fixed-income securities. In this case, the sponsor can eliminate all investment risk by investing in securities that match the promised benefits (Bodie, 1990b). If, for example, the plan sponsor has to pay $100 per year for the next five years, it can provide this stream of benefit payments by buying a set of five zero-coupon bonds each with a face value of $100 and maturing sequentially. By so doing the sponsor eliminates the risk of a shortfall. This is called immunization of the pension liability.

As of 1987, the law in the U.S. specifies that the employer owns all surplus pension assets as long as specific standards are satisfied (Van-Derhei, 1988). Regardless of current law, however, representatives of organized labor, some politicians, and even a few pension professionals

1. The relevant law is the Omnibus Budget Reconciliation Act (OBRA) of 1987.
2. See Bodie et al. (1987) for a more complete discussion of the financial slack motive for funding a pension plan.

believe that the sponsor does not have a right to the entire surplus (Bulow and Scholes, 1983). Some are actively trying to change the law to require sponsors to use surplus assets to provide cost-of-living adjustments for retirees.

In light of these tax and risk considerations, there is an empirical puzzle regarding the investment policy of defined benefit plans in the U.S. By investing 100 percent in fixed-income securities, a sponsor could both maximize the tax advantage of funding the pension plan and minimize the risk-adjusted cost of guaranteeing the defined benefits. But on average sponsors invest from 40 percent to 60 percent of their portfolios in equity securities (Bodie and Papke, 1990). There are several possible explanations for this practice:

1. Management views the pension plan as a trust for the employees and manages fund assets as if it were a defined contribution plan. Believing that a successful policy of investing in stocks will result in extra benefits for employees, management may decide to take the risk.

2. Since the expected rate of return is higher on stocks than on bonds, some sponsors think that they can contribute less to the pension fund by investing more in stocks. They reason that since pension obligations are long term, stocks are not really riskier than bonds. Therefore, they need only match the stock market averages in order to reduce pension costs. But such reasoning is a fallacy (Bodie, 1990b). The only way to reduce risk-adjusted pension costs by investing in stocks is to beat the market, not merely match it.

3. For an underfunded plan of a corporation in financial distress, PBGC insurance may unintentionally create an incentive to invest in stocks and other risky assets. The PBGC's insurance of pension benefits, in effect, transfers much of the downside risk from the sponsor to the government. The value of PBGC insurance increases with the risk of the underlying assets, but the cost to the sponsor does not (Harrison and Sharpe, 1983). Before the Single-Employer Pension Plan Amendments Act of 1986, even healthy firms with underfunded pension plans had some incentive to exploit PBGC insurance by voluntarily terminating an underfunded plan. The new law has eliminated this possibility (Utgoff, 1988). Firms in financial distress, however, still have an incentive to invest pension fund money in the riskiest assets, just as troubled thrift institutions insured by the government have had similar motivation with respect to their loan portfolios.

Pension Funding and Benefit Security

While defined contribution plans are by definition fully funded, defined benefit plans can be funded to any degree. In Germany and Japan, for example, most corporate pension promises are unfunded. How does pension funding affect benefit security? First, consider why it might not affect benefit security.[3] Suppose sponsors have completely unfunded defined benefit pension plans. Each year benefits accrue to the plan participants. These benefits are guaranteed by the sponsor. Thus, the pension plan beneficiaries have a claim on the sponsor similar to the claim of other creditors. The pension liability is collateralized by the assets of the sponsor. If the plan sponsor is a good credit risk, then the promised benefits are secure. Even if the sponsor is not a good credit risk, the promised benefits can be secure if they are guaranteed by a third party like the Pension Benefit Guaranty Corporation (PBGC).

Now assume full funding of the plans. Assume that sponsors fund their plans by issuing stocks and bonds to other sponsors. Each pension trust will now hold a diversified portfolio of securities issued by the other plan sponsors. In the aggregate no new saving takes place and no new real assets are created as a result of funding. Funding in this case simply amounts to the transfer of securities among plan sponsors, but does not change the value of the benefits. If the government is insuring pension benefits, funding will shift much of the cost of providing this insurance away from the government to the plan sponsors.

How, then, can funding affect benefit security? Suppose benefits can be represented as a perpetual annuity of $B per year. The present value of that perpetual annuity is $B/(r + \delta)$ where r is the risk-free interest rate and δ a risk premium reflecting the default risk of the benefits. Funding can increase the present value of benefits in two ways.

First, if there is funding, the pension obligation is collateralized by a more diversified portfolio of assets, thus reducing the risk of default on the pension obligation. Therefore, δ is reduced and the present value of benefits increases. This assumes that government insurance of pension benefits is only partial. If government insurance is full then, as stated already, funding just shifts the cost of providing it from the government to the sponsors.

Second, if benefits are funded, it is possible that the sponsor will increase B voluntarily. For example, ad hoc benefit increases during periods of high inflation may be related to the pension surplus.[4] If true, this would also increase the present value of benefits.

3. Some of the ideas discussed in this section can be found in Tepper (1982).

The Nature of the Pension Liability

The pensions offered under defined benefit plans in the U.S. are best viewed as annuities that offer a guaranteed minimum nominal benefit determined by the plan's benefit formula. This guaranteed benefit is permanently enriched from time to time, at the discretion of management, depending on the financial condition of the plan sponsor, the increase in the living costs of retirees, and the performance of the fund's assets.[5]

The evidence in support of this "guaranteed minimum" contention is that many plans have voluntarily given ad hoc benefit increases to plan participants in the past.[6] While many have interpreted these increases as evidence of implicit cost-of-living indexation, in actuality they are very different from a formal COLA (cost-of-living adjustment).[7] Rather, they are an implicit claim of the employees on the plan sponsor resembling a profit-sharing arrangement.

The implicit pension obligation is a complex contingent claim, in both the economic and legal senses. One way to view this contingent claim is as an employee ownership share in the pension fund surplus. In the case of corporate pension plans, it seems clear that if the sponsoring corporation does not do well financially, then employees cannot expect to receive anything more than the minimum guaranteed formula benefit.

There is mounting evidence that U.S. corporations facing severe financial difficulties, either because of low profitability or because of a threat of hostile takeover, will terminate their overfunded pension plans and give employees only the legal minimum.[8] On the other hand, if the corporation is doing well financially, and if retired employees face inflation, then there is evidence that the corporation will help them out with ad hoc benefit increases.

In order to measure and compare the degree of funding across plans, it is necessary to establish an accepted and uniform measure of pension benefit (or liability). Since the value of implicit benefits varies by firm, they cannot be uniquely characterized. However, the explicit

---

4. See Allen, Clark, and Sumner (1984), and Allen, Clark, and McDermed (1990) for a discussion of ad hoc benefit increases and inflation.

5. Once a sponsor increases the benefit under a defined benefit plan, it is never reduced. This distinguishes it from a variable annuity.

6. See Clark, Allen, and Sumner (1983) for a discussion of these ad hoc increases.

7. See, for example, Cohn and Modigliani (1985) or Ippolito (1986).

8. See, for example, VanDerhei and Harrington (1989), Petersen (1989), and Pontiff, Shleifer, and Weisbach (1989). Mitchell and Mulherin (1989) present evidence that terminations of overfunded plans may reflect efficient corporate restructuring rather than the transfer of wealth from plan participants to shareholders.

pension obligation, a guaranteed nominal floor, can be easily measured and compared across plans.

In the U.S., both the Financial Accounting Standards Board (FASB) and Congress have adopted the present value of the guaranteed nominal floor as the appropriate measure of a sponsor's pension liability. In FASB Statement 87, the rule-making body of the accounting profession specifies that the measure of corporate pension liabilities to be used on the corporate balance sheet in external reports is the accumulated benefit obligation (ABO)—that is, the present value of pension benefits owed to employees under the plan's benefit formula absent any salary projections and at a nominal rate of interest.[9] In its Omnibus Budget Reconciliation Act (OBRA) of 1987, Congress defined the current liability as the measure of a corporation's pension liability and set limits on the amount of tax-qualified contributions a corporation could make as a proportion of the current liability. OBRA's definition of the current liability is essentially the same as FASB Statement 87's definition of the ABO.

The use of the ABO as the balance sheet measure of a corporation's pension liability has encountered widespread resistance. To quote one critic: "The ABO Must Go!"[10] The essence of the criticism is that the ABO only measures the liability in the event of a plan termination but is irrelevant in a going-concern context. In addition to the ABO, therefore, the Financial Accounting Standards Board recognized another measure of a defined benefit plan's liability—the projected benefit obligation (PBO). The PBO is a measure of the sponsor's pension liability that includes projected increases in salary up to the expected age of retirement. Statement 87 requires corporations to use the PBO in computing pension expense reported in their income statements.

The projected benefit method is not an appropriate way to measure the contingent pension obligation of the corporate sponsor. The adjustments made by actuaries to account for the possibility of employee turnover do not capture the nature of the contingent indexing of benefits under a defined benefit plan. The PBO would be the correct number to use if benefits were tied to some index of prices or wages up to the age of retirement independently of whether the employee stays with the employer. Because private plans in the U.S. do not offer such automatic indexation, however, it is a mistake to use the PBO as the measure of what the sponsor owes.

In contrast to the situation in the U.S., current law in the U.K.

---

9. FASB Statement 87 also requires that U.S. multinational corporations value the liabilities of their foreign pension plans in the same manner as their domestic plans.
10. Ambachtsheer (1989).

requires pension sponsors to index accrued pension benefits for inflation to the age of retirement.[11] Thus even a terminated employee has
indexation for general inflation up to retirement age, as long as the
benefit is vested. Under the U.K. system, the PBO is the appropriate
measure of the sponsor's liability.

Pension Funds and the Capital Markets

Since the mid-1970s, the investment policies of pension funds have
had a profound effect on the capital markets, affecting the rate and
direction of financial innovation, the behavior of security prices, and
the policies of the corporations whose securities they hold. The tightening of fiduciary standards in the U.S. under the Employee Retirement Income Security Act (ERISA) of 1974 and a large increase in the
volatility of interest rates that started at about the same time made it
important for defined benefit pension funds in the U.S. to find efficient
ways to hedge their liabilities.

In response to the hedging demands of pension funds, the financial markets have produced a variety of innovative products (Bodie,
1990b). The success of new financial instruments such as zero coupon
bonds, collateralized mortgage obligations (CMOs), guaranteed investment contracts (GICs), and interest rate futures contracts can be
viewed, at least in part, as due to the active participation of pension
funds.

Pension funds have also pioneered in the development of index
trading. Indexing consists of managing a portfolio in order to match
the performance of some broad market index of stocks, bonds, or a
combination of both. (This market indexing of pension assets should
not be confused with inflation indexing of pension benefits.) Since it
has proven to be less expensive to implement index trades in the futures and options markets, the growing popularity of indexing among
pension funds has fueled the development of new markets for index
futures and options contracts. Pension funds that write call options on
individual stocks or on stock indexes are in effect converting some of
their investment in equities into short-term fixed-income investments.

Pension funds now own a substantial portion of the stock in U.S.
corporations. Their voting powers can profoundly affect corporate
policy. In that power, some political activists see an opportunity to use
pension funds as a means of achieving social and political objectives
seemingly unrelated to the primary goal of providing retirement bene-

---

11. This so-called preservation of pension benefits is subject to a cap of 5 percent per
year.

fits. Examples include the promotion of economic growth in depressed regions or industries, the protection of the environment against pollution, the battle against apartheid in South Africa, or the support of trade unions. This practice of linking retirement goals with social and political objectives is called social investing. In the U.S. and Canada social investing has had its greatest impact on government and union pension funds (Deaton, 1989). Even there, however, the practice has had very limited impact.

Perhaps as significant as the capital market innovations that have occurred because of pension funds are the innovations that have not. Chief among the missing innovations is a market for long-term inflation-protected instruments like CPI-linked bonds. Had pension funds demanded them there is little doubt that such a market would have come into existence. Indeed, several attempts to issue CPI-linked bonds have withered and died because of lack of demand for them, not a shortage of willing issuers. The failure of pension funds to show any significant interest in inflation-protected investment products such as CPI index-linked bonds and CDs may be evidence that they do not view their liabilities as indexed for inflation.[12]

Pension Investment and Public Policy

Pension funds are a large influence in the markets, and their investment policies have been the subject of public discussion and some criticism. We provide an overview of these issues below.

Excessive Churning and Speculation

Recently pension funds have come under criticism for excessive churning and short-sightedness. Some critics argue, for example, that the investment practices of pension funds are partly responsible for short-sightedness on the part of American business. They maintain that this short-sightedness jeopardizes American productivity and our competitive position in the world economy.[13] It is difficult for most finance professionals to understand the basis for these criticisms. There is no

12. These securities had been issued by Franklin Savings Association. See Bodie (1990c) for a discussion.

13. The Excessive Churning and Speculation Act of 1989 (S.1654), sponsored by Senators Dole and Kassebaum, is intended to reduce stock market turnover by taxing short-term capital gains of pension funds. In explaining the rationale for the proposed law, Senator Kassebaum has said: "The legislation is designed to encourage pension fund managers to adopt a better long-term investment strategy. . . . Absent such a change, we face the stark prospect of losing our status as a major industrial player."

economic motive on the part of managers for "excessive churning." More likely, this type of criticism stems from a misunderstanding of how managers select investments.

Most pension fund equity managers search for stocks whose intrinsic values (based on long-run expectations of cash flow) exceed their current price, and they sell them when they believe their prices exceed intrinsic value. Professional equity managers usually employ discounted cash flow models that incorporate estimates of corporate outflows and inflows well into the future.[14] It is, therefore, not unusual for firms with little or no current earnings or net cash inflow to command substantial prices for their stock (biotech firms are a good example). Also, managers react quickly to news such as earnings announcements—this process is the method by which stock prices incorporate all available information.

Using data on portfolio turnover (sale of assets) from selected years, McCarthy and Turner (1989) find that passively managed funds earned a higher rate of return than did pension plans that were actively managed. Plans with extremely low turnover (less than 15 percent) averaged a rate of 8.1 percent, while those with greater turnover (over 70 percent) averaged 7.8 percent. Ippolito and Turner (1987) and Berkowitz Logue (1986) have made a similar calculation and concluded that an active management strategy diminished fund performance. However, this finding is consistent with the notion that defined benefit plans are pursuing a type of portfolio insurance or contingent immunization. If so, then protecting against downside risk comes, it appears, at the cost of a slightly lower rate of return.

Pension Funds and Corporate Control

A criticism of pension funds and other institutional investors is that they do not become sufficiently involved in the management of the corporations whose stock they own. Typically, if a pension fund disapproves of a corporation's actions, it will simply sell its stock, rather than challenge the corporation's top executives.

In the recent environment of hostile takeovers, the fear of losing shareholder support has been a powerful force pushing management of target firms to take actions to please their institutional investors. But it is not at all clear that either the national interest or the interests of plan beneficiaries would be better served if pension funds became more actively involved in corporate management. A recent attempt by

---

14. See Chapters 17 and 18 of Bodie, Kane, and Marcus (1989) for an explanation of these models.

several public pension funds to exercise greater control over the top management of General Motors was decisively rejected by GM's Board of Directors.

Unfunded Liabilities and Stock Market Valuation

Several economists have studied the extent to which the market value of a firm's shares reflects the funding status of its pension plan.[15] The interest in this issue is in determining whether unfunded corporate pension plans depress national saving. If the unfunded liability is not reflected in a lower market value for the firm, the pension plan would create the appearance of an asset from the worker's point of view without a signal to the firm's owners that they are poorer.

While in the published studies the measured effects are in the right direction, their precise magnitude is open to question. In particular, these studies ignore the effect of a plan's asset allocation. As we have discussed, the asset mix can be an important determinant of the sponsor's shareholder value. This remains an issue for future research.[16]

Reversions, Mergers, and Acquisitions

VanDerhei and Harrington (1989) analyze the large number of terminations of overfunded plans that occurred in the 1980s. Their interpretation of their findings is broadly consistent with a financial slack motive of pension overfunding, that is, plan sponsors may overfund their plans in part to create a contingency fund.

Excess pension assets have also been identified as a possible lure for corporate raiders. Mitchell and Mulherin (1989) analyze pension plan terminations associated with corporate takeovers during 1980–87. Citing Jensen's (1986) free cash flow idea and the market for corporate control, the authors argue that excess funds may represent inactive assets and that plan terminations are another aspect of efficient financial restructuring. However, their results are open to alternative explanations, and no conclusion seems warranted.

Sources and Limitations of Pension Finance Data

Data on single employer, multi-employer, and public pension plans come from a variety of sources. This section discusses the major data

---

15. See, for example, Feldstein and Morck (1983) or Bulow, Morck, and Summers (1987).
16. See Bodie and Papke (1990).

sources of pension funding and asset allocation and summarizes recent empirical findings.

The assets of private pension plans can be broadly characterized into two types of funds—trusteed funds and insured funds. Pension plan assets can be held exclusively in trusteed or insured accounts or a combination of the two. Trusteed funds are managed by a trustee appointed by the plan sponsor. The trustee may be an employee of the sponsor or may be a bank or trust company. Contributions are made to the trust, and the trustee is to manage the investment of those funds in the sole interest of the beneficiaries.

Insured pension funds are managed by life insurance companies. Under a contractual agreement, the sponsor pays premiums to the insurance company which in return guarantees payment of future benefits. The sponsor may transfer all investment risk to the insurer, or share in the investment gains and losses. The guarantee may be backed by the insurance company's general accounts, which also back life insurance and other commitments, or they may be backed by separate accounts invested exclusively for pension liabilities.

A primary source for economy-wide estimates of private and state and local government pension assets is the Federal Reserve Board's (FRB) Flow-of-Funds Accounts (FOF). Private noninsured assets, as well as a total amount of insured pension assets, are reported. Most assets are reported at book value, while equities are based on market value. All assets are valued as of the end of the calendar year.

Data from the American Council of Life Insurance (ACLI) can be used to determine the appropriate portion of life insurance companies' assets allocable to group pensions. The ACLI data on insured pensions are difficult to classify since equities are at market value, but all other assets are at statement value which may differ from book value. For an illustration of estimating pension assets from the ACLI data, see Hoffman (1989).

The Internal Revenue Service's (IRS) Form 5500 is a plan-level source of pension finance data. A sponsor of a plan with more than 100 employees is required to file a Form 5500 with the IRS and Department of Labor.[17] These reported data include private noninsured (trust fund) assets valued at market value. The Form 5500 includes the total value of unallocated insurance contracts, but, unlike the FRB, does not report allocated insurance amounts. It does contain some data items not included in the FRB data, primarily noninvestment and

17. Smaller plans file a Form 5500-C form every three years, and Form 5500-R (a short registration form) in between Form 5500-C filings.

nonfinancial items.[18] Assets values are reported as of the beginning and end of the plan fiscal year, which varies by plan (about 70 percent of plan fiscal years coincide with the calendar year).

One serious drawback of the Form 5500 data for determining pension asset mix is the treatment of bank-pooled funds. Pooled funds are the combined contributions of many plans which are managed by one or more banks. Pooled funds are reported in total on each Form 5500; that is, the separate allocation into equity, bonds, cash, and other assets is not available. Pooled funds average about 20 percent of all financial assets. The Employee Benefit Research Institute (EBRI) publishes the *Quarterly Pension Investment Report* (QPIR) which provides tabulations of assets and rates of return for both trusteed and insured pension funds and for state and local government pension plans. Their tabulations are based on both the FOF and Form 5500 data for private trusteed pension funds, the ACLI data for private insured pension funds, and the FOF data for state and local plans.[19]

Empirical Findings: Corporate Pension Funding

While there is some evidence that the profitability and tax status of corporations influence their pension funding and asset allocation policies, it does not seem to be in precisely the ways predicted by the integrated balance sheet theory (integrated in the sense that the sponsor owns all the fund surplus). Friedman (1983) finds that pension decisions are related in a general way to other aspects of corporate financing decisions. His findings lend support to the notion that the balance sheet of the corporation and the pension plan are integrated in some way.

Using a 1980 sample from FASB Statement 36 filings, Bodie, Light, Morck, and Taggart (BLMT, 1987) find that the choice of a discount rate used to value liabilities is negatively related to firm profitability. Lower assumed actuarial discount rates increase the present value of the liability. This enables sponsors to manipulate IRS limits on contributions and thus make larger contributions to the plan. This suggests that profitable firms may have been using their pension fund as a tax shelter.

Since the profitable firms in their sample systematically choose lower discount rates, in order to evaluate the plans' funding policy, BLMT

18. These include accounts receivable, real estate, and buildings and property, for example.
19. See the Appendix of *QPIR*, 1989.

adjust the funding ratios (plan assets to the present value of either vested or accrued liabilities) to a common discount rate. They find evidence that the level of pension funding is positively related to firm profitability, but find no relationship between the degree of funding and risk or tax-paying characteristics.

Bodie and Papke (1990) reexamine these relationships with a 1981–1984 panel of Compustat firms. Compustat data consist of information reported by corporations and made public in 10-K (annual) reports filed with the Securities and Exchange Commission. Since 1981, Compustat lists at least five data items relevant to pension finance—vested and accrued liabilities, value of plan assets, the interest rate used to calculate the plan liability, and the reporting date.

They find that most plans are overfunded by either measure of the funding ratio. After the discount rate adjustment, the average asset to vested liability ratio in their sample is 2.22. The average asset to total liability ratio is 1.68. The relationships between funding and profitability found by BMLT for 1980 persist in this four-year sample as well. Warshawsky (1989) reports a funding ratio of 1.51 for a sample of 96 large Compustat firms in 1986.

Empirical Findings: Corporate Pension Asset Allocation

BMLT find that 10 percent of their FASB 36 firms invest as the tax advantage and shared-surplus theories predict—entirely in fixed-income securities. The proportion of assets allocated to fixed-income securities is positively related to the level of funding. They find no statistically significant relationship between investment policies and risk or tax-paying characteristics.

Bodie and Papke (1991) analyze the asset allocation of defined benefit plans from 1981 to 1987 using the IRS Form 5500 plan-level data. They divide assets into four categories: fixed-income securities, equities, pooled funds, and other, and find that, for all defined benefit plans, the proportion invested in fixed-income securities averaged 50 percent while about 23 percent is invested in equities. Pooled funds account for about 20 percent of all assets. Larger plants typically invest slightly less in fixed-income securities.

This defined benefit asset mix is somewhat similar to that found for defined contribution plans. There are two categories of defined contribution plans—profit-sharing and money purchase plans. In profit-sharing plans (the vast majority) employer contributions are made from profits and may be based either on a formula or discretionary basis. Defined contribution profit sharing plans average about 41 percent fixed income, 33 percent equities, and 17 percent pooled funds.

In a money purchase plan, the employer's contributions are determined by formula, usually a percentage of compensation. As with other defined contribution plans, however, money purchase plans do not specify benefit levels. Money purchase plans over this period hold 51 percent fixed-income, 12 percent equity, and 26 percent pooled funds. If the defined contribution is classified by the Department of Labor as primary (that is, there is no accompanying defined benefit plan) it typically invests a larger fraction of assets in fixed-income securities. Money purchase plans are almost all the primary defined contribution plan.

Multiemployer plans, both defined benefit and defined contribution, invest a larger fraction in fixed-income securities than single employer defined benefit plans. On average, they invested 67 percent in fixed-income securities and 17 percent in equities.

Bodie and Papke were unable to allocate the reported value of pooled funds, and this is a limitation of the study. Unfortunately, there is no other source of data of the universe of plans with which to compare the results. A small private compilation is published annually by Greenwich Associates. It reports personal interviews with approximately 1000 larger plan sponsors. For 1987, Greenwich reports a breakdown of 57 percent in equities and 35 percent in bonds and fixed-income securities.

The QPIR data on asset mix are difficult to compare directly with the Form 5500 breakdown findings because, for example, in reporting asset mix by plan type, QPIR's Other category includes bank-pooled funds, private mortgages, guaranteed investment contracts (GICs), mutual funds, and real estate. Since there is little difference between bonds (and mortgages and GICs) nearing maturity and cash, Bodie and Papke add these assets (except bank-pooled funds) to the fixed-income category.

EBRI receives data on the asset breakdown of bank-pooled funds from the Federal Financial Institution Examination Council on an annual basis. Unfortunately, the asset categories EBRI reports in the QPIR are aggregated across defined benefit and defined contribution plans and across size of plan. With bank-pooled funds allocated, the latest QPIR reports overall asset allocation for defined benefit and defined contribution plans into about 40 percent in equity and about 40 percent in fixed-income for 1982–84.[20]

Do plan sponsors fully immunize their liabilities, as predicted by the shared-surplus theory? While the Form 5500 contains no questions about investment strategy, it is possible to determine the strategy for

20. See *QPIR*, 1989, Table 4, Section I, p. 13.

underfunded plans. Bodie and Papke find some evidence that under-to just-fully-funded plans are fully immunized (about 28 percent of all plans).

It is not possible to determine the investment strategy for over-funded plans (which are the majority) from data on the static asset mix because a sponsor of an overfunded plan need not invest in a 100 percent fixed-income portfolio to minimize the cost of the corporate pension guarantee. Management can invest surplus pension assets in stocks, provided it reduces the proportion so invested when the market value of pension assets comes close to the value of the pension liability. Therefore, for an overfunded plan, the proportion of a fund invested in stocks at any point in time tells us little about the fund's dynamic strategy.

This technique described above is called contingent immunization, and it is a specific type of portfolio insurance strategy designed to guarantee a minimum rate of return, yet achieve some of the upside potential of the stock market. To understand how contingent immu-nization works, consider a very simple version of it that makes use of a stop-loss order. Imagine that the present value of the pension liability is $100 and that the fund has $120 of assets entirely invested in stocks. The fund can protect itself against downside risk by maintaining a stop-loss order on all of its stocks at a price of $100. This means that should the price of the stocks fall to $100, the fund manager would liquidate all of the stocks and immunize the liability. A stop-loss order at $100 is not a perfect hedge because there is no guarantee that the sell order can be executed at a price of $100. However, if the policy is to place a series of stop-loss orders at prices starting well above $100, the result is even better protection against downside risk.

Often the most efficient way to implement such a strategy is to use stock and bond index futures contracts rather than stocks and bonds themselves (see Leland and Rubinstein (1988)). Unfortunately, the Form 5500 does not separate futures contracts from stocks, so it is not possible to determine if fund managers are using futures in such a strategy.

Bodie and Papke find some evidence that underfunded plans whose sponsors are in financial distress do invest a smaller proportion in fixed-income securities, as our discussion of PBGC insurance suggests.

Public Pension Plans

Assets of state and local pension plans were 25 percent of the total pension assets in 1987 (Hoffman, 1989). Public Employee Retirement Systems (PERS) are not subject to federal oversight or much reporting standardization. Indeed, standards for disclosure of pension information were only recently issued by the Government Accounting Standards Board (Statement 5, 1986). Since states and localities can levy taxes to meet pension expenses, retirement security may not be the main issue in the funding of public pension plans.[21] However, pension cost deferral is often used as a short-run budget balancing service. This means that current taxpayers are receiving the services of public employees whose pensions will be paid for by a subsequent generation of taxpayers. In effect, in a public system, deferral pushes the liability onto another sponsor, that is, a later generation of taxpayers.

This deferral has implications, as discussed by Inman (1982) for the efficient allocation of local public resources. With mobile taxpayers, the pressure is to underfund local pensions and shift the burden onto future generations. The underfunding operates as an implicit subsidy from future to current taxpayers for the purchase of public services— this reduction in labor costs may stimulate excessive provision of public services.[22]

Some degree of funding at the state and local level is both feasible and desirable to enforce fiscal responsibility on the part of current residents. In addition, state and local governments may avoid the higher interest costs of low credit ratings in financial markets stemming from unfunded liabilities.[23]

Assessing the funding adequacy of public pension plans is difficult because valuation methods for both assets and liabilities differ across plans and sponsors.[24] The Bureau of the Census conducts a quarterly survey of the 104 public employee retirement systems in the U.S. with the largest amounts of cash and security holdings. Revenues, benefit payments, cash and security holdings, and membership are included. Annual totals for the nation, states, and largest PERS are published in "Finances of Employee-Retirement Systems of State and Local Governments."

As of the quarter ending June 30, 1989, major retirement systems covering employees of state and local governments held $541 billion in cash and investment securities. About 32 percent is invested in equities, and 54 percent in fixed-income securities. These proportions

21. See Tepper (1982) for a comparison of the importance of funding in private corporate and public pension plans.

22. If pension underfundings are fully capitalized into land values, however, then all allocative inefficiencies disappear. Reliable estimates of the degree of capitalization are not currently available.

23. See Munnell and Connolly (1980) for a detailed discussion of these points.

24. See Gustman and Segal (1977) and Munnell and Connolly (1980) for funding estimates.

should not be compared to the asset allocation of private plans, because public plans often report security values at cost rather than at market value.

Information on actuarial assumptions must be obtained by survey. The most recent survey to provide insights into actuarial methods, investment practices, and funding ratios of PERS was developed by the staff at the Government Finance Research Center (GFRC).[25] Two hundred and nine systems from a stratified random sample (designed to include state, city, county, special district, school district, and hospital systems) represent a cross-section of the nation's PERS. In principle, this survey contains the actuarial assumptions and valuation methods required approximately to adjust reported assets and liabilities to a common base for comparison purposes.

Most of the respondents in the GFRC sample (77 percent) provide defined benefit plans, 14 percent offer defined contribution plans, and 10 percent offer plans that combine characteristics of both. Most of the defined benefit plans fund benefits on an actuarial basis. Of these, most conduct actuarial valuations on an annual basis, and almost all conduct them at least once every three years. The ratio of plan assets to accrued liabilities averaged 81 percent.

Two additional surveys contain qualitative information about PERS. The Retirement Research Committee of Wisconsin surveyed 85 major public pensions (77 statewide and 8 local) in the U.S. in 1984 and 1988. A survey of investment practices was completed in October of 1989 by the National Conference of State Legislatures and the National Association of Legislative Fiscal Officers.

Conclusion

Some of the unresolved issues in pension fund finance could be addressed with improved data. By adding several questions to existing government forms filed regularly by plan sponsors (like the IRS Form 5500), we could acquire this data relatively efficiently. In this concluding section of the essay we make several specific recommendations.

With regard to funding strategy, it would be useful to ask pension plan sponsors a question designed to determine whether their funding target is the ABO, the ABO with an implicit COLA, or something else. Are they offering supplementary defined contribution plans? Is their purpose to offer inflation protection or to achieve some other replacement goal?

With regard to investment policy it would be useful to get some information about goals, strategies, and tactics. Are they employing an

25. See Zorn and Hanus (1987).

immunization strategy? If so, how are they implementing it? Why are they investing in equities?

It would be useful to researchers to have the reporting period for Form 5500 be the same as the sponsor's fiscal year. In the surveys of public plans conducted by the Bureau of the Census, sponsors should be encouraged to report liabilities using a standardized set of assumptions and to report assets at market value.

References

Allen, Steven G., Robert L. Clark, and Ann A. McDermed. 1990. "Post-Retirement Benefit Increases." Presented at the International Conference on Private Pension Policy and Statistical Analysis, U.S. Department of Labor, February 21, 1990.

Allen, Steven G., Robert L. Clark, and Daniel A. Sumner. 1984. "Comparisons of Pension Benefit Increases and Inflation, 1973–1979." *Monthly Labor Review* (May 1984): 45.

Ambachtsheer, Keith P. 1989. "Fixing the Accounting Standards for Pension and Health Care Benefits: Advice for FASB." *Ambachtsheer Letter*, July 31, 1989.

Arnott, Robert D., Frank Fabozzi, Robert M. Lovell, and David L. Rice. 1990. "The Many Dimensions of the Pension Fund Asset Allocation Decision." In Frank Fabozzi, ed., *Managing Institutional Assets.* New York: Ballinger, 1990, pp. 23–24.

Berkowitz Logue and Associates, Inc. 1986. "Study of the Investment Performance of ERISA Plans." Prepared for the Office of Pension Welfare Benefits, U.S. Department of Labor, July 21, 1986.

Black, F. 1980. "The Tax Consequences of Long Run Pension Policy." *Financial Analysts Journal* (September–October 1980): 17–23.

Black, F. and M. P. Dewhurst. 1981. "A New Investment Strategy for Pension Funds. *Journal of Portfolio Management* (Summer 1981).

Bodie, Zvi. 1990a. "Pensions as Retirement Income Insurance." *Journal of Economic Literature* (March 1990).

———. 1990b. "Managing Pension and Retirement Assets: An International Perspective." *Journal of Financial Services Research* 4 (1990): 419–60.

———. 1990c. "Inflation, Index-Linked Bonds, and Asset Allocation." *Journal of Portfolio Management* (Winter 1990).

Bodie, Zvi, Alex Kane, and Alan J. Marcus. 1989. *Investments.* Homewood, IL: R.D. Irwin, 1989.

Bodie, Zvi, Jay O. Light, Randall Morck, and Robert A. Taggart, Jr. 1987. "Corporate Pension Policy: An Empirical Investigation." Chapter 2 in Bodie, Shoven, and Wise, eds. (1987).

Bodie, Zvi, Alan J. Marcus, and Robert C. Merton. 1988. "Defined Benefit vs. Defined Contribution Pension Plans: What Are the Real Tradeoffs?" Chapter 5 in Bodie, Shoven, and Wise, eds. (1988).

Bodie, Zvi and Leslie E. Papke. 1990. Report to the U.S. Department of Labor, contract J-9-P-8-0097, 1990.

———. 1991. "Pension Fund Finance: Theory and Evidence." Unpublished report, 1991.

Bodie, Zvi and John B. Shoven, eds. 1983. *Financial Aspects of the U.S. Pension System.* Chicago: University of Chicago Press, 1983.

Bodie, Zvi, John B. Shoven, and David A. Wise, eds. 1987. *Issues in Pension Economics*. NBER Project Report. Chicago: University of Chicago Press, 1987.

————, eds. 1988. *Pensions in the U.S. Economy*. Chicago: University of Chicago Press, 1988.

Brennan, Michael and Eduardo Schwartz. 1979. *Pricing and Investment Strategies for Guaranteed Equity-Linked Life Insurance*. Monograph 7, Huebner Foundation, University of Pennsylvania. Homewood, IL: R.D. Irwin, 1979.

Bulow, Jeremy I. 1982. "What Are Corporate Pension Liabilities?" *Quarterly Journal of Economics* 97 (August 1982).

Bulow, Jeremy I., Randall Morck, and Lawrence Summers. 1987. "How Does the Market Value Unfunded Pension Liabilities?" Chapter 4 in Bodie, Shoven, and Wise, eds. (1987).

Bulow, Jeremy I. and Myron Scholes. 1983. "Who Owns the Assets in a Defined-Benefit Pension Plan?" Chapter 1 in Bodie and Shoven, eds. (1983).

Clark, Robert L. 1990. "Cost of Living Adjustments in International Perspective." In John A. Turner, ed., *Pension Policy: An International Perspective*. Washington, DC: U.S. Government Printing Office, 1990.

Clark, Robert L., Steven G. Allen, and Daniel A. Sumner. 1983. "Inflation and Pension Benefits." Final report for the U.S. Department of Labor, contract J-9-P-1-0074, 1983.

Cohn, Richard A. and Franco Modigliani. 1985. "Inflation and Corporate Financial Management." Chapter 13 in Edward I. Altman and Marti G. Subrahmanyam, eds., *Recent Advances in Corporate Finance*. Homewood, IL: R.D. Irwin, 1985.

Deaton, Richard L. 1989. *The Political Economy of Pensions*. Vancouver, BC: UBC Press, 1989.

Dorsey, Stuart and John A. Turner. 1987. "Union-Nonunion Differences in Pension Fund Investments and Earnings." Washington, DC: Department of Labor, November 1987.

Employee Benefit Research Institute. 1987. "Pension Portability and What It Can Do for Retirement Income: A Simulation Approach." *EBRI Issue Brief* 65 (April 1987).

————. 1989. *EBRI: Quarterly Pension Investment Report* 4, 1 (June 1989).

Feldstein, Martin and Randall Morck. 1983. "Pension Funding Decisions, Interest Rate Assumptions, and Share Prices." Chapter 7 in Bodie and Shoven, eds. (1983).

Friedman, B. M. 1983. "Pension Funding, Pension Asset Allocation and Corporate Finance: Evidence from Individual Company Data." In Bodie and Shoven, eds. (1983).

Greenwich Associates. 1988. "Greenwich Reports: More Policy, Less Tactics: Large Corporate Pensions." Unpublished report, 1988.

Gustman, A. L. and M. Segal. 1977. "Interstate Variations in Teachers' Pensions." *Industrial Relations* 16, 3 (October 1977).

Harrison, M. J. and W. F. Sharpe. 1983. "Optimal Funding and Asset Allocation Rules for Defined Benefit Pension Plans." Chapter 4 in Bodie and Shoven, eds. (1983).

Hoffman, A. J. 1989. "Pension Assets and the Economy." In Turner and Beller, eds. (1989).

Inman, R. P. 1982. "Public Employee Pensions and the Local Labor Budget." *Journal of Public Economics* 19 (1982): 49–71.

Ippolito, Richard A. 1986. "The Economic Burden of Corporate Pension Liabilities." *Financial Analysts Journal* (January/February 1986): 22–34.

Ippolito, Richard A. and John A. Turner. 1987. "Turnover, Fees, and Pension Plan Performance." *Financial Analysts Journal* (November/December 1987): 16–26.

Jensen, J. C. 1986. "Agency Costs of Free Cash Flow, Corporate Finance, and Takeovers." *American Economic Review* 76 (May 1986): 323–29.

Leibowitz, Martin L. 1986. "The Dedicated Bond Portfolio in Pension Funds." *Financial Analysts Journal* 42, 1–2 (Jan/Feb–Mar/April 1986).

Leland, Hayne E. and Mark Rubinstein. 1988. "The Evolution of Portfolio Insurance." Chapter 1 in Donald Luskin, ed., *Portfolio Insurance*. New York: John Wiley & Sons, 1988.

Leonard, H. B. 1986. *Checks Unbalanced: The Quiet Side of Public Spending*. New York: Basic Books, 1986.

McCarthy, D. D. and John A. Turner. 1989. "Pension Rates of Return in Large and Small Plans." In Turner and Beller, eds. (1989).

Merton, Robert C. 1969. "Lifetime Portfolio Selection by Dynamic Stochastic Programming: The Continuous Time Case." *Review of Economic Statistics* 51, 3 (August 1969).

———. 1971. "Lifetime Consumption and Portfolio Rules in a Continuous Time Model." *Journal of Economic Theory* (1971).

Merton, Robert C. and Paul A. Samuelson. 1977. "Fallacy of the Log-Normal Approximation to Portfolio Decision-Making over Many Periods." In Irwin Friend and James L. Bicksler, eds., *Risk and Return in Finance*. New York: Heath Lexington, 1977.

Mitchell, M. L. and J. H. Mulherin. 1989. "Pensions and Mergers." In Turner and Beller, eds. (1989).

Munnell, Alicia H. and A. M. Connolly. 1980. "Financing Public Pensions." *New England Economic Review* (Jan/Feb 1980).

Petersen, Mitchell. 1989. "Pension Terminations and Worker-Stockholder Wealth Transfers." Working Paper, Massachusetts Institute of Technology, 1989.

Pontiff, Jeffrey, Andrei Schleifer, and Michael Weisbach. 1989. "Reversions of Excess Pension Assets After Takeovers." Working Paper, June 1989.

Samuelson, Paul A. 1963. "Risk and Uncertainty: A Fallacy of Large Numbers." *Scientia* 6th ser. 57th year (April/May 1963): 1–6.

———. 1969. "Lifetime Portfolio Selection by Dynamic Stochastic Programming." *Review of Economics and Statistics* 51, 3 (August 1969): 239–46.

———. 1971. "The Fallacy of Maximizing the Geometric Mean in Long Sequences of Investing or Gambling." *Proceedings of the National Academy of Science* 68 (1971): 207–11.

———. 1989. "The Judgement of Economic Science on Rational Portfolio Management: Timing and Long-Horizon Effects." *Journal of Portfolio Management* (Fall 1989): 4–12.

Sharpe, W. F. 1976. "Corporate Pension Funding Policy." *Journal of Financial Economics* (June 1976): 183–93.

Tepper, I. 1981. "Taxation and Corporate Pension Policy." *Journal of Finance* (March 1981): 1–13.

———. 1982. "The Future of Private Pension Funding." *Financial Analysts Journal* (Jan/Feb 1982).

Treynor, J. 1977. "The Principles of Corporate Pension Finance." *Journal of Finance*. (May 1977): 627–38.

Turner, John A. and Daniel J. Beller, eds. 1989. *Trends in Pensions, 1988*. U.S. Department of Labor, Pension and Welfare Benefits Administration. Washington, DC: U.S. Government Printing Office, 1989.

Utgoff, Kathleen P. 1988. "Pension Reform Strengthens Defined-Benefit Plans." *Compensation and Benefits Management* (Summer 1988).

VanDerhei, Jack. 1988. "Plan Termination Insurance for Single-Employer Pension Plans." Chapter 51 in Jerry S. Rosenbloom, ed., *The Handbook of Employee Benefits*. 2nd edition. Homewood, IL: Dow-Jones-Irwin, 1988.

VanDerhei, Jack L. and S. E. Harrington. 1989. "Pension Asset Reversions." In Turner and Beller, eds. (1989).

Warshawsky, M. J. 1989. "The Adequacy of Funding of Private Defined Benefit Pension Plans." In Turner and Beller, eds. (1989).

Zorn, P. and M. Hanus. 1987. "Public Pension Accounting and Reporting: A Survey of Current Practices." Public Pension and Benefits Consortium, Government Finance Research Center of the Government Finance Officers Association, December 1987.

Comments by Irwin Tepper

The essay by Zvi Bodie and Leslie Papke analyzes strategic decisions facing pension plan sponsors and public policy issues. It contains both analytical and empirical material. This discussion focuses on the analytical portions of the essay.

Building on a very well researched body of literature, the central unifying thesis of the essay is that defined benefit pension liabilities are participating annuities. In this characterization pension benefits have guaranteed floors equal to the legally accrued benefit. This benefit may be enriched by the plan sponsor from time to time. A good example of this phenomenon is an ad hoc cost-of-living adjustment (COLA) to the benefits of retirees. An equivalent way to characterize these participating annuities is as contingent claims, as defined in the theoretical literature on options. The contingent claim analogy and participating (annuity) characterizations will be used interchangeably.

The essay shares with much of the prevailing literature the uncomfortable feature that its conclusions are, in many instances, contrary to what we observe in practice. One explanation for this is that the theories are seriously flawed. This discussion will present some of the possible criticisms of the essay and will also try to extend the authors' arguments in rebuttal. The issues to be addressed are as follows:

1. The guaranteed floor, approximated by the accountant's accumulated benefit obligation (ABO), is the correct target liability for developing funding and investment strategies. This liability is fixed in nominal terms since it contains no projections of benefit increases beyond the current accrued benefit.

2. Since the target obligation is a benefit fixed in nominal terms, the optimal investment policy is a 100 percent allocation to a fixed income portfolio that hedges the ABO (that is, a portfolio with the same duration as ABO). Any other strategy introduces risk of shortfall which will have to be guaranteed by the sponsor. This guarantee has an economic cost which should be avoided.

3. Since the target is fixed in nominal terms, the plan sponsor does not have to worry about inflation.
4. Not related to the characterization of the target liabilities, and contrary to what many practitioners believe, equities do not provide an almost risk-free way to reduce the cost of providing benefits. That is, they cannot be counted upon either to be superior to fixed income or to be free of losses over the long term.

Pension Benefits as Contingent Claims

Figure 1 presents the characterization of pension benefits as contingent claims. The vertical axis is the level of pension benefit; the horizontal axis is the value of the pension fund taken together with the health of the company. The definition of the horizontal line is fuzzy since either the performance of the pension fund and/or the performance of the company can induce actions that change pension benefits. Where reference is made below to the performance of the pension fund, it should be interpreted to mean the joint performance of the fund and the company. The scaling of both axes should be interpreted as indices, each starting at 100. A hedge strategy would maintain the neutral position (100/100) in the absence of any external influences.

The horizontal line portrays a pure fixed benefit similar to ABO that is not affected by the performance of the fund. For retirees it is the current benefit. For active employees it is the accrued benefit calculated using current service and current salary. The 45-degree line is a pure defined contribution plan; the benefit tracks the performance of the fund. The difference between the lines is either the surplus or the shortfall that results from performance relative to the fixed benefit, depending upon which side of neutral we are looking at.

The remaining line is the contingent claim characterization of the benefit. If the fund does well, the benefit is enriched and the plan sponsor shares some of the surplus with the plan participant. This could come about as a result of an ad hoc cost-of-living adjustment to retirees. It could also come about as a result of pay increases to active employees in a pay-related pension plan. Sharing of the surplus might result from explicit decisions of the sponsor or it might arise from legislation that effectively transfers ownership of surplus from the plan sponsor to the participant. If the fund does poorly, there is the possibility of plan termination where all of the accrued benefit may not be guaranteed.

What Is the Correct Liability Target?

Is it more appropriate to set funding and investment policies using the fixed benefit or the contingent claim benefit as the target? While it may

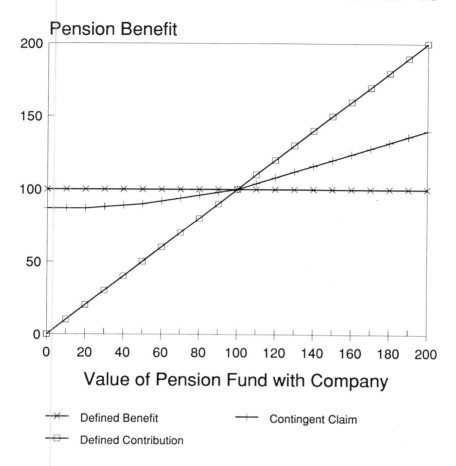

Pension Benefits Viewed as Contingent Claims

Figure 1

seem reasonable not to anticipate ad hoc COLAs in measuring liabilities, the omission of future expected pay increases in the calculation
of the liabilities for active employees may seem less correct. The ABO
definition ignores these expected pay increases and measures the benefit using the current age and pay in the plan's benefit formulas. The
accountant's alternative definition that is used to determine pension

expense, projected benefit obligation (PBO), includes the expected future pay increases in the benefit calculation.

The proponents of including future expected increases in liability argue that they are implicit obligations of the employer; both the employee and the employer anticipate that pay will rise and with it the accrued benefit. Those who oppose including future expected increases argue that pay increases are *contingent* upon the employee continuing to work. This, in turn, will be contingent upon the plan sponsor having a volume of business that will make it profitable to continue to employ the employee. To be profitable, the employer must generate enough revenues each year in the future to cover the total cost of compensation in that year. Total compensation cost in each year is equal to the pay in the year plus the increase in pension liability that accompanies the pay increase. The future revenues are a "shadow" asset that covers future compensation cost and are properly attributable to the years of occurrence. Since future revenues cover benefit increases, current policies should address current liabilities.

To take the argument further, the contingent claims viewpoint suggests that PBO is an illogical stopping point in defining pension liability. Since future benefit increases due to pay increases are contingent upon the employee continuing to work, the definition of liability that includes future pay increases should include future service as well.

Is an ABO Hedge Strategy the Minimum-Cost Asset Allocation Strategy?

Whatever measure of liability is adopted as a target, should a plan sponsor absorb the risk of a mismatch between this liability and the plan's assets? The nature of the liability may affect the desirability of risk taking in the following way.

For a company that views the possibility of termination as remote, but believes that some of the surplus will be captured by the plan participant, the gains and losses from investment policy are asymmetrical. The contingent claim jargon for this situation is that the plan participant has a call option on the fund. This call option is the obligation of the sponsor, and the best way to minimize the value of this call is to reduce the volatility of the investment strategy relative to the liabilities. In this case, the authors' ABO hedge strategy would be optimal.

For a plan sponsor that believes that the level of benefits is largely independent of the performance of the fund, the gains and losses are symmetrical and the minimum risk hedge strategy does not dominate all other policies.

Are Equities the Dominant Investment Vehicle over the Long Term?

The issues about which liability to target and whether or not to hedge would be moot if it were virtually certain that equities will outperform bonds over the relevant target-time horizon for the plan and if the plan sponsor were willing to absorb some interim volatility along the way. If this is the case, there is virtually no likelihood of being on the left-hand side of neutral in Figure 1.

Equities have outperformed bonds over virtually all time horizons of ten or more years since 1926. This superior performance is seen as being consistent with efficient market pricing since investors in equities are absorbing interim volatility. In addition to empirical support, the hypothesized superiority of equities is, as the authors describe, also attributable to an incorrect application of the statistics of the law of large numbers.

Figure 2 presents the statistical arguments. It is a lognormal projection of investment performance for time horizons of one to twenty years. I have used the authors' expected risk premium and standard deviation of 8 percent and 20 percent, respectively. Returns are, therefore, relative to the risk-free investment which may also be thought of as the ABO hedge. Losses are measured relative to this neutral position. The following percentiles are displayed as we move from the bottom of each chart to the top: 1 percent, 25 percent, mean, 75 percent, 99 percent. The chart on the right shows the average compound rate of return. The potential loss *decreases* from −30 percent (or more) to about −10 percent as the time horizon is lengthened. The gap would continue to shrink if we went out further in time. The fallacy of the law of large numbers is to interpret this phenomenon as a demonstration that the risk from investing in stocks declines as the investment is held for long time periods.

The chart on the left shows what the value of $100 would be if invested at these rates of return. The loss in the "worst case" *increases* as the time horizon is lengthened. The reason why the rate of return and unit value graphs present a different picture is a "good news/bad news" story. The good news is that the *average* loss declines with time horizon; the bad news is that the investment is being exposed to this inferior rate of return for a longer time. Thus, the average annual loss is cumulating over a longer time frame.

Proponents of the "dominance of equities" thesis (those that do not fall into the fallacy trap) argue that the value chart does not correctly portray what *has* happened in the past or what *can* happen in the

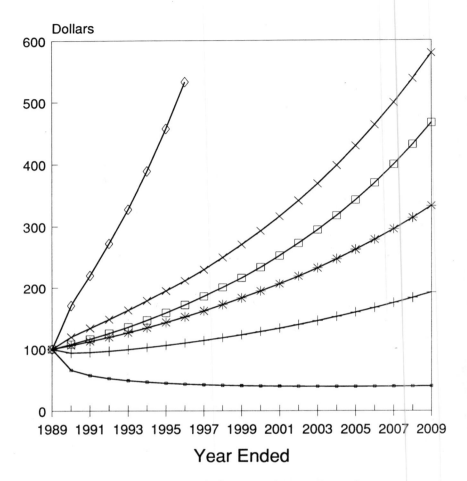

Value of $100 Invested
For Different Time Horizons

Figure 2

future. They disagree with one key assumption that was used in producing the projections—the (statistical) independence of returns from one year to the next. They argue that reversals take place to ensure that owners of capital are compensated over the long term. While the chart correctly portrays the magnitude of possible losses in the short term,

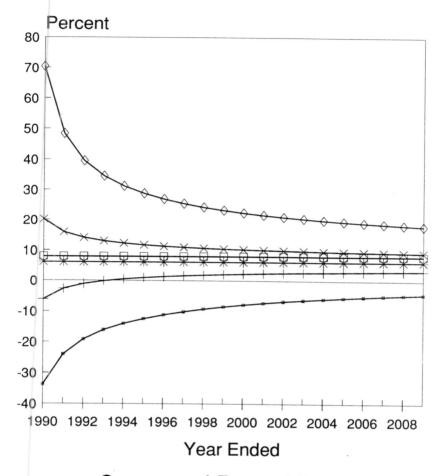

Compound Rate of Return
For Different Time Horizons

they contend that the projected magnitude of long-term losses would have dire consequences for the capitalist system.

Chapter 5
Pension Taxes and the U.S. Budget

David C. Lindeman and Kathleen P. Utgoff

Introduction

Qualified plans are retirement plans given special treatment in the Internal Revenue Code. They are governed by their own subchapter[1] with their own accounting rules and conditions. Their treatment—which they share with some other provisions[2]—represents the clearest preference in the tax code relative to normal income tax rules. In addition to being the single largest tax preference in the individual income tax, qualified plans afford an opportunity for the clearest form of tax arbitrage in what has been described as our "hybrid" tax system.[3]

Note that the reference point here is an income tax. If one takes as the reference point a consumption tax, then the notion of a preference for pension or other retirement savings is not relevant. The special rules that now apply to qualified plans would become the universal rules for all savings in a consumption tax world.[4]

The views expressed here are the authors' and do not reflect the views of the Pension Benefit Guaranty Corporation or Groom and Nordberg, Chartered.

1. Subchapter D, Sections 401 et seq. Also see Section 72 for taxation of annuities from qualified plans and otherwise, and Section 219 for deduction rules for IRAs.

2. As discussed later, the so-called deferral associated with qualified plans translates into a complete exemption of property income within those plans. A similar result occurs with respect to the limited capital gains exemption for the sale of homes by taxpayers over the age of 55, the exemption for the inside build-up of life insurance products that pass to the beneficiaries, and the step-up basis given inheritors of appreciated property. In addition, the Congress has enacted an exemption on the gains from U.S. savings bonds used to finance higher education. The Administration currently is recommending a broadening of that model in the form of Family Savings Plans.

3. Henry J. Aaron, Harvey Galper, and Joseph A. Pechman, eds. 1988. *Uneasy Compromise: Problems in a Hybrid Income-Consumption Tax* (Washington, DC: Brookings Institution, 1988), Introduction, pp. 1–13.

4. For a discussion of the difficulty of defining what is a tax preference in a hybrid tax system, see William D. Andrews and David F. Bradford, "Savings Incentives in a Hybrid Income Tax." In Aaron, Galper, and Pechman (1988) (note 3), 269–97.

The still dominant type of qualified plan is the defined benefit pension—that is, a promise by an employer to pay an annuity (or a lump-sum equivalent) according to a formula, usually based on age and service. The other type is the defined contribution plan. Defined contribution plans take different forms. Many plans operate by the employer contributing a percentage of wages or salaries to the employees' accounts. That percentage can be fixed; more often, it varies with the firm's yearly profits. Increasingly prevalent, however, is the kind of defined contribution plan that also depends on the individual saving decision of each employee. Although savings plans that matched after-tax employee contributions long existed, the "401(k)" option effectively made employee contributions deductible within limits. This added deductibility has greatly popularized plans that permit and depend on discretionary employee saving, although typically these plans contain some employer matching.[5]

The underlying economics of defined benefit and defined contribution plans are different. Defined benefit plans have incentives that both depend on and are independent of their tax treatment[6]; on the other hand, defined contribution plans are essentially just tax-preferred savings accounts.

Tax Treatment of Qualified Plans

The tax preference for qualified plans has two components. The first is the difference between (1) how income would be taxed in a cash-flow consumption tax and (2) how income would be taxed in an income tax that had no exceptions. The second is what may be called lifetime income averaging.

In an income tax, savings come from after-tax compensation. In theory, all capital income should be taxable on an accretion basis. In practice, current property income—rents, interest, dividends—are taxed annually; capital gains are taxed when realized. Withdrawals are nontaxable. Those withdrawals therefore have the following value:

$$(1 - t)W(1 + (1 - t)r)^n   ,$$

5. Individual Retirement Accounts (IRAs), though not qualified plans, follow similar tax rules.

6. Defined benefit plans may be analogous to long-term corporate bonds. The firm promises a stream of payments after retirement in return for the worker's long-term placement of his labor, much like the promise a firm makes to its investors for the long-term investment of their capital. See Richard A. Ippolito, *Pensions, Economics and Public Policy* (Homewood, IL: W.D. Irwin for the Pension Research Council, 1986), Chapter 10, for a discussion of how underfunding pre-ERISA and inflation post-ERISA convert defined benefit plans into long-term bond contracts.

where $(1 - t)W$ is the after-tax compensation placed into savings and $(1 + (1 - t)r)^n$ is an after-tax return after n years.

In a cash-flow consumption tax, savings are deductible from the tax base, capital income accumulates tax free, and withdrawals are added to the tax base. These rules mean that capital income is not taxed. Just before withdrawal, savings have the value

$$W(1 + r)^n \quad ,$$

where W is deductible compensation placed into savings and $(1 + r)^n$ is a tax-free return after n years. After withdrawal, those savings have the value

$$(1 - t)W(1 + r)^n \quad .$$

If the taxpayer's tax rates at the times of contribution and withdrawal are the same, then the result is as if the compensation were initially taxed, invested, and never taxed again.[7] This portion of the tax advantage can be summarized as the present value of the difference between $(1 - t)W(1 + r)^n$ and $(1 - t)W(1 + (1 - t)r)^n$. Note that this tax advantage would exist even if the normal income tax rule were a flat tax on capital income.

The second tax advantage—income averaging—can exist in either an income tax or a cash-flow consumption tax. If the taxpayer's tax rate at withdrawal (t_2) is lower than when the compensation is first earned (t_1), then the effective tax rate on that compensation is lowered. This portion of the tax advantage can be summarized as the present value of $(t_1 - t_2)W$. Some have suggested that the difference in the second and first period tax rates causes the treatment for qualified plans to be a net subsidy. Others have suggested that it provides a form of lifetime income averaging for wage income.[8]

By allowing a tax exclusion or deduction for the increment of earnings placed into savings, society becomes a co-investor with the worker. If $t_1 = t_2$, the government is indifferent in a present-value term: $t_1(W) = PV\, t_2(W)(1 + r)^n$. The government will share both in extraordinary returns and in losses. Provided government accounting allowed for such a practice, some portion of this deferred tax could be treated as a receivable on the government's books. For example, if we knew all

7. For a more thorough discussion of tax equivalents, see David F. Bradford and U.S. Treasury Tax Policy Staff, 1984 *Blueprints for Basic Tax Reform,* 2nd ed. (Arlington, VA: Tax Analysts, 1984), 123–24.

8. C. Eugene Steuerle, *Taxes, Loans and Inflation* (Washington, DC: Brookings Institution, 1985), 16–17. For a different view, Ippolito (1986) (note 6), 17–20.

pension participants would be at least in the 15 percent bracket at the time of retirement, then 15 percent of the forgone tax on contributions to qualified plans could be treated as a receivable.

The application of these simple equations to a defined contribution plan is straightforward. From the account holder's perspective, he accumulates retirement wealth at a before-tax, rather than an after-tax, return.

In defined benefit plans, the application is more complicated. Under current law, employers make contributions to a special trust. These contributions are based on aggregate assumptions about wage growth, turnover, and death. Until a given worker separates or retires from the plan, it cannot be said with any certainty how that individual benefited from the tax preference. A further complication is that a defined benefit plan typically contains assets that exceed what is legally owing its participants if it were terminated. These excess amounts represent liabilities of the plan that will be realized only if the plan remains ongoing. Holding promised benefits constant and assuming the firm's tax rate remains constant over time, earlier deductions for these excess amounts has the same present value as the later deductions the firm eventually would have to make. Present-value equivalence is maintained, however, only by allowing the excess amounts to earn a before-tax rate of return within the nontaxable pension trust. If the firm were forced to anticipate its future liabilities in an after-tax solution, it is generally believed that promised benefits would be lower as a result.

Policy Concerns

The tax breaks for qualified plans are exceptional—in particular, the effective exemption of capital income. To a greater or lesser extent, these preferences are valuable to all taxpayers, but they are most valuable to higher-income taxpayers. At a minimum, society does not want these preferences hoarded by a select few for whom the advantages are most valuable. More ambitiously, qualified plans are viewed as a mechanism for forced saving and possible redistribution of the costs of that saving.

In the context of a tax system that is neither an income tax nor a consumption tax, qualified plans (along with IRAs) also offer opportunity to engage in what has been called "pure" tax arbitrage. This is the advantage to a taxpayer of borrowing at an immediately deductible interest rate (for example, against one's home or business) and investing a comparable amount in a tax-free solution. When both the investment and the obligation mature, the former is used to satisfy the latter. Provided the transaction does not push income into a higher tax rate period and provided that the spread between an individual's borrowing rate and return on assets is sufficiently low, tax arbitrage increases after-tax wealth. The individual who engages in successful tax arbitrage may have consumed the higher after-tax income, saved it, or both. Thus, even after an individual may have satisfied his retirement goals, there remain strong tax motivations to accumulate even greater amounts in tax-free accounts with offsetting borrowing.

Tax arbitrage with qualified plans also can exist at the firm level. As discussed earlier, current tax law allows sponsors of defined benefit plans to anticipate the cost of their future obligations in a tax-free trust. By carefully choosing interest rate, mortality, and turnover assumptions, those obligations can be computed in ways that exceed expectations. The firm can increase its borrowing against its business assets by equivalent amounts. Eventually, the plan's assumptions will be adjusted to lower required contributions, and the firm will use the difference between its old and new contribution rates to pay off its larger indebtedness. In the meantime, the firm has lowered its effective tax rate.

These policy concerns have caused Congress to place a great number of complex conditions and limits on the use of qualified plans. The conditions include nondiscrimination rules for participation, coverage, and the distribution of contributions and benefits. In recent years, the conditions have expanded to include spousal rights. The limits, which are our principal concern here, apply to deductions at the firm level (Section 404) and the individual level (the Section 415 limits). Relatively new excise taxes have been applied to make nondeductible contributions prohibitive (Section 4979), to discourage large lifetime accumulations in qualified plans (Section 4980A), and to encourage recognition within the taxpayer's lifetime (Section 4974). In addition, when a firm discontinues an ongoing plan and recovers amounts in excess of termination benefits ("reversions"), the transaction is subject to both ordinary income taxation (recovery of the tax benefit of the previous deduction) and a special excise tax (Section 4980). This excise tax is designed to capture the value of the tax-free build-up on the remainder—that is, the difference

$$(1 - t)R(1 + r)^n - (1 - t)R(1 + (1 - t)r)^n \quad ,$$

where R is the reversion.

Current Tax Expenditure Accounting

We do not now measure tax preferences for qualified plans in present-value terms. Consistent with overall federal government accounting, tax expenditures are measured on a cash-flow basis. In the case of qualified plans, the measure assumes that a given year's contributions are taxable wages or salary income, and that property income earned at the trust or account level is taxable income to workers. The tax applied to these amounts is the weighted average marginal tax rate for covered workers. From this amount is subtracted the tax paid on the same year's distributions from qualified plans. In the most recent estimates of federal tax expenditures, the Joint Committee on Taxation has scored the tax preference at some $283 billion for fiscal years 1991–95 ($52 billion in FY 1991 growing to $61 billion in FY 1992). This surpasses all other tax expenditures (compare, for example the five-year totals for mortgage interest deductions at $180 billion, excess depreciation allowances at $104 billion, the nontaxability of employer-paid health insurance at $210 billion, and the partial nontaxability of Social Security benefits at $121 billion).[9]

In addition to the annual tax expenditure analysis, the protocols of revenue scoring are important. Each year the Congressional Budget Office (CBO) estimates the base line. This a prediction of tax receipts within the forecast period assuming, with minor exceptions, that current tax law continues. The Joint Committee on Taxation (JCT) then estimates the effects of changes in the tax law—departures from the base line—as tax measures are considered over the course of the year. Though data sources, models, and macroeconomic assumptions between the two agencies are generally compatible, they are not precisely the same. The JCT and the CBO on the one hand, and the Treasury on the other, though they will differ in some assumptions from time to time, try to maintain consistent methods.

Both tax expenditure estimates and revenue scoring are the most inexact when the exercise involves information not ordinarily collected on tax returns. With key exceptions, such as the ongoing debate on the effects of capital gains changes, estimates and scoring do not try to incorporate behavioral effects, especially those that take place over the long run.

Problems with Using a Cash-Receipts Measure

Though the tax expenditure estimate for the overall pension system does assume that pensions are deferred wages, it probably underestimates the taxes that will eventually be paid. Distributions to current retirees is a poor proxy for the eventual taxes that will be collected on the contributions for current workers. At least in the near term we can

9. U.S. Congress, Joint Economic Committee, *Estimates of Federal Tax Expenditures for Fiscal Years 1991–1995* (Washington, DC: U.S. Government Printing Office, 1990).

expect continuing expansion of the pension system from greater life-time coverage rates and an expanding population. By reflecting an immature system, the current measure overstates the long-term costs. By the same token, the effects on such future taxes is ignored in revenue estimating. For example, the tax gain from holding down current year contributions is not offset by the coincident loss of future contributions.

In addition, in the environment of Gramm-Rudman-Hollings, all attention has been focused on getting beneath the target in the next fiscal year. Consequently, current tax policy is now being driven by cash-receipt accounting. A few examples of the distortions caused by such accounting are described below.

Funding Limits

In 1987, the Omnibus Budget Reconciliation Act (OBRA) contained a provision that reduced the maximum amount that can be contributed to a defined benefit pension plan. Prior to 1987, employers were allowed to take anticipated wage increases (largely inflation) into ac-count in making contributions. A typical defined benefit plan promises a retirement benefit that is a specified fraction of wages at the end of a career. This fraction increases with years of service. Consequently, each year the firm accrues a marginal cost that depends not only on current wages but on future wage growth between the current period and when each worker separates from the plan. Before 1987, employers were allowed to fund the anticipated full marginal cost of each year's benefit by including an assumption for future wage growth in the funding calculation. OBRA reduced the total amount that could be contributed to an amount equal to 150 percent of the benefit liability, with no allowance for future wage growth. The new limits reduced the amount that could be contributed to plans, particularly for plans with a high percentage of young workers.[10]

Because the new limits reduced the amount in tax-qualified pension plans, this provision of OBRA was expected to raise several billion dollars in tax revenues over three years. But a three-year horizon is much too short for measuring the revenue impact of changes in the tax rule for pensions. Contributions were not reduced but merely delayed for many plans. The only real saving from the new limits for these plans was due to the prevention of tax-free accumulation.

In the OBRA case, the absence of present-value accounting led to an

---

10. *After* the legislation was passed, the Department of Labor commissioned a study of the effects of the new limit: Hustead, Hustead and Selles, "OBRA 1987: The Impact of Limiting Contributions to Defined Benefit Plans," Hay/Huggins Company, Inc.

overestimate of tax receipts from a measure that has no merit, other than its impact on the budget. When the legislation was passed, little or no attention was paid to the effect on national savings or increased risks to the PBGC or to the impact on the attractiveness of defined benefit plans relative to defined contribution plans.[11] Defined contribution plans are still allowed to contribute the marginal cost of pension accruals for each year of service, which is by definition equal to the contribution. But since 1987, defined benefit plans can do so only if long-term wage growth is zero.

Asset Reversions

Under current law, when an employer terminates a pension plan, any assets that remain after benefits have been provided for through the purchase of annuities reverts to the employer. Such a transaction is called an asset reversion. Although reversions are relatively rare and will become even rarer with the new funding limits, these transactions have caused a storm of controversy. Several bills have been introduced to end reversions or to force employers to share the excess funds with employees, but to date, none of these bills have been enacted. One of the major roadblocks this legislation has faced is that it is scored as a revenue loser on the budget. Because employers pay income tax and an excise tax on the reversion amount, anything that restricts reversions loses revenue.

This revenue impact is either a blessing or a curse; if you support the status quo, it is a blessing, and if you want legislation, it is a curse. The question addressed here is whether the tax benefit of restricting reversions is accurately measured by cash-receipts accounting.

We ignore here the widely held belief that a restriction on reversions would lead to lower funding levels and a switch from defined benefit to defined contribution plans. These effects are induced behavioral changes that are rarely included in revenue estimates. The primary focus here is on the difference between cash-receipts and present-value accounting.

The revenue impact of reversions is measured on a cash-receipts basis—how much tax revenue is lost over the few years of the budget horizon. But cash-receipts accounting overstates the amount of revenue from asset reversion because some companies engage in reversions to reduce the present value of their taxes even though their

---

11. No hearings were even held on the funding limit changes contained in OBRA. Like many recent changes in pension law, the funding limit changes were only a tiny part of massive budget legislation; consequently, they received scrutiny only after the legislation was passed.

current taxes may increase. Two cases when reversions are engaged in for net long-term tax reductions are when companies have expiring net operating losses (NOLs) and in leveraged buyouts (LBOs).

When NOLs are about to expire, companies can effectively extend them by taking a reversion, which allows the expiring NOLs to be applied to the income from the reversion. This transaction increases the tax-deductible amount that can be contributed to a pension plan, in effect, extending the NOLs for roughly fifteen years.

LBO transactions create a similar opportunity. The debt used to finance an LBO produces high deductions for companies. When these deductions cannot all be used within the allowable period, a reversion is an effective way to extend the tax advantages offered to debt financing.

The use of reversions to extend the tax advantages of NOLs and LBOs demonstrates the importance of present-value accounting when changes in our pension system are evaluated. Corporations clearly use present-day accounting. When the government does not, distortions can occur.

Health Benefit Transfers

The prefunding of retiree health benefits on a tax-preferred basis is much more limited than the prefunding of pension benefits. In addition, some companies have pension funds that are so overfunded that they will not be able to make tax-deductible contributions for many years due to the full-funding limits described above. These companies want to be able to transfer funds from pension trusts to health trusts without paying the normal income and excise taxes associated with reversions. Legislation that allows these tax-free transfers has been considered several times by Congress.

Although this legislation has the potential for expanding tax preferences available to pension and health trusts taken together, the immediate impact on the budget is positive. The transfer to health plans reduces current expenses and increases reported income. This happens because, when companies pay health benefits from a tax-qualified trust, they do not get the expense deduction that would be allowed for their normal source of payments, which is current income. This is equivalent to submitting the transfer to ordinary income taxation. Thus, some companies that are seeking this legislation would actually pay *higher* taxes if employee transfers were allowed. Apparently the present value of the extra money in pension plans is so low that companies are willing to forgo arbitrage opportunities. Also important is that the transfer is not subject to the excise tax for several years. In effect, health benefit transfers are an indirect way of distributing tax-preferenced funds in the pension plans to shareholders.[12] This is ignored because the companies are seeking legislation that will increase tax receipts in the short run and lead to a desirable budget scoring result.

This situation does not apply to all companies, however; for some companies, the present value of additional taxes paid if health benefit transfers were allowed would be negative because of the increase in total tax-preferred funding. In the case of retiree health transfers, the negative long-term tax consequences (present-value accounting in our terminology) is clearly recognized. Because Congress has been trying to limit the tax preference for both health and pension plans for many years, all proposed pension legislation is scrutinized to make sure that it does not relax existing limits. The way Congress deals with this problem of short-term gain and long-term loss is not through present-value accounting but through restrictions that limit long-term tax losses. The health transfer proposals that have been considered by Congress have been modified to limit the amount that is transferred or to limit the availability of the transfers to a narrow window period.

It is clear from the experience of retiree health transfers that some long-term tax consequences of pension law are recognized in the legislative process. Even though they are not reflected in budgetary accounting, they are evident in complex legislative restrictions and window periods.

Accounting Rules and Major Structural Changes

The previous examples have all dealt with micro-changes within the pension system, but our budgetary accounting rules are equally influential and equally distortionary in the overall design of our pension system. Many political leaders say that they want to increase national savings and believe that they can accomplish this objective by expanding the availability of Individual Retirement Accounts (IRAs). However, the budgetary costs of expanding IRAs in their current form are daunting because current IRAs allow an immediate deduction from taxable income. This deduction increases the current budget deficit.

Taking advantage of our budget myopia, recent proposals for expanding IRAs have shifted the timing of the tax. These new IRAs would change the tax-preferred period from the period it was contrib-

12. The opposition of unions to this proposal may seem surprising at first, but viewed in this light it is not.

uted to the period it was withdrawn. These new IRAs are essentially tax-exempt savings.[13]

New IRAs and old IRAs have the same impact using present-value accounting if personal tax rates are the same in the contribution and withdrawal period. But the two different IRAs look vastly different in our cash-receipts budget system. Cash-receipts accounting causes several problems:

1. If legislation for the new IRAs is enacted and used by savers, future taxes will fall. But, because the price of future tax breaks does not show up in cash-receipts accounting, the new IRAs may obscure future tax changes or spending adjustments that will be necessary to compensate.
2. Because tax rates may not be the same in the contribution and withdrawal period, the new IRAs and old IRAs may have different effects. But this difference, the only difference between the two proposals, is completely ignored under current budgeting rules.
3. To the extent that personal savings can be increased through the tax system, the new IRAs may be less effective than the old IRAs. Individuals do not respond to future tax promises as readily as they do to current deductions. Part of this is undoubtedly due to suspicion over whether the promise of lower tax rates in the withdrawal period can be kept. Some would argue that individuals see through the facade of cash-receipts accounting and surmise that the promise of tax-free withdrawal will not be kept.

The United States is not the only country where cash-receipts accounting rules influence pension design. In 1988, the Australian tax on pensions was completely revamped to bring the taxation of pension income forward. Tax on employer-provided pensions was changed from tax at the individual level on withdrawal to one where employer contributions were taxed when contributed but were tax-free upon withdrawal. The Australian government made the rationale for change explicit:[14]

13. Two examples are the 1989 Packwood-Roth proposal and the Administration's Family Savings Plan.
14. See *A Guide to the Reform of the Taxation of Superannuation,* (Canberra: Australian Government Publishing Service, May 1988), 6. The reforms included several other changes in addition to those described above. A tax was imposed on earnings of pension funds which was offset to a large degree by the extension of dividend imputation to pensions. One reason that the government wanted to lower tax rates through pension reform was because the labor unions had been promised lower tax rates in exchange for wage moderation.

In effect, the existing tax on benefits which would be collected well into the future is brought forward for payment now by the funds. This reduces the current cost to the Budget of the superannuation tax concessions, but most importantly without any reduction in the after-tax benefits of fund members.

The report also states that:

The revenues gained from this reform will be used to cut personal tax rates, and so will reduce tax on other income including other forms of savings.

Rarely is the difference between present-value and cash-receipts accounting so apparent. In this case, cash-receipts accounting was used to achieve a tax cut from a change that had no effect on the present value of resources available to the government. No tax cut could have been justified under present-value accounting.

Modeling and Data Needs

Other chapters in this volume point out the deficiencies in data that exist in the field of pensions. Our focus is, however, more on society's deficiencies in tax and retirement modeling—that is, the failure to use data that do exist to build models that would shed some light on the longer-term consequences of changes in pension policy, especially the revenue consequences.

Unless the General Accounting Office and others prevail in their proposals to shift the U.S. government away from cash-flow accounting, it is unlikely, however, that current practices in tax expenditure accounting for qualified plans will soon change. Alternative measures nonetheless would be helpful in addressing some persistent policy debates over qualified plans and helping legislators make more informed decisions.

Ideally, a model is needed that projects today's pension system into the next several decades. That model has to be flexible enough to accommodate different assumptions about lifetime coverage rates, mobility, and such. The more the model is based on actual wage histories, the more reliable the extrapolations.

This type of modeling has been tried in the past, in some cases more successfully than others. Several different versions of DYNASIM have been developed, though their recent use for pension simulation has been limited. ICF, a Washington-based consulting firm, also has developed a lifetime pension model, which was used by both Employee Benefit Research Institute (EBRI) and the Congressional Budget Office for their studies on the size and distribution of lifetime tax expenditures.

These modeling enterprises have languished, partly because of the lack of persistent attention and funding. They are complicated exercises that require a merging of data from several sources. A severe impediment has been the lack of access to Social Security wage information. An unintended result of information reporting requirements in the 1970s was to put these records within the purview of the privacy section of the Internal Revenue Code. Trying to achieve consensus among the competing privacy views of the IRS, the Social Security Administration, and the Census Bureau is nearly impossible.

In addition, more specific information at the firm level and the plan level would be useful in addressing specific proposals, such as the retiree health transfer proposal. The Pension Benefit Guaranty Corporation is developing a library of the Form 5500 filings that will be linked over time. This should help on some of these issues, though a recent use of these filings has revealed many data entry and employer identification problems when they are used at this level.

A recent request by the Ways and Means Committee to the General Accounting Office (GAO) gives some hope that the Congress may be increasing its demand for information on a present-value basis. That request asked whether the current tax on reversions adequately recaptures the value of past deductions and, more important, the value of the inside build-up within the tax-free trust. The GAO, uniquely expert in creating specific data bases, has built a simple tax simulation model for this purpose and started to use it on a small sample of filers.

Also hopeful has been the request to the Pension Benefit Guaranty Corporation to examine the relationship of leveraged buyouts (LBOs) and reversions. Thanks to a data base that the Securities and Exchange Commission (SEC) had developed for some similar questions, it was possible to match reversion activity between firms that had undergone an LBO and a control group. Unfortunately, this study has revealed the costs associated with such a labor intensive activity.

Probably no amount of data collection and modeling will be able to resolve some of the fundamental issues in pension policy. We are unlikely to know how the costs of defined benefit plans get passed back to participating workers. Nor are we ever likely to know what effects the nondiscrimination rules are having.[15] On the savings front, firm

---

15. Do the nondiscrimination rules force savings among lower-income and younger workers that would not otherwise take place? To the extent that some workers are reluctant participants in these plans, do they successfully resist coincidental reductions in current compensation, thereby forcing higher-income and older workers to absorb at least some of the costs of the reluctant participants? Does this intra-workforce cross subsidy become sufficiently large that rates of return effectively converge between those in higher and lower tax brackets?

conclusions may also be elusive: do the preferences change the relative demand for immediate and deferred consumption? It may be that we will never know conclusively whether these tax breaks are even contributing to retirement wealth.[16] But, within this overall agnosticism, better tax accounting nonetheless might help. Some issues that seem relevant to these debates are:

1. The tax rate changes in the 1986 Tax Reform Act, along with the growing inclusion of Social Security in taxable income, have lowered the advantages of tax rate shifting. Nonetheless, from the perspective of the joint lives of a worker and the surviving spouse, at least some of the deferred wage likely will be received during years in which tax rates will be relatively low or nonexistent. Assuming that this preference does get passed forward to participants, a better sense of the magnitude of what is left of income tax shifting and when during the life cycle it occurs most would help in deciding whether we should any longer regard it as a significant tax expenditure. Put another way, the government's receivable may be so large that it makes sense to disregard this "preference."

2. Under any circumstances, the difference between the before-tax in a qualified plan and the normal after-tax return of an income tax will remain a significant preference. To what extent is it compensated? The government now forgoes collecting taxes on this accumulating capital income. If those taxes are compensated by, say, higher taxes on current consumption, and the extra value in the pension plans does get passed forward, pension participants and society are wealthier. If, on the other hand, government debt merely goes up by the amount of the forgone taxes, society is no wealthier, although there will have been some shift in the distribution of the tax burden.

3. To what extent is pure tax arbitrage a substantial problem in the use of qualified plans? The tax arbitrage phenomenon pervades our current hybrid tax system and cannot be completely resolved without going to a comprehensive consumption tax or a truly broad-based income tax, either of which would involve considerable transition problems. Absent those changes, however, what are the comparative effects of addressing this matter through limits on interest deductibility, rather than limits on qualified plans?[17]

16. Have the tax preferences for qualified plans, like so many other tax breaks, become internalized in market operations, such that net (after-tax) lifetime compensation is unaffected and the tax preference gets passed back in the form of lower prices?

17. For some suggestions along these lines, see Andrews and Bradford (1988) (note 4), 295–97.

4. Tensions exist between the Treasury's desire to hold down deductions and minimize tax-free build-up and the Pension Benefit Guaranty Corporation's desire for greater pension funding and, thus, less exposure for its pension insurance program. Modeling that concentrated on the longer term would highlight the real, permanent costs of the tax-free build-up, rather than the transitory costs of when deductions are recognized. Those permanent losses could then be contrasted to alternative claims scenarios for the insurance program, thereby allowing Congress to make a clearer choice between revenues and contingent liability.

As both of this chapter's commentators indicate, there is no single temporal perspective that is always right for the legislator. When we come to questions of retirement income and national savings, though, some perspective that goes beyond the next three years of a budget agreement is needed. Of course, the assumptions involved in long-term models are heroic, especially when those models use, as they must, what always will be incomplete data. These models, however, are no less heroic when we attempt to model Social Security or Medicare for the next twenty-five, even seventy-five, years. Nor, despite that added perspective, are those programs less immune from debates about their immediate effects on the budget, as witness the perennial arguments over Social Security cost-of-living increases or whether it is desirable or possible to "save" payroll tax surpluses. Nonetheless, Congress makes more deliberate and balanced decisions about these programs because it has these alternative perspectives. We need more of that same balance when it comes to the private sphere of retirement saving.

Comments by Lawrence H. Thompson

I have spent a major part of my career as an analyst working for and with policy makers, and will use this experience as the basis for a few observations about the use of data in policy debates, whether or not they are budget-related debates. I then want to note my agreement with what I take to be the key point in the chapter by Kathleen Utgoff and David Lindeman and discuss another example of that point. As they explain, for purposes of preparing and debating the budget, conceptual issues are probably more important than are data issues. How one chooses to think about a matter and present data concerning it can often have a much greater impact than refining an estimate.

The Use of Data in Policy Debates

In my experience, data analyses are used in three different ways in the policy process: (1) to isolate emerging issues for the public policy agenda; (2) to analyze particular legislative proposals; and (3) to develop impact (usually cost) estimates.

The first use encompasses the role played by most academic studies. Researchers conduct studies of phenomena they believe are important and, in the process, help to identify and explore larger social issues. These studies tend to be communicated to policy makers (and would-be policy makers—such as those running for political office) through several kinds of intermediaries, including analytically oriented staffers and journalists who popularize current academic thinking.

At least in the social sciences, the process of knowledge development and dispersion tends to have a democratic aura. No single study is taken as definitive. Instead, topics are moved onto public policy agendas after a number of studies seem to agree that a particular topic or set of topics deserves greater public policy consideration.

Most policy makers are not analysts. They do not have the training or skills necessary to differentiate between a methodologically sound study and a less well-conceived analysis. For this reason, it is especially helpful if the policy prescription that emerges from these studies is a relatively simple and logical response to the problem identified. In contrast, it is especially unhelpful if the prescription is cloudy because the researchers are engaged in a heated debate over arcane points.

The kind of work that influences policy agendas is the kind of work undertaken by people like those reading this volume. In this work, developing the correct conceptual framework and using the appropriate data probably have roughly equal importance. But the data needed for these kinds of studies are the same sorts of data that have been discussed in earlier chapters on research data uses.

The second use is the development of particular statutory provisions within the context of broader legislative packages. This is the task of Congressional staff and the policy analysts in the executive branch.

These days, most legislative changes represent relatively minor adjustments to existing rules—for example, changes in certain details of the vesting rules applicable to top-heavy plans. The changes usually have both proponents and opponents, each preparing analytical studies through which they attempt to persuade agency leaders and members of Congress to their point of view. The worth of these studies depends on their being both timely and easily understood. As a consequence, the more analytical of these studies tend to be cross tabular analyses built on existing data bases. Cross tabs are used because nontechnical decision makers can understand them; existing data bases are used because the life span of most policy debates is less than the time required for any but the most primitive original data collection.

This policy use requires the maintenance of data bases containing some general, reasonably accurate micro level data. In my experience, attempts to collect specific, policy-relevant data usually fail; the issues anticipated when designing the data collection strategy have been replaced by other concerns by the time the data are ready to use.

The third use is for cost estimates. In the current budget climate, these estimates play a vital role in determining which proposals are considered seriously or which of two competing proposals is adopted. Although I have no direct experience as a cost estimator, my impression is that their data needs are similar to the policy analysts' needs—general data upon which plausible estimates of the impact of a variety of possible changes can be prepared on short notice.

The Importance of Conceptual Frameworks

As noted earlier, I agree with Utgoff and Lindeman that for many public policy purposes the conceptual framework is as important as precise numbers. I will use the current budget deficit problem to illustrate this point.

Table 1 shows federal budget results for four years: actual numbers for recent years, and the CBO base line projections prepared in the spring of 1990 for future years. These numbers are arrayed in two different ways. The first set of numbers (Table 1A) is the standard format used over the last twenty years; all receipts from all sources are lumped together and compared to all expenditures from all sources. The deficit represents the amount by which total expenditures exceed total receipts. Note that the numbers in 1A showed steady, if not spectacular, progress in reducing the federal deficit. It was reduced by some $60 billion between fiscal year 1985 and fiscal year 1989 and, in these figures, falls by another $35 billion by fiscal year 1995. The numbers suggest that some combination of modest revenue increases and outlay reductions (for instance, a 4 percent change in each) could bring the budget into balance by fiscal year 1995.[1]

Many federal receipts are earmarked for particular purposes, however, including Social Security taxes and federal taxes to support airport and highway construction. The collection of these receipts generates (politically, if not legally) pressure for future matching expenditures and, in recognition of this, the receipts are credited to and outlays are charged to specific federal trust funds. In other cases, current operations create future liabilities, most importantly in the case of civilian and military pensions. Increasingly, federal agencies are charged for the cost of future pensions on an accrual basis. The amounts charged against individual agency budgets are credited to trust funds against which the future retirement benefits will also be charged.

The second set of numbers (Table 1B) shows the same budget results formatted to reflect separately the operations of the various special trust funds and of the general operating fund of the federal government. Presenting the same numbers in a different format changes the picture substantially. First, note that all of the apparent deficit reduction between fiscal year 1985 and fiscal year 1995 comes from rising trust fund surpluses; the fiscal results of the general operations of the government actually deteriorated over the ten-year period.

Of particular concern is the fact that the largest portion of the growing trust fund surpluses occurs in the Social Security funds. But under the current Social Security financing plan, these balances are only temporary. Early in the next century they will be drawn down to finance retirement benefits. At that time, the social security trust funds will begin to run large deficits. Most of the rest of the growing trust

---

1. Since these projections were developed, the deficit picture has deteriorated. Major contributors include escalating costs for bailing out insolvent savings and loans and slowing growth in revenues.

TABLE 1   Alternative Budget Presentations (billions of dollars)

	FY 85	FY 89	FY 91[a]	FY 95[a]
A. *Federal deficit (standard format)*				
Receipts	734	991	1,137	1,438
Outlays	946	1,143	1,275	1,555
Total deficit	−212	−152	−138	−118
B. *Federal deficit by fund type*				
General fund	−267	−275	−273	−303
Trust funds	54	123	136	185
Total deficit	−212	−152	−138	−118

[a]Congressional Budget Office, Baseline Estimates, 1990, from *The Economic and Budget Outlook: Fiscal Years 1991–1995* (Washington, DC: U.S. Government Printing Office, 1990).

fund surplus reflects the advance funding of the retirement benefits of an increasing fraction of federal employees.

Second, note that the general fund deficit does not look nearly as manageable in the 1B number set. Eliminating the $303 billion fiscal year 1995 general fund deficit is a considerably more challenging task. Moreover, the realization that the major revenue shortfall is concentrated in the general fund raises questions about the appropriateness of revenue and outlay changes (such as delaying Social Security COLAs) that would increase the trust fund surpluses rather than reducing the general fund deficit.

Table 2 arrays the fiscal year 1989 numbers a third way; it represents an approach to thinking about the budget deficit first brought to my attention by Senator Terry Sanford. The operations of the major retirement trust funds are shown separately. Other federal fiscal operations are further divided into the amount the general fund must pay annually for interest on general fund debt and the remaining operations of the federal government (referred to here as current operations).

Table 2 shows that the retirement accounts had revenues of $499 billion and outlays of $389 billion, producing a surplus of $109 billion in fiscal year 1989. (All the other federal trust funds combined ran a $14 billion surplus that year, producing the total fiscal year 1989 trust fund surplus shown in Table 1B.) The interest account had no receipts and had expenditures of $243 billion, for a deficit of $243 billion. The rest of the operating budget ran a deficit, but only $19 billion.

The picture emerging when the numbers are displayed this way shows that the current deficit problem is neither in the retirement accounts nor primarily in the current operation accounts. These numbers suggest that the problem is excessive debt service charges. Con-

TABLE 2   Fiscal Year 1989 Federal Deficit by Expenditure Type
(billions of dollars)

	Retirement accounts	Interest expense	Current operations	Total budget[a]
Receipts	499	—	842	991
Outlays	389	243	861	1,143
Surplus/deficit	109	−243	−19	−152

[a]Total receipts and total outlays differ from the sum of the receipts of outlays of the component parts because of interfund transactions.

trary to conventional wisdom, the American people have been willing to pay enough taxes to cover the current cost of the federal government. But taxes have not been sufficiently high to deal with the current year implications of prior year fiscal shortfalls. Following this line of reasoning, an appropriate deficit reduction approach might be to eliminate the relatively modest deficit on current operations through expenditure cuts and then to levy a new tax whose receipts would be dedicated to debt service.

The Importance of the Conceptual Framework

I suspect there is no single correct way to present the budget numbers. My point is simply to show that the way they are arrayed can affect dramatically what one conceives as the basic problem. And, in turn, the conceptual framework employed to define the problem can have a major impact on the types of solutions that appear appropriate.

Consider the effect that better data or better estimating procedures might have had on this analysis. Suppose that the availability of both would have produced an estimate for fiscal year 1991 that the trust fund surplus would be $15 billion less than shown in these numbers; that the interest payments would be $10 billion higher than reflected in these numbers; that income tax revenues would be $15 billion lower than these numbers reflect. Would any of these changes have altered the fundamental picture? I think not. As Utgoff and Lindeman have argued, the key here is the conceptual framework, not the precise numerical estimates.

Comments by Gary Burtless

David Lindeman and Kathleen Utgoff have written an essay on the need for better data in thinking about pensions, taxes, and policy making. By my reading the chapter has four substantive parts:

(1) A concise survey and handy algebraic derivation of the tax preference to pensions.
(2) A discussion of the proper way to assess the effects on government revenue of these preferences as well as a discussion of the actual way that assessment is now made in Washington. (No one will be surprised to learn there is a difference between the right way and the Washington way.)
(3) A fascinating catalogue of instances in which use of the "Washington way" has misled policy makers.
(4) A discussion of implications for wise and beneficent data-gathering policy.

If I were the type of nit-picking discussant who assigned letter grades to essays—which of course I'm not—I would give the authors uneven marks for the four parts of their paper: A, B−, A+, and "Incomplete." But, as I said before, I'm not that kind of discussant. It might suggest I know as much as the authors about what they're writing. Nonetheless, let me say something about each of the topics treated.

The first section of the paper, which shows the nature and size of the tax preference for pensions, earns high marks for conciseness. You could find the same derivations elsewhere, usually developed at tedious length. Lindeman and Utgoff kindly cut to the chase and tell us what we need to know.

According to U.S. Treasury calculations, the tax preference for employer pensions is unquestionably important. It causes a more sizable loss of revenue than any other preference in the tax code, including far better known preferences, such as the deductibility of mortgage interest payments.

The next section of the paper deals with how the tax preference for pensions—and reforms in the preference—should be calculated and treated in policy making. The authors distinguish two basic approaches: a "present value" calculation and a scoring technique (apparently used by the Treasury and Congress) known as "cash-flow" accounting.

Under the first approach, which is the preferable one according to the authors, we establish some idealized version of the tax system (such as pure income taxation). And then we calculate the present value of the tax shortfall from that system after the preference is enacted. Alternatively, if we are considering modifications in the current preference, we calculate tax liabilities of workers and firms in all future periods under the reformed and current systems and then determine the present value of the *difference* between these two flows, that is, the sum of annual differences discounted to the present.

By assumption, there is no behavioral response to the reform. Thus, we can project future behavior with perfect confidence based on tax returns and observed behavior in the recent past.

One way to look at this technique is as follows: The income of firms and individuals in all future periods is calculable and predetermined. The tax code at any point in time defines how that income is divided between the government, on the one hand, and tax filing units (workers and firms), on the other. A reform in the tax code changes the way income is divided between the government and filing units. It changes the fraction going to the government in a different way in each future year. The goal of "present-value" calculations is to discount these changes to the present.

Now, of course, what the Treasury and Congress do falls short of this ideal. As I understand it, they make the required calculations for only a fixed number of years—say, the next three or five. And they do not discount the tax revenue changes within that fixed time horizon. To limit the *long-run* consequences of their reform, Congress and the President put arbitrary rules into the tax code that limit the ultimate tax losses the government will sustain.

The difference between the ideal accounting system (present-value) and the current system (cash-flow) boils down to this: the present-value calculations require infinite (or at least very long) time horizons, while cash flow requires only a three- to five-year horizon. And present-value calculations require discounting, while cash flow does not.

I suspect cash-flow scoring is a bit more sophisticated than the authors imply. First, cash flow is just a very simple discounting procedure. Discounts of zero percent applied to revenue changes in the next three or five years and rates of 100 percent to revenue changes after that. In addition, members of Congress and OMB directors are very keen on the exact timing of the revenue changes over the next three or five years. To meet October's Gramm-Rudman targets, they place low discount factors on next year's revenue gain and huge discounts on the gains or losses after the next election. As I say, a very sophisticated discounting technique.

What bothers me about this section of the paper is that the authors are persuasive about the shortcomings of cash-flow accounting, but they do not tell the reader the extent of data requirements for full-fledged present-value accounting. Even if we restrict attention to the next fifty years—which may not be enough, in this context, because workers' careers, including retirement, can last seventy to seventy-five years—the data requirements and the number of calculations are awesome. The calculations do not simplify to a simple algebraic formula in practice. They require sophisticated year-by-year calculations for a wide variety of firms, pension plans, and assumed turnover rates.

Where can the information come from? A sensible person might throw up his or her hands, restrict attention to the next few years, and let the distant future take care of itself. I am persuaded that we can do better, but where will the data come from? This paper does not suggest an answer.

A second problem only lightly touched upon is the assumption under present-value accounting that the distant future is knowable and predictable. The necessary calculations, for example, would assume that all provisions in the tax code are fixed except the provision that tightens or loosens the preference for pensions. But of course, this is hardly a safe assumption.

The Accelerated Cost Recovery System (ACRS), enacted in 1981, permitted businesses to depreciate their plant and equipment more rapidly than was possible in the 1970s. From a present-value standpoint, this simply moved their deductions for depreciation forward in time. Eventually their deductions would fall below the levels permitted under the old law, and their tax liability would rise. From a present-value standpoint the revenue loss from ACRS was therefore far below the loss during the first three to five years after enactment, when deductions were huge.

The problem is the tax code was reformed again in 1986. Tax rates were sharply lowered. Firms that enjoyed windfalls or tax gains between 1982 and 1986 found that, when their deduction for depreciation fell sharply later on during the useful life of a particular piece of capital equipment, the cost to them of the lower depreciation fell as well. From the government's standpoint, the *delay* in collecting taxes as a result of ACRS became, in effect, a permanent revenue loss. Because of lower tax rates after 1986, the government never got back the taxes whose collection had been delayed between 1982 and 1986. Arguably, cash-flow accounting would have measured the tax loss more reasonably than present-value accounting.

The bottom line is this: a "temporary" tax loss or tax gain next year because of a change in law could easily turn out to be the *permanent* loss or gain, since the tax law could easily be changed again the following year. That is why the short time horizon in cash-flow accounting might make some kind of perverse sense.

The third section of the paper is the most fascinating and entertaining, at least to the jaded policy analyst. The authors give us a sorry catalogue of folly in tax policy making, attributable in some measure to reliance on cash-flow accounting. I highly recommend this section to teachers in public policy schools.

The authors give us instructive vignettes, showing how the wrong time horizon and analytical procedure can lead policy makers astray and attempt to persuade us that the motto of the Kennedy School— "Better policy through better analysis!"—is justified. But while I understand their logical point, I wonder where we will get the information—in practice—to do a better job.

This brings us to what we should be considering in this volume, and what the authors deal with in their last section—namely, data requirements. I have already noted that the data requirements for their preferred present-value methodology are enormous and the assumptions are heroic.

If I have a single criticism to make of this very interesting chapter it is that the authors do not spell out those data requirements very clearly. What do we need to know? How can it be obtained? How likely are we to get it? What "second best" alternatives can they suggest?

Any revision of this chapter should attempt to answer these questions clearly, or at least the authors should tell us why they are not important. Unkind readers might otherwise grade this chapter "incomplete."

Chapter 6
The Use of International Private Pension Statistics for Policy Analysis

Lorna M. Dailey and John A. Turner

Study of pension policies and pension statistics for other countries with similar pension systems provides a new perspective on the U.S. pension system, suggests new policy options for the U.S., and provides a broader range of experience against which theory concerning pensions can be tested. Comparative private pension statistics, however, are in the early stages of development, with no consistent international reporting system having been developed. There are about a dozen countries with well-developed private pension systems. With reference to these countries, the five subject areas covered by the earlier chapters are revisited to provide an international perspective on U.S. pension policy issues.

Traditionally, families have provided for their nonworking elderly, often in multigenerational households. In the last half of this century in many countries, the social function of families taking care of their elderly has been partially replaced by government social security programs. In part due to increased geographic mobility and decreased family size, multigenerational households have become much less common and reliance on government programs has consequently increased.

Because of the aging of populations in developed countries, social security programs are providing old age benefits for an increasingly large share of the population. This growing dependency burden is causing further change in the provision of retirement income. The legislated reduction of Social Security benefits starting in the year 2000 in the United States and reductions in future social security benefits in the United Kingdom and Japan are examples of the policy response.

In most western democracies, private pensions predated social security, but only covered a small fraction of the labor force. As a further result of population aging, in Japan and Western Europe as well as the

United States and Canada, the importance of private pensions as a source of retirement income is growing.

In the United States, retirement income is now provided through private pensions, private savings, Social Security, and employer- and government-provided retiree health insurance. When viewed in world perspective, this type of retirement income system, a modern version of the so-called "three-legged stool," is not used in many countries. Although virtually all countries have some form of social security, and in most countries private savings or family support are relied on, private pensions currently play an important role in providing retirement income in only about a dozen countries.

In countries where private pensions have developed, however, similar problems have arisen. In these countries the growing importance of private pensions and the need to address the risks associated with the receipt of pension benefits have fostered increasing regulation. Because of the similarities in the problems facing pension systems in different countries, an international perspective on pension policy would be useful, but a lack of comparative statistics has hampered pension policy analysts from gaining an international perspective. No system has been developed for regularly collecting and publishing internationally comparable pension statistics. By contrast, comparative statistics for social security have been available for decades.

In discussing the need for international pension statistics, each of the five major aspects of private pensions discussed in the context of the United States in preceding chapters is revisited.

I. The Need for Internationally Comparable Private Pension Statistics

What can be learned from international pension statistics? International pension statistics provide a more precise understanding of the pension policies of different countries than would be available from a purely verbal description of the policies. This may aid policy development in several ways.

First, by providing a new perspective, internationally comparable private pension statistics may promote a better understanding of one's own private pension system. A new perspective may provide greater clarity for viewing one's own system by causing analysts to look at their pension system in a different way and may call into question practices that have been taken for granted.

Second, by promoting a better understanding of alternative policies pursued by other countries, such statistics may help to expand the range of policy options. Aggregate pension statistics can provide information on the magnitude of the effects of pension policies and institutions in other countries, allowing analysts to judge the efficacy of pension policies, and thus providing new insights as to feasible policy alternatives.

Third, by providing a broader range of experience for analysis, the availability of internationally comparable pension statistics may further the development of theory concerning private pension policy. Cross-sectional and time series private pension data from different countries provide a new source of data for testing theories on the effects of pensions in capital and labor markets. Statistical variability in broad national policies can be gained through the use of international data.

Fourth, internationally comparable private pension statistics may be useful for examining competitiveness in international trade. Data on pension costs will help determine the cost competitiveness of industries in international trade. Data on government subsidies to pension plans in different industries would allow an assessment of the comparative subsidies on export products by different countries.

Fifth, along with the move to standardize other laws, there is a trend toward regulating certain features of the national pension laws of European Community members, such as equal treatment of male and female participants. Such a trend increases the need for comparable pension statistics for the enforcement of pension laws and regulations.

Internationally comparable pension statistics are more likely to advance policy analysis when a few guidelines are followed. Comparisons are more likely to be useful for U.S. policy making when the countries compared have well-developed private pension systems within the context of democratic institutions, free market economies, and a tradition of reliance on the private sector.

Private Sector Uses of Internationally Comparable Pension Statistics

The growing internationalization of both capital and labor markets has increased the private sector's need for private pension statistics from other countries.

The removal by 1992 of many national barriers to the flow of labor and capital in Western Europe among the twelve countries of the European Community increases the need for standardized pension reporting and statistics. With a single European market, labor mobility across countries (including labor mobility within firms across countries) will increase the need for international pension portability, which will require an understanding of private pensions in different countries.

The worldwide internationalization of capital markets raises the need for internationally comparable statistics on financial aspects of pensions. For example, with investment in foreign stocks, there is an increased need to understand pension accounting in different countries in order to evaluate the effect of pension liabilities of foreign firms on their long-run profitability.

A change in accounting practice in the United States has increased the need in the United States for financial statistics on foreign pension plans. The Financial Accounting Standards Board (FASB) sets rules for accounting practice in the United States. FAS87 requires that for the purposes of financial reporting, U.S. multinational companies value the liabilities of their foreign pension plans in the same manner as they value the liabilities of their U.S. pension plans.

In summary, both at the macro level for government policy making and at the micro level for decision making by individual firms, there is an increasing need for internationally comparable pension statistics.

II. What We Have Learned

The U.S. Department of Labor (USDOL) has undertaken a project to study private pension policy in other countries with similar pension systems. To support an international exchange of knowledge on pension policy, part of this project involves encouragement of the development of internationally comparable private pension statistics. Comparative private pension statistics are in the early stages of development, with no consistent international pension reporting system having been developed.

In the USDOL International Pension Statistics Project, countries with private pension systems similar to those in the United States were chosen. All countries chosen are governed by democratic institutions, all have market economies, all have mixed public-private systems for the provision of retirement income, and all are highly developed, high-income countries.

The countries chosen in the USDOL project are the United States, Australia, Canada, France, Japan, the Netherlands, Switzerland, the United Kingdom, and West Germany. All of these countries, except France, have private pension systems, with a structure similar in most respects to that of the United States. France was included as an example of a country with a comprehensive private system, but which is funded on a pay-as-you-go basis.[1] These nine countries contain a large majority of the worldwide private pension assets and participants.

---

1. The French pension system is referred to as a "repartition" or "distribution" system which pays benefits out of current contributions. Pension assets consist of about one

Though some other small countries, such as Sweden, have relatively high private pension coverage rates, no other countries have large numbers of private pension participants. In most other countries, private pensions have low coverage rates. In Italy and Spain, for example, where social security replaces a high percentage of earnings, private pension coverage is very low.

Lorna Dailey of Bedford Research Consultants, under a contract to the Pension and Welfare Benefits Administration of the U.S. Department of Labor, has made a preliminary attempt at constructing internationally comparable private pension statistics. Her statistics are based on published statistics for the nine countries in the USDOL project.[2]

The analysis of statistics for these countries over the period 1970–86, undertaken by Dailey and Turner (1989), provides an indication of the type of policy-relevant information that can be learned from international pension statistics. Rather than focusing on the complexities of the different pension institutions, this analysis examines the outcomes of the institutions as described by their statistics.

In using international private pension statistics, it is helpful to understand different terminology used in different countries. The terms "occupational schemes," "private retirement schemes," and "superannuation funds" all refer to what in the United States are called private pension plans.

Private pension plans do not include all employer-provided pension plans or occupational pension plans, however, because private plans exclude plans for public-sector employees. Where they can be separately identified in the data, plans for public-sector employees are excluded, as are plans for self-employed workers. Plans in which only a single individual can participate (e.g., Individual Retirement Accounts in the U.S., Registered Retirement Savings Plans in Canada, and Personal Pensions in the United Kingdom) are also excluded.

The involvement of government in pension institutions differs across countries, sometimes blurring the distinction between public and private pensions and making it important in international comparisons to indicate clearly the characteristics that separate public and private

---

year's worth of contributions held as a reserve. There is also an element of "compensation" which refers to sharing among the various pension funds. If one pension fund has an unfavorable age structure, for example, and is unable to cover all the required benefits, other funds are required to make up the deficit.

2. Dailey's findings are published in Lorna M. Dailey and John A. Turner, "U.S. Pensions in World Perspective," and Lorna M. Dailey, "Private Pensions Statistics in Nine Countries," both in John A. Turner and Daniel J. Beller, eds., *Trends in Pensions* (Washington, DC: U.S. Government Printing Office, 1989). Updated and expanded statistics appear in John A. Turner and Lorna M. Dailey, *Pension Policy: An International Perspective* (Washington, DC: U.S. Government Printing Office, 1991).

pension plans. A private pension plan is an employer-sponsored plan or an employee-group-sponsored plan which provides retirement benefits to private-sector employees. Such plans may be voluntary or mandatory. The mandatory pension plans in France and Switzerland, for example, are considered private pension plans because the assets of those plans remain under private-sector control. France, however, provides a good example of the blurred distinctions between public and private plans, since its mandatory pay-as-you-go system is closer to the U.S. Social Security system than to its private pension system.

It is also important to distinguish between pension plans and other types of saving plans. The primary purpose of a pension plan is to provide retirement benefits. Some types of defined contribution plans, such as profit-sharing plans, are frequently cashed out before retirement in the United States, with the cash-out frequently being used for a purpose other than to provide retirement benefits. Similarly, it is also important to distinguish between severance benefit plans and retirement plans. In Japan, its Tax Qualified Pension Plans are generally cashed out in the form of a lump-sum payment if a worker leaves the employer before retirement. In both cases, however, the plans are used primarily for providing retirement income rather than as savings vehicles for pre-retirement purchases, and therefore they are classified as pension plans. While some types of plans are used for multiple purposes, if a plan is used primarily to provide retirement benefits it is classified as a pension plan.

Overview of Findings[3]

Because of the large size of its labor market and the requirement that its private pensions be fully funded, the United States has a large percentage of the participants (44 percent) and an even larger share of the pension assets (70 percent) that can be accounted for in the nine countries in the USDOL project (Tables 1 and 3). France and Japan, the next largest countries in terms of participants, both have about a third as many pension participants as does the United States, while the United Kingdom and Japan, the next largest countries in terms of pension assets, have pension assets equal to 13 percent and 9 percent those of the United States. In nearly all countries, however, over the past fifteen years private pension coverage and assets have grown relative to the size of the national economies.

How Good a Job Are Pensions Doing in Providing Retirement Income?

Beneficiaries. There have been large increases in the number of pension beneficiaries in the countries for which data are available, due in

3. See note 2.

TABLE 1 Active Participants in Private Pension Plans, 1970–86 (thousands)

Year	Australia	Canada	France	Germany	Japan	Netherlands	Switzerland	United Kingdom	United States
1970	—	1,552	10,583	—	5,905[a]	1,592	1,142	7,125[b]	26,100
1975	—	2,046[c]	15,183	—	9,424[d]	1,729	1,247	6,000	30,738
1980	—	2,505	16,502	—	11,200	2,109	1,359	6,025[e]	35,939
1981	—	—	16,494	—	11,810	2,106	1,419	—	36,912
1982	—	2,682	16,414	—	12,440	2,063	1,498	—	37,481
1983	—	—	16,407	—	12,830	2,059	1,586	5,800	38,971
1984	—	2,536	15,823	—	13,430	2,083	1,616	—	39,713
1985	1,014	2,559[f]	15,509	—	14,030	2,137	—	—	40,444
1986	1,160	2,582	15,324	—	14,620	2,205	—	—	41,343
Percent change									
Total 1970–1986	—	66	45	—	148	39	—	—	58
Five year periods									
1970–1975	—	32	43	—	60	9	9	–16.0	18
1975–1980	—	22	9	—	19	22	9	.4	17
1980–1985	—	2	–6	—	25	1	—	—	13

[a] Data are interpolated by the author for this year from data available for 1967 and 1972.
[b] Data are interpolated by the author for this year from data available for 1967 and 1971.
[c] Data are interpolated by the author for this year from data available for 1974 and 1976.
[d] Data are interpolated by the author for this year from data available for 1972 and 1977.
[e] Data are interpolated by the author for this year from data available for 1979 and 1983.
[f] Data are interpolated by the author for this year from data available for 1984 and 1986.
— Data not available.
Source: See Chapter 13, John A. Turner and Daniel J. Beller, eds., *Trends in Pensions* (Washington, DC: U.S. Government Printing Office, 1989).

TABLE 2   Active Participants in Private Pension Plans as a Percentage of the Private-Sector Labor Force, 1970–86 (percent)[a]

Year	Australia	Canada	France	Germany	Japan	Netherlands	Switzerland	United Kingdom	United States
1970	—	26	80	—	20	50	47	38	42
1975	—	28	100	—	29	49	52	32	44
1980	—	29	100	—	31	59	57	31	45
1981	—	—	100	—	32	58	58	—	45
1982	—	30	100	—	33	56	62	—	45
1983	—	—	100	—	33	56	66	30	45
1984	—	28	100	—	34	57	68	—	46
1985	20	28	100	—	35	59	—	—	46
1986	22	27	100	—	36	59	—	—	46

— Data not available.

[a]Caution should be used in comparing coverage rates among countries as there are significant differences in the categories of participants included. A consistent private-sector labor force number is not available from published sources for all countries, partly due to the complexity of distinguishing private-sector from public-sector employment in many countries (e.g., the government may own a majority share of corporations or banks which otherwise operate as private-sector entities). The distinction between private-sector and public-sector employment is not considered important in other countries, so that the appropriate data are not collected by these categories.

For Table 2, the private-sector labor force number was constructed by taking the "business-sector civilian labor force" provided by the Organisation for Economic Co-operation and Development (OECD) from its internal database, subtracting the self-employed and unpaid family labor statistics taken from the OECD publication *Labor Statistics 1966–86*, and adding the figures for the unemployed from the same publication. Some additional adjustments were made for the Netherlands and Switzerland.

This method of calculating the base private-sector labor force numbers may cause some discrepancies in the final plan participant percentages. For example, the split between public- and private-sector pension plan participants may not be exactly the same as the labor force split.

The percentages in Table 2 have been calculated as participants from Table 1, divided by the base labor force number calculated as described above. The country notes for Table 1 should also be read in conjunction with Table 2 in order to understand the participant data for each country.
Source: See Table 1.

TABLE 3   Total Assets of Private Pension Plans, 1970–86 (millions of U.S. dollars)

Year	Australia	Canada	France	Germany	Japan	Netherlands	Switzerland	United Kingdom	United States
1970	—	—	1,244	—	—	5,032[a]	—	10,704	149,500
1975	—	—	3,782	14,681[b]	6,739[c]	18,070[a]	22,234	21,422	289,600
1980	—	42,066	8,866	31,468	28,563	46,393	51,716	78,000	621,800
1981	—	44,286	7,948	29,646	36,168	41,864	48,065	79,635	659,200
1982	—	51,761	7,443	30,248	39,092	44,677	50,651	90,695	781,600
1983	—	63,371	7,252	31,528	49,533	46,734	53,671	102,071	923,200
1984	—	65,816	7,411	—	59,141	46,339	51,148	106,223	994,100
1985	15,362	74,173	8,238	—	69,857	49,384	—	130,960	1,186,000
1986	—	81,927	11,859	—	115,941	72,848	—	176,634	1,339,600

[a]Data are partially estimated by the author.
[b]Data are interpolated by the author for this year from data available for 1973 and 1978.
[c]Data are partially estimated by the author for this year from data available for 1976.
— Data not available.
Source: See Table 1. Assets for the Netherlands and for the United Kingdom include only non-insured private pension plans. Assets for Germany include support funds, pensionskassen and direct insurance. Assets for Switzerland include both private pension plans and plans for government employees.

part to the maturing of the pension systems. An increase in pension beneficiaries relative to the population aged 65 and older has occurred in all countries examined for which beneficiary data are available.

In Japan only 8 percent of the older population received annuity benefits from a funded plan in 1986, although other retirees received benefits from unfunded plans; receipt of lump-sum payments at retirement is also common. In the United States, 29 percent of the population aged 65 and older received a pension benefit. The percentage is 68 percent for France, 21 percent for the United Kingdom, and 2 percent for Australia (which has a relatively young private pension system and where lump-sum payments are frequently taken).

Comparison across countries reveals that the prevalence of lump-sum payments as the form of benefit receipt may have a large effect on pension statistics of beneficiaries and benefits. Receipt of lump-sum benefits is generally counted in pension statistics only in the year of receipt. Receipt of benefits in the form of lump-sum payments has been common in Japan and in Australia due to tax laws favoring this type of benefit.

Benefits. How do U.S. pension benefit levels compare with those in other countries? Average private pension benefits in national currency units provide the basic data for making international comparisons of benefit levels. These benefits can be converted to U.S. dollars by use of foreign exchange rates. Adjusting by foreign exchange rates provides data in a common currency, but valued at different sets of prices, since exchange rates are not affected by the prices of nontraded goods.

Taking into account purchasing power parity provides a better measurement of the actual comparative purchasing power of pension benefits in a given year, since it provides data in a common currency and at a common set of prices. Purchasing power parity for private consumption expenditures accounts for international differences in the price of nontraded goods and services which affect the living standards of the beneficiaries. With the purchasing power parity calculations, benefits are expressed in terms of the dollar value of what they can purchase in each country. This correction is particularly important for Japan, where government policies and institutional factors keep the price of food and housing high, thereby reducing the domestic purchasing power of the currency. With the purchasing power parity correction, the value of annual private pension benefits in Japan is reduced 19 percent in 1986 compared to its value when calculated using foreign exchange rates. The correction raises the value of annual pension benefits in Canada by 11 percent in 1985. The value of pension benefits is unchanged in the United States, since prices in the United States are the base to which other countries' prices are being compared.

Average annual private pension benefits in the United States were $4,530 in 1984, which is high by world standards and equals or exceeds the average benefits for other countries. Switzerland and Canada also have relatively high private pension benefits, but the statistics are biased upwards because they include the benefits of government workers. Countries with high coverage rates, such as France, have relatively low average pension benefits in part because low-wage workers, who have low benefits, are covered in those countries but are generally not covered in others. Annual pension benefits from funded pensions are relatively low in Japan ($1,201 in 1986), which may be explained by the popularity of lump-sum payments and unfunded benefits not counted in the measure of annual pension benefits.

International comparisons provide perspective on the preferred form in which pension benefits are received. In the United States, it is generally thought that pensions should be received as an annuity to assure that people will not spend down their savings too fast. Japan, where pension benefits are generally received as a lump sum, is known for the high savings rate of its population. The difference between Japan and the United States in the receipt of lump-sum distributions may reflect important cultural differences in attitudes towards saving which need to be taken into consideration when analyzing pension policies in different countries.

Pension benefit levels rise over time due to inflation. Thus, to make meaningful comparisons over time as to the purchasing power of pension benefits, it is necessary to adjust benefit levels for the effect of inflation by expressing them in terms of a constant price level across years. Doing this indicates that, in constant dollars, average pension benefits in the United States have risen only 5 percent over the sixteen years from 1970 to 1986.

This surprisingly small increase for pension benefits in the United States may be explained by the increasing percentage of older workers receiving pension benefits. For example, in 1962, 17 percent of men and 5 percent of women aged 65 or older were receiving income from private pensions or annuities. By 1986, these rates had increased to 33 percent for men and 13 percent for women. When a private pension system is started, high-income workers are generally the first to be covered and receive benefits. When lower-income workers are later covered, their benefits, which tend to be lower than average, depress average benefit levels even though the benefits for all workers are increasing. This sample selection effect causes aggregate data to understate the growth in pension benefits experienced by the typical worker during periods when the percent of older workers receiving pension benefits is increasing. In France, over the years 1970 to 1986, real average benefits increased only 0.7 percent, and in Switzerland over the years 1970 to 1984, real average benefits increased only 6 percent.

The post-retirement indexation of benefits is a policy concern in all countries because even a low inflation rate over a twenty-year or longer retirement will significantly erode the real value of benefits. There is very little data on post-retirement adjustments of benefits. However, it is known that few companies in any country provide automatic post-retirement cost-of-living adjustments.

Even when effort is made to measure pension benefits appropriately, care should be taken when drawing conclusions from cross-country comparisons of benefit levels. The finding that one country has higher private pension benefits than another does not necessarily indicate that the first country has a more successful retirement income system. The finding may simply indicate differing roles for the public and private sectors in the two countries. The adequacy of benefit levels in a country can only be determined by examining all sources of retirement income.

Influence of Pensions on Labor Force Activity

The pension coverage rate in the United States has been stable for a number of years at roughly half the labor force, and some policy analysts have concluded that steps should be taken to expand coverage. Pension coverage rates in most countries with private pension systems are considerably higher now than they were at the end of World War II. Even among countries chosen because they have relatively well-developed private pension systems, however, few countries have private pension systems that cover a majority of the private-sector workforce. The United States, the United Kingdom, Canada, and Australia had coverage rates in 1986 of 48 percent, 30 percent, 27 percent, and 22 percent (Table 2). The pension coverage rate for funded pensions in Japan was 36 percent in 1986 (which rate is greatly understated because the data do not include employees who will receive a lump-sum benefit from an unfunded plan). Although the United States has by far the most participants in private pension plans, its pension coverage relative to its labor force is considerably lower than France, with 100 percent coverage, and Switzerland, with 59 percent coverage in 1986.

While in most countries the decision to provide a pension plan is made voluntarily by employers and the decision to work for a company offering a pension plan is made voluntarily by workers, that is not the case in all countries. France and Switzerland are the only countries included in the USDOL project that had mandatory systems in 1990, but Sweden and Finland also have mandatory systems.

A similar pattern of pension coverage is observed in most countries with voluntary systems. Because of tax incentives, higher-paid workers are more likely to be covered than lower-paid workers. For that reason, and because of economies of scale in administration, workers are more likely to be covered by a private pension if they work in a large firm than if they work in a small firm. In most countries, collective bargaining agreements have been important in the development of private pensions and consequently workers covered by collective bargaining agreements have higher pension coverage rates than do other workers.

Pensions and Saving

The net saving that occurs within pension plans can be calculated as the change in pension assets between two years. Whether or not the net savings in pension plans is a net contribution to national savings is a complex issue. Although the United States lags behind Japan in its overall saving rate, the per-participant saving within private pension plans is more than twice as high in the United States than in Japan. Private pension saving per participant over the period 1980–86 was $5,000 in Japan and $12,000 in the United States. Private pension saving is thus a considerably more important aspect of saving in the United States than in Japan.

The net saving that occurs within private pension plans depends in part on the funding of the plans. In France, where nearly all private pensions are funded on a pay-as-you-go basis, pension plans are a source of little saving. In West Germany, private pensions are generally funded on a book reserve basis with at most a small trust fund, the pension "assets" with book reserve funding being equal to liabilities on the books of the sponsoring firm. With pay-as-you-go funding and book reserve funding, there is little or no accumulation of assets in a pension trust and little or no occurrence of pension saving, although saving presumably does occur within the firm in order to provide for the promised payment of future benefits.

What Are the Appropriate Funding Strategies for Pensions?

Even though all countries with well-developed private pension systems have a policy concern for the riskiness of the promise of future pension benefits, and funding is one way to reduce this risk, the extent and methods of plan funding vary considerably across countries. The pay-as-you-go private pension system in France arose from the experience of French pensions following World War II. The high inflation of that period greatly eroded the value of assets in French pension funds; and a pay-as-you-go system was adopted, in part because it is not directly subject to financial market risk. Such a system is subject, however, to demographic risk due to changes in the population age structure.

With book reserve funding in West Germany and Japan, the pension plan is in a sense funded with non-tradeable debt of the sponsoring corporation. The assets of a plan funded by the book reserve method are in effect non-tradeable, interest-bearing corporate notes issued by the sponsoring corporation.

In the United States, the United Kingdom, and Canada, all plans are required to be funded and most plans are required to reduce portfolio risk by diversifying. The requirement of diversification does not apply, however, to some types of defined contribution plans in the United States, such as Employee Stock Ownership Plans (ESOPs). ESOPs are similar to plans funded using book reserve funding in that they are undiversified, both types being basically invested in a single asset. In the case of ESOPs, the asset held by the plan is corporate equity of the sponsoring firm rather than corporate debt.

In most countries, plans have the option of eliminating the financial risk they face by investing in insurance company products (where, barring the failure of the insurance company, the financial risk is borne by the insurance company) or by offering defined contribution plans (where the financial risk is borne by the workers).

Assets per participant differ considerably across countries, in part reflecting different policies towards funding of pensions. In 1986 in the United States, assets per participant were $26,800, which was roughly equal to that for Switzerland and the Netherlands, the countries sharing with the U.S. the highest value of assets per participant. Among countries with funded pensions, Japan has the lowest amount of assets per participant at $7,400, a low value explained by the popularity of pay-as-you-go plans and plans wholly or partially funded on a book reserve basis.

The analysis of pension funding is greatly affected by whether a plan is a defined benefit plan or a defined contribution plan. Defined contribution plans are by definition always fully funded, while in defined benefit plans assets and liabilities generally differ. Defined benefit plans are the predominant plan type worldwide; only in the United States and Australia are defined contribution plans common. While a number of arguments can be made concerning the relative merits of defined benefit and defined contribution plans, the clear worldwide preference of plan sponsors (and presumably participants) is for defined benefit plans.

In all countries, employer pension contributions exceed employee contributions as a source of funding. Employers in the United States pay 87 percent of total pension contributions, versus 13 percent for employees. The share of pension contributions paid by employers is considerably higher in the United States than in all other countries except Japan. The high percentage of contributions paid by employers in the United States probably occurs because employee contributions are tax deductible only if they are made to a 401(k) plan and thus are not tax deductible for the participants in most plans. In Japan, pension benefits and severance benefits have traditionally been funded entirely by employers.

Implications of Pension Plans for the Federal Budget

In the nine countries considered, tax treatment of private pension plans differs considerably. The effect of private pensions on government budgets depends on the amount of tax deductions and other tax preferences granted to pensions. That amount depends both on the tax laws of the country and the size of its private pensions.

In all countries except Australia and New Zealand, tax deductions are allowed for employer contributions to tax-qualified private pensions. In 1986, New Zealand eliminated the tax deductibility of pension contributions, and in 1988 Australia levied a 15 percent tax on contributions. In Japan and West Germany, a tax deduction is allowed even when no contributions are made, so long as a reserve is listed on company books that is specified as being set aside for the purpose of paying future pension benefits.

The ability to earn a before-tax rate of return on pension assets is an important aspect of tax preferences. In most countries, the earnings on assets invested by pension funds are tax exempt. In Japan, however, there is a tax of 1.173 percent on pension assets, and in Australia there is a 15 percent tax on certain pension investment earnings.

The extent of the ability to earn a before-tax rate of return is affected by the degree to which advance funding is allowed. The greater the advance funding, the higher is the total tax subsidy. In France no advance funding is allowed, but in all other countries at least some advance funding is required. The United States has recently reduced allowable advanced funding (through the OBRA87 funding limitations), and other countries have made changes to limit advance funding. As pension assets grow in importance, the tax-favored treatment they receive is increasingly likely to come under scrutiny.

*   *   *

This chapter has analyzed existing data from the nine countries covered in the USDOL International Pension Statistics Project: Australia, Canada, France, West Germany, Japan, the Netherlands, Switzerland, the United Kingdom, and the United States. The International Bibliography that follows describes the sources of such data.

International Bibliography on Pension Statistics and Retirement Income Policy

This International Bibliography includes selected books, articles, and conference papers on pension statistics, pension surveys, retirement income policy, pensions and labor mobility, and the effect on national savings of the financing method used for a retirement system, plus major descriptive works on the pension and social security systems of twenty-four countries.

References to articles and books are arranged alphabetically by country first. Only two basic U.S. references included as U.S. sources are well covered elsewhere. No single-country or primarily U.S. directories, databases, or periodicals are included. The International section includes items covering more than one country. A final section lists international databases.

The Bibliography has been produced from the Bedford Index, a proprietary computer database developed and maintained by Bedford Research Consultants, covering international social security, pensions, and human resources issues. Reproduction of a portion of this Bibliography requires the permission of the University of Pennsylvania Press and Bedford Research Consultants.

Note: The distribution of some consultants' publications listed may be restricted to clients or survey participants.

Australia

Association of Superannuation Funds. *Survey of Superannuation Funds*. Sydney, February 1989.
> A detailed survey of the provisions of pension plans published about every four years. February 1989 survey covers 187 companies.

"Australia: Industrywide Superannuation—Survey." *IBIS Briefing Service*, October 1989, p. 3.
> Basic statistics on industry-wide pension plans in Australia.

Australian Bureau of Statistics. *DIRECT: The Directory of Social, Population and Labour Statistics*. Canberra. Basic volume and annual updates.

Bibliography of Australian statistical publications on demographics, labor, and social issues.

———. *Employment Benefits, Australia.* Canberra. Annual. 24 pp. (Catalogue no. 6334.0)

Survey of all employee benefits including participant data only for insured and non-insured pension plans.

———. *The Labor Force, Australia.* Canberra. Monthly. (Catalogue no. 6203.0)

———. *Labour Mobility, Australia.* Canberra. Annual. (Catalogue no. 6209.0)

———. *Public Sector Superannuation Funds and Schemes, Australia, 1986–87.* Canberra, 1990. 15 pp. (Catalogue no. 5511.0)

Statistics on pension plans for government employees.

———. *Retirement and Retirement Intentions, Australia.* Canberra, November 1989. 24 pp. (Catalogue no. 6238.0)

Statistical survey includes reasons for retirement and sources of income of retirees.

———. *Superannuation, Australia.* Canberra, April 1989. 26 pp. (Catalogue no. 6319.0)

Analyses persons covered and not covered by a pension plan. Results of a special supplementary survey to *The Labor Force, Australia.*

———. *Superannuation Funds, Australia, 1985–86.* Canberra, September 1988. 18 pp. (Catalogue no. 5649.0)

Comprehensive statistics on both insured and non-insured, private-sector and public-sector pension plans.

Foster, Chris. *Towards a National Retirement Incomes Policy.* Woden, ACT: Department of Social Security, 1988. 253 pp. (Social Security Review, Issues Paper 6)

Discussion of income of retirees, retirement age, social security, means tests for benefits, private pension plans, and directions for reform.

Gunasekera, Michelle and John Powlay. *Occupational Superannuation Arrangements in Australia.* Woden, ACT: Department of Social Security, 1987. 55 pp. (Social Security Review, Background/Discussion Paper 21)

A compilation of pension statistics from other sources with commentary.

Manning, I.G. and S. A. King. *Incomes and Housing Costs of Older Australians.* Woden, ACT: Department of Social Security, October 1988. (Social Security Review, Background/Discussion Paper 26)

Mendelsohn, Ronald, ed. *Finance of Old Age.* Canberra: Australian National University, Centre for Research on Federal Financial Relations (distributed by ANUTECH, Canberra), 1986. 366 pp.

Includes twenty-four papers covering social security, private- and public-sector pensions, private savings, taxation of pensions, and government policy relating to retirement income, along with proposals for the future.

Moore, Jim and Peter Whiteford. *Trends in the Disposable Income of Australian Families, 1964–65 to 1985–86.* Woden, ACT: Department of Social Security, December 1986. 103 pp. (Social Security Review, Background/Discussion Paper 11)

Parliament of the Commonwealth of Australia. *Income Support for the Retired and Aged: An Agenda for Reform.* Canberra: Australian Government Publishing Service, August 1988. 424 pp. (Report of the Senate Standing Committee on Community Affairs)

Extensive inquiry into all issues relating to retirement income conducted from 1983 through 1988. The Committee conducted public hearings and reviewed written submissions.

Stemp, P.J. *Tax Concessions for Occupational Superannuation: Implications for Aggregate Saving.* Canberra: The Australian National University, Centre for Economic Policy Research, 1988. (Discussion Paper 185)

Watts, Rob. *The Foundations of the National Welfare State.* Sydney/Boston: Allen and Unwin, 1987. 169 pp.

Austria

Brooks, Robert. "Interaction Between Pensions and the Labour Market: The Austrian Experience." In *Conjugating Public and Private: The Case of Pensions,* International Social Security Association, pp. 161–70. Geneva, 1987.

Brazil

MW-de Montigny Woerner Ltda. *Survey of Benefit Practices.* Sao Paulo, 1989.
    Survey of employee benefits as of January 1989 in 190 companies in Brazil including Brazilian, multinational, and government-owned companies.

TPF&C Ltda. *Ninth Annual Survey of Benefit Practices—1988.* Sao Paulo, 1989.
    Survey of employee benefits practices in 201 companies, 35% of which have a pension plan.

Canada

Archibald, T. R., C. P. Lanfranconi, B. Portis, and D. A. Robertson. *Survey of Pension Plans in Canada.* 7th ed. Toronto: Financial Executives Institute Canada, 1988. 88 pp.
    Survey of 198 private pension plans; includes indexation and surplus asset data and other financial and actuarial information. Survey conducted on an irregular basis.

Conklin, David W. "Pension Policy Reforms in Canada." In *Pension Policy: An International Perspective,* edited by John A. Turner and Lorna M. Dailey. Washington, DC: U.S. Government Printing Office, 1991.

Coward, Laurence E. *Mercer Handbook of Canadian Pension and Welfare Plans.* 9th ed. Don Mills: CCH Canadian Ltd, 1988. 337 pp.
    Handbook on customary practice and legislation for pension and group insurance plans in Canada.

Department of National Health and Welfare. Policy Planning and Information Branch. *Inventory of Income Security Programs in Canada—July 1985.* Ottawa, 1986. 330 pp.
    Description and summary of statistics on all federal and provincial government-sponsored income security programs.

Goodman, Catherine. "Changing Structures of Retirement Income in Canada." In *Conjugating Public and Private: The Case of Pensions,* International Social Security Association, pp. 105–22. Geneva, 1987.

Hewitt Associates. *Canadian SpecBook.* Lincolnshire, IL. Annual.
    Benefit plan specifications for salaried plans at 253 companies in Canada. *Canadian SpecBook Summary* published separately.

Ministry of Financial Institutions. *Building on Reform: Choices for Tomorrow's Pensions.* Toronto, March 1989. 117 pp.
> The Ontario Government's proposals for mandatory indexation of private pension benefits and other changes to pension legislation.

Report of the Task Force on Inflation Protection for Employment Pension Plans. Toronto: Queen's Printer for Ontario, 1988. 4 vols.
> Report and three volumes of research studies compiled by the Task Force during its study of indexation for pension plans in Ontario.

Report to the Treasurer of Ontario on the Financing of Benefits Under the Superannuation Adjustment Benefits Act and Associated Superannuation Plans. Prepared by Laurence E. Coward. Toronto: Ontario Government Bookstore, 1987. 120 pp.
> Study of pension benefits and indexation for the public-sector employees and teachers in Ontario.

Revenue Canada. *Taxation Statistics: Analyzing the Returns of Individuals for 19.. Taxation Year & Miscellaneous Statistics.* Ottawa. Annual. (Catalogue no. Rv 44-19..)
> Includes number of pension beneficiaries, total amount of pensions reported as income, and number of persons contributing to a RRSP; split by age categories; pensions from private-sector and public-sector employers cannot be separated.

Statistics Canada. *Financial Institutions: Financial Statistics.* Ottawa. Quarterly. (Catalogue no. 61–006)
> Includes assets of Registered Retirement Savings Plans and insured pension plans.

———. *Guide to Federal Goverment Labour Statistics.* Occasional. (Catalogue no. 72–512)
> Source guide to the numerous government publications on Canadian labor statistics.

———. *Pension Plans in Canada.* Ottawa. Biennial. (Catalogue no. 74–401)
> Analysis of insured and non-insured pension plans in both the public and private sectors with numerous tables. Data from Statistics Canada pensions database. 1988 data published in 1990.

———. *Trusteed Pension Plans: Financial Statistics.* Ottawa. Annual. (Catalogue no. 74–201)
> Financial statistics for non-insured pension plans only, in both the public and private sector.

Stouffer, David and Nicholas Simmons. *Report for the Treasury Board on the Financial Position of the Public Service Pension Arrangements, Inflation Adjustment Methods, Investment Strategy and Plan Management.* Toronto: William M. Mercer Ltd., 1985.
> Study of public-sector pension plans in Ontario.

Task Force on the Investment of Public Sector Pension Funds. *In Whose Interest?* Toronto: Queen's Printer for Ontario, 1987. 397 pp.
> Report of the Task Force on the investment of seven major public-sector pension funds in Ontario.

Wolfson, Michael C. "An Overview of Statistics Relating to Private Pension Plans in Canada." In *Pension Policy: An International Perspective,* John A. Turner and Lorna M. Dailey, eds. Washington, DC: U.S. Government Printing Office, 1991.
> Discussion of pension statistical agencies and list of statistical sources for Canada.

China

"Mutual Assistance Funds Expand in China." *Ageing International* (June 1989): 21–22.
>Report on voluntary, contributory, social welfare funds established in some villages in China to provide pensions, medical care, and other social services to village members.

Denmark

Beretning fra Finanstilsynet. *Livsforsikringsselskaber m.v., Bilag 2.* Copenhagen. Annual.
>Volume 2 of six-volume 1989 annual report of the Supervisory Authority of Financial Affairs contains statistics on private- and public-sector pension funds and insurance companies. In Danish.

Pensionsforsikringsanstalten A/S. *PFA-Information.* Copenhagen. Looseleaf.
>Manual covering social security and private pension practice in Denmark including financial methods, published by a major insurance company.

Finland

Central Pension Security Institute. *Report.* Annual.
>Major source of statistics on mandatory pension plans.

Hytti, H. "Vanhuss- ja tyokyvyttomyyselakkeensaajien tulot 1980." *Kansane-lakelsitoksen julkaisuja* M:42. Helsinki. 1983.
>Survey of the income sources of retirees, in Finnish. English-language summary included in Riska, 1986.

Kalimo, Esko and Pekka Siren. "Trends in the Composition and Level of Retirement Income in Finland." In *Conjugating Public and Private: The Case of Pensions*, International Social Security Association, pp. 123–37. Geneva, 1987.

Ministry of Social Affairs and Health. *Social Insurance in Finland.* Helsinki, 1986. 48 pp.

Riska, Elianne, Seppo Ruotsalainen, and Esko Kalimo. "Social Science Research on Social Security in Finland." In *Sociological Research and Social Security: Proceedings of the European Institute for Social Security*, pp. 275–87. Deventer: Kluwer, 1986. (EISS Yearbook 1984)
>Describes several Finnish studies on incomes, retirement, and other social security issues.

France

AGIRC Retraite des Cadres: Bulletin Trimestriel. Paris. Quarterly. (New title: *Le Point sur la retraite des cadres*)
>May 1987 issue includes article "Quarante années de chiffres" with 40 years of statistics for AGIRC funds (complementary pension funds for managers). Updated in various quarterly issues.

ARRCO. *Rapport d'activité.* Paris. Annual.

Financial and participant statistics for all ARRCO pension funds (complementary pension funds for non-managers).

Carbonel. *Employee Benefits Handbook for France*. Paris, 1988.
Comprehensive description of the pension and labor laws of France with related historical statistics.

Commission des Comptes de la Sécurité Sociale. *Les Comptes de la sécurité sociale: résultats, prévisions, tous régimes*. Paris, December 1987. 468 pp.
Comprehensive statistics on all social security funds, plus basic statistics on the complementary pension system.

Lynes, Tony. *Paying for Pensions: The French Experience*. London: London School of Economics and Political Science, 1985.
Description of the French pension system with some comparison with the pension system of the United Kingdom.

Germany, Federal Republic of

"Betriebliche Altersversorgung in der Bundesrepublik Deutschland," *Der Betrieb*. Dusseldorf: Handelsblatt GmbH, October 1976 and October 1978.
Commentaries on the government pension surveys of 1976 and 1978.

Deutsche Bundesbank. *Monthly Report of the Deutsche Bundesbank*. Monthly.
Assets and asset mix of pensionkassen only.

Deutsche Bundestag, 10. Wahlperiode. *Unterrichtung durch die Bundesregierung: Bericht der Bundesregierung über die Situation und Entwicklung der betrieblichen Altersversorgung.* . . . (Drucksache 10/2681), January 2, 1985.
Report of the government-sponsored pension survey conducted in 1984.

————, 8. Wahlperiode. *Unterrichtung durch die Bundesregierung: Bericht der Bundesregierung über die Erfahrungen bei der Durchführung des Gesetzes zur Verbesserung der betrieblichen Altersversorgung.* (Drucksache 8/2377), December 11, 1978.
Report of the government-sponsored pension survey conducted in 1978.

Heissmann, Prof. Dr. Ernst, ed. *Steuerrecht der betrieblichen Altersversorgung mit arbeitsrechtlicher Grundlegung*. Cologne: Verlag Dr. Otto Schmidt KG, 1985.
A compilation of German pension statistics, mainly from earlier government surveys. Includes estimates of value of book reserves.

Hewitt Associates. *Financing Pensions in West Germany*. Lincolnshire, IL.
Description of various pension financing methods in Germany including the impact on cash flow, taxation, accounting requirements, and benefit security.

Schiller, Bradley R. and Randall D. Weiss. "The Impact of Private Pensions on Firm Attachment." *Review of Economics and Statistics*, Vol. 61, pp. 369–80.

Schmahl, Dr. Winfried. "Public and Private Pensions for Various Population Groups in the Federal Republic of Germany: Past Experience and Tasks for the Future." In *Conjugating Public and Private: The Case of Pensions*, International Social Security Association, pp. 57–79. Geneva, 1987.
Includes statistical tables from various surveys.

————. "Labour Force Participation and Social Pension Systems." In *Workers Versus Pensioners: Intergenerational Justice in an Ageing World*, edited by Paul Johnson et al., pp. 137–61. Manchester: Manchester University Press, 1989.

Greece

Kremalis, Dr. Konstantinos. "Sociological Research and Social Security." In *Sociological Research and Social Security: Proceedings of the European Institute for Social Security*, pp. 289–302. Deventer: Kluwer, 1986. (EISS Yearbook 1984)
Describes several Greek studies on income, old age, and social security issues.

Ireland

Keogh, G. and B. Whelan. *National Survey of Occupational Pension Schemes*. 1985. (unpublished)
Survey of pension plans conducted for the Department of Social Welfare.
Report of the Commission on Social Welfare. Dublin: The Stationery Office, July 1986. 530 pp.
Analysis of all social security and welfare programs in the Republic of Ireland. Includes brief statistics from the *National Survey of Occupational Pension Schemes* above.

Israel

Central Bureau of Statistics. *Labour Mobility Survey*. (Special Publication No. 749)
Labor survey, in Hebrew.
Cohen, Shlomo and Nira Shamai. "The Pension System in Israel: The Present Situation and Future Prospects." In *Conjugating Public and Private: The Case of Pensions*, International Social Security Association, pp. 91–104. Geneva, 1987.
"Successful Aging: Relevance of the Israel Kibbutz." *Ageing International* (June 1989): 38–40.
Report of a conference organized by the Project for Kibbutz Studies, Center for Jewish Studies, Harvard University. Includes discussion of employment opportunities for the elderly on kibbutzim.

Japan

Clark, Robert L. *Retirement Systems in Japan*. Homewood, IL: Business One Irwin, 1991.
"Japan: Book Reserves—Data." *IBIS Briefing Service*, February 1990, p. 15.
Tax statistics which show the total for tax-deductible book reserves for paying pensions.
Hijikata, Heidi, Anna M. Driscoll, and James M. Fatheree. *The High Japanese Savings Rate: Causes and Prospects*. New York: Committee for Economic Development, 1988.
An analysis of the reasons for the high Japanese household savings rate. Authors are from the Office of Trade and Investment Analysis, International Trade Administration, U.S. Department of Commerce.

Japan Federation of Employers' Associations. *Current Labor Economy in Japan.* Tokyo, 1989. 60 pp.
>   Includes section on Japan's aging society, along with discussions of wage and employment issues. Comparative tables of labor statistics including Japan and major foreign countries.

The Life Insurance Association of Japan. *Summary of Life Insurance Business.* Tokyo. Annual. 300+ pp.
>   Comprehensive statistics on all life insurance companies in Japan including pension assets under management.

Murakami, Kiyoshi. *Retirement Benefits and Pension Plans in Japan.* Tokyo: Sophia University, Institute of Comparative Culture, 1988. 36 pp. (Business Series, No. 118)

———. "Severance and Retirement Benefits in Japan." In *Pension Policy: An International Perspective*, edited by John A. Turner and Lorna M. Dailey. Washington, DC: U.S. Government Printing Office, 1991.
>   Description of Japan's retirement, including statistics from several Japanese sources.

Pension Fund Association. *Corporate Pension Plans in Japan.* Tokyo, April 1989.
>   Description of the Japanese retirement system, including a compilation of statistics.

Shinohara, M. "The Determinants of Post-War Savings Behavior in Japan." In *The Determinants of National Saving and Wealth*, edited by Franco Modigliani and Richard Hemming. London: Macmillan, 1983.

Social Insurance Agency. *Outline of Social Insurance in Japan.* Tokyo. Annual. 135+ pp.
>   Description and statistics of Japan's social security system.

Yumiba, Yoshihiro. "Pension Policy Statistics in Japan." In *Pension Policy: An International Perspective*, edited by John A. Turner and Lorna M. Dailey. Washington, DC: U.S. Government Printing Office, 1991.
>   Paper includes historical pension statistics, description of agencies publishing pension statistics, and list of pension statistics sources.

Mexico

Hewitt Associates. *Mexico Manual of Benefits, Perquisites and Compensation Practices.* Lincolnshire, IL.
>   Description of customary benefit and compensation practices in Mexico, including labor law and social security.

Netherlands

Algemeen Burgerlijk Pensioenfonds. *Jaarverslag.* Heerlen. Annual.
>   Annual financial report of the Civil Service Pension Fund covering national and local government employees including teachers, police, and firefighters.

De Nederlandsche Bank. *Quarterly Bank Bulletin.* Dordrecht: Martinus Nijhoff Publishers. Quarterly.
>   Includes non-insured private- and public-sector pension assets and asset mix.

Keizer, Piet J. C. "Pension Policy Statistics in the Netherlands." In *Pension*

Policy: An International Perspective, edited by John A. Turner and Lorna M. Dailey. Washington, DC: U.S. Government Printing Office, 1991.

Discussion of pension statistics in the Netherlands, statistical tables, and list of sources.

Verzekeringskamer. *Financiële gegevens pensioenfondsen*. Apeldoorn. Annual.

Financial and participant statistics of non-insured pension plans, both company and industry-wide, as reported to the Insurance Chamber. In Dutch with English-language summary.

New Zealand

The Association of Superannuation Funds of New Zealand. "Superannuation Survey." *Super Benefits* (October 1989): 4.

Results of a survey of 183 pension plans.

"Government Actuary's Analysis of Superannuation Schemes—March 1989." *Super Benefits* (October 1989): 9.

Official statistics on number of plans, participants, assets and contributions to private and individual pension plans.

Ministry of Finance. *Consultative Document on Superannuation and Life Insurance.* 2 vols. Wellington: Government Printer, March 1988.

Description of taxation of life insurance and pension plans and the government's proposals for change. Includes basic statistics on private pension funds, life insurance companies, the Government Superannuation Fund, the National Provident Fund, and individual pension plans.

Norway

Central Bureau of Statistics of Norway. *Credit Market Statistics: Life and Non-Life Companies, etc.* Oslo. Annual.

Includes assets and asset mix of private- and public-sector pension funds.

Hvidsten, Vetle. "Household Saving and Debt Burden." (*Norges Bank*) *Economic Bulletin* 3 (1986): 210–15.

South Africa

Registrar of Pension Funds. *Statistics.* Irregular. (unpublished)

South African Reserve Bank. *Bulletin.* Monthly.

Assets of private and public-sector pension funds.

Sweden

Allmaenna Pensionsfonden. *Report.* Annual.

Financial data on the social security funds of Sweden.

Betzel, R. and L. Berg. "The Role of Demographic Factors as a Determinant of Savings in Sweden." In *The Determinants of National Saving and Wealth*, edited by Franco Modigliani and Richard Hemming. London: Macmillan, 1983.

Discusses the relationship between wealth and age including savings of retirees.

Palmer, Edward. *Household Saving in Sweden and its Composition: An Empirical Analysis*. Stockholm: Almqvist & Wiksell International, 1985.

———. "Public and Private Pensions and Savings in Sweden." In *Conjugating Public and Private: The Case of Pensions*, International Social Security Association, pp. 237–54. Geneva, 1987.

Pontusson, Jonas. *Public Pension Funds and the Politics of Capital Formation in Sweden*. Goteborg: Tryckt va Graphic Systems AB, 1984.

Switzerland

Gilliand, Pierre. "Recherche sociologique et sécurité sociale en suisse." In *Sociological Research and Social Security: Proceedings of the European Institute for Social Security*, pp. 193–234. Deventer: Kluwer, 1986. (EISS Yearbook 1984)
Describes numerous Swiss studies on income, old age, and social security issues.

Mattei, A. "Épargne et sécurité sociale." *Revue Suisse d'Économie Politique et de Statistique* (March 1985).
Examines the impact of social security contributions on savings in Switzerland.

Office Fédéral de la Statistique. *Institutions de prévoyance en Suisse: statistique suisse des caisses des pensions 1987*. Bern, 1990. In French and German.
First major survey of mandatory private pension funds (BVG funds) in Switzerland since they were required on January 1, 1985.

———. "Prévoyance professionelle vieillesse, survivants et invalidité," in *La Vie économique*. Bern. Monthly.
Summary of statistics of both public- and private-sector pension plans. Usually published in the April or May issue each year until 1986.

Segalman, Ralph. *The Swiss Way of Welfare*. New York: Praeger, 1986. 205 pp.
Discussion of the social security and welfare system of Switzerland. Private pensions covered briefly.

Thailand

"Thailand: Statistics on Approved Provident Funds." *IBIS Briefing Service*, October 1989.
Basic statistics on approved private pension plans.

Union of Soviet Socialist Republics

U.S. Central Intelligence Agency. *USSR: Estimates of Personal Incomes and Savings*. Springfield, VA: National Technical Information Service. [n.d.] (Central Intelligence Agency Monographs).

United Kingdom

Association of British Insurers. *Insurance Statistics 1984–1988*. London, 1989.
Booklet of insurance statistics including basic statistics on insured pension plans.

Board of Inland Revenue. *Improving the Pensions Choice: Proposed Tax Rules for the New Pensions Arrangements.* London, November 1986.
A consultative document.
———. *Inland Revenue Statistics, 1989.* London: HMSO. Annual.
Compilation of tax statistics.
Central Statistical Office. *Financial Statistics.* London: HMSO, monthly.
Includes assets and asset mix of private and public sector non-insured pension plans.
Daykin, Christopher D. "United Kingdom Pension Statistics." In *Pension Policy: An International Perspective,* edited by John A. Turner and Lorna M. Dailey. Washington, DC: U.S. Government Printing Office, 1991.
Discussion of private pension statistics, extensive tables, extracted from U.K. statistical sources, and list of sources.
Department of Employment. *Family Expenditure Survey, 1989.* London: HMSO, 1990.
Department of Health and Social Security. *Population, Pension Costs and Pensioners' Incomes.* London: HMSO, 1984.
A background paper on the provision of retirement income.
———. *Reform of Social Security.* London: HMSO, 1985. 3 vols. (Cmnd 9517–9519)
Green Paper on social security and private pensions issues.
———. *Reform of Social Security: Programme for Action.* London: HMSO, 1985.
White Paper on Goverment's plans for changes to the social security and private pension systems.
———. *Reforming Social Security.* London, November 1986–February 1987. 4 vols.
Four sets of draft regulations concerning changes to personal and occupational pensions to be made under the *Social Security Act 1986.*
Department of Social Security. *Protecting Pensions: Safeguarding Benefits in a Changing Environment: A Report by the Occupational Pensions Board in Accordance with Section 66 of the Social Security Act 1973.* London: HMSO, February 1989. 101 pp.
Report covering pension issues upon takeover of a company, disclosure of information, trusteeship, etc. Basis of government's proposals for change in 1990.
Department of Trade and Industry, Business Statistics Office. *Business Monitor MQ5: Insurance Companies' and Pension Funds' Investment.* London: HMSO. Quarterly.
More detailed assets and asset mix of private- and public-sector non-insured pension plans than published in *Financial Statistics.*
Government Actuary. *Occupational Pension Schemes, 1987: Eighth Survey by the Government Actuary.* London: HMSO, 1991.
Analysis of public- and private-sector, insured and non-insured pension plans conducted by the Government Actuary about every four years.
National Association of Pension Funds. *Annual Survey of Occupational Pension Schemes.* London. Annual.
Detailed survey of the characteristics of 800+ U.K. private- and public-sector pension plans.
Office of Population Censuses and Surveys. *Labour Force Survey, 1987.* London: HMSO, 1989 (Series LFS no. 7)
———. Social Survey Division. *General Household Survey, 1987.* London: HMSO, 1989 (Series GHS no. 17)

Phylaktis, K. *Finance: Financial Data of Banks and Other Institutions*; and Geraldine Kaye. *Life Assurance and Pension Funds*. Published for the Royal Statistical Society and Economic and Social Research Council. New York: Pergamon Press, 1987. 495 pp. (Vol. XXI, Reviews of United Kingdom Statistical Sources)

> Major source of information on pensions, life insurance, and banking statistics in the United Kingdom.

United States

Turner, John A. and Daniel J. Beller, eds. *Trends in Pensions*. Washington, DC: U.S. Government Printing Office, 1989. 489 pp.

> Comprehensive historical statistics on U.S. private pension plans, plus some data on Social Security, public-sector plans, Individual Retirement Accounts, and individual annuities. Includes commentary.

U.S. Congress. Senate. Special Committee on Aging. *Aging America: Trends and Projections (Annotated)*. Washington, DC: U.S. Government Printing Office, February 1990. 152 pp. (An Information Paper to the Special Committee on Aging)

> Compilation of pension, Social Security, retirement income, and health statistics for the U.S. with commentary.

International

Ageing International. Washington, DC: International Federation of Ageing. 2 issues per year.

> Worldwide coverage of retirement, health, demographics, social services and income of the eldery. Good coverage of Third World countries.

Barro, Robert J. and Glenn M MacDonald. "Social Security and Consumer Spending in International Cross-Section." *Journal of Public Economics* II (June 1979): 275–89.

Benefits & Compensation International. London: Pension Publications Ltd. Monthly.

> Comprehensive articles on private pension practice, social security, and other investment and human resources issues in many countries. For benefits professionals.

Boylan, Peter, compiler and editor. *Directory of International Benefits*. 2nd ed. London: AP Information Services Ltd, 1990. 536 pp.

> Directory information for companies, associations and government agencies in the international benefits field in thirty-six countries. Basic background information (demographic and economic statistics, structure of pension and social security systems, legal holidays and vacation, insurance regulations, stock market and taxation) for each country. Glossary of international benefit terms.

Cartwright, William S. "Saving, Social Security, and Private Pensions." *International Social Security Review* 37, 2 (1984): 123–38.

Centre for Policy on Aging. *World Directory of Old Age*. London, 1989.

> Directory of organizations concerned with aging in 158 countries. Includes some demographic statistics and national profiles on pensions and health care for many countries.

Dailey, Lorna M. "Private Pension Statistics in Nine Countries." Chapter 13 in *Trends in Pensions*, edited by John A. Turner and Daniel J. Beller. Washington, DC: U.S. Government Printing Office, 1989.

> Sixteen tables of comparative pension statistics covering nine countries (Australia, Canada, France, Germany, Japan, Netherlands, Switzerland, United Kingdom, United States) with extensive explanation of the data sources.

Dailey, Lorna M. and John A. Turner. "Issues in the Development of Internationally Comparable Pension Statistics." *Benefits & Compensation International* (August 1989): 16–23.

> Discussion of issues in developing comparable pensions statistics including specific examples from various countries, plus sources of U.S. pension data.

––––––. "Private Pensions in Nine Countries: 1970–1988." Chapter 2 in *Pension Policy: An International Perspective*, edited by John A. Turner and Lorna M. Dailey. Washington, DC: U.S. Government Printing Office, 1991.

> Comparative pension statistics revised and updated from those first published in *Trends in Pensions*.

––––––. "U.S. Pensions in World Perspective." Chapter 2 in *Trends in Pensions*, edited by John A. Turner and Daniel J. Beller, eds. Washington, DC: U.S. Government Printing Office, 1989.

> Overview of how the United States pension system compares to that of other countries, based on data collected in the DOL international study.

Eekelaar, John and David Pearl. *An Ageing World: Dilemmas and Challenges for Law and Social Policy.* Oxford/New York: Oxford University Press, 1989. 900 pp.

Employment Conditions Abroad. *A Survey of Social Security Contributions and Demographic Change in OECD Countries.* London, 1989.

> Covers 23 industrialized countries.

Feldstein, Martin S. "International Differences in Social Security and Saving." *Journal of Public Economics* 14 (October 1980).

––––––. "Social Security and Private Savings: International Evidence on an Extended Life Cycle Model." In *The Economics of Public Services*, edited by Martin Feldstein and Robert Inman. New York: MacMillan, 1977.

Foster, Howard, ed. *Employee Benefits in Europe.* London: Longman Group, 1989. 600 pp.

> Description of the social security and private pension systems in seventeen European countries and the United States, plus financing pensions, comparative costs, expatriate benefits, reciprocal agreements.

Fuery, Michael, Peter Huta, Karen Gauntlett, and Annabelle Murrary. *Occupational Superannuation Arrangements in Overseas Countries.* Woden, ACT: Department of Social Security, October 1988. (Social Security Review, Background/Discussion Paper No. 25)

Gordon, Margaret. *Social Security Policies in Industrial Countries: A Comparative Analysis.* New York: Cambridge University Press, 1988. 377 pp.

> Analysis of the historical development of the social security systems of all major countries; includes chapter on employer-provided pensions. Arranged by topic with examples from various countries. Extensive bibliography.

Hannah, Leslie. *Pension Asset Management: An International Perspective.* Homewood, IL: R.D. Irwin, 1988. (Published for the Pension Research Council)

Heller, Peter S., Richard Hemming, Peter W. Kohnert, et al. *Aging and Social*

Expenditure in the Major Industrial Countries, 1980–2025. (Washington, DC: International Monetary Fund, September 1986. (Occasional Paper no. 47) Includes a statistical appendix.

Hewitt Associates. *International SpecBook.* Lincolnshire, IL. Annual.
Benefit plan specifications of ten representative companies in fifteen countries, plus social security and other mandatory benefits.

———. *Summaries of Statutory Compensation and Benefits.* Lincolnshire, IL.
Separate reports on the social security contributions and benefits, labor laws, mandatory benefits and taxation of benefits for over 80 countries. Updated regularly.

Holzmann, Robert. "On the Relationship Between Retirement and Labor Market Policy." In *Structural Problems of Social Security Today and Tomorrow: Proceedings of the European Institute of Social Security*, pp. 133–74. Leuven: Acco, 1988. (EISS Yearbook 1987)
Has a particular emphasis on early retirement programs including summaries of the early retirement programs of major countries.

IBIS Briefing Service. Chicago: Charles D. Spencer and Associates, Inc. Monthly.
Brief descriptions of new pensions and social security legislation, benefits and compensation surveys, benefit and contribution rates for social security, taxation of benefits, and related areas. Arranged by country. For benefits professionals.

IBIS Review. Chicago: Charles D. Spencer and Associates, Inc. Monthly.
Brief articles on international benefits issues.

Insurance Research Letter. Camden, ME: International Research Services. Monthly. (Four regional editions)
Translations and summaries of insurance statistics for all countries of the world. Pensions statistics included when separately identified in insurance data.

International Benefits Information Service. *Reference Manuals and Profiles.* Chicago: Charles D. Spencer. Looseleaf.
Ten Reference Manuals describing the social security and private pension systems in Australia, Belgium, Canada, France, Japan, Mexico, Netherlands, Switzerland, United Kingdom, United States. Covers contribution and benefit rates, private pension practice including the financing of plans. Intended for benefits professionals. Also briefer profiles on Brazil, Denmark, Finland, Ireland, Italy, Luxembourg, New Zealand, Norway, Portugal, Spain, Sweden, and Switzerland with similar information.

International Labour Office. *The Cost of Social Security.* Twelfth International Inquiry, 1981–1983. Geneva, 1988. 110 pp.
Comparative tables covering receipts and expenditures for social security and mandatory benefits systems for over 60 countries of the world.

———. *Economically Active Population 1950–2025.* Geneva, 1986. 6 vols.
For comparative population and labor force statistics, by country, sex, and age bracket.

———. *From Pyramid to Pillar: Population Change and Social Security in Europe.* Geneva, 1989. 187 pp.
Discussion of the effects of aging populations on the social security systems in Europe.

International Social Security Association. *Conjugating Public and Private: The Case of Pensions.* Geneva, 1987. 261 pp. (Studies and Research No. 24)
Papers from an expert group meeting on the relationships between public and private pension plans held in Baltimore from May 6–8, 1986. In-

cludes papers on Austria, Canada, Finland, Germany, Israel, the Netherlands, Sweden, the United Kingdom, and the United States.

————. *Occupational Pension Schemes.* Geneva, 1984.

International Social Security Review. Geneva: International Social Security Association. Quarterly.

Articles and news items on the social security systems of all countries.

InterSec Research Corp. *Global Pension Asset Study.* London. 11 vols.

Major analysis of pension funds in 11 countries, covering asset statistics, asset mix, investment regulations, asset management, and foreign investments. Includes ranked lists of money managers with assets under management, a directory of pension funds with addresses and assets, translations of pertinent pensions legislation. Available to InterSec clients only.

Johnson, P., C. Conrad, and D. Thompson, eds. *Workers Versus Pensioners: Intergenerational Justice in an Aging World.* Manchester: Manchester University Press, 1989.

Kinsella, Kevin. *Aging in the Third World.* Washington, DC: U.S. Government Printing Office, 1988. (Published for the U.S. Bureau of the Census; International Population Series P–95, No. 79)

Includes statistics on life expectancy, health, and social services.

Kohler, Peter A. and Hans F. Zacher. *The Evolution of Social Insurance, 1881–1981: Studies of Germany, France, Great Britain, Austria, and Switzerland.* New York: St. Martin's Press, 1982.

Kopits, George and Padma Gotur. *The Influence of Social Security on Household Savings: A Cross-Country Investigation.* Washington, DC: International Monetary Fund, 1980. (Staff Paper No. 27)

Kosela, Erkki and Matti Viren. "Social Security and Household Saving in an International Cross-Section." *American Economic Review* (March 1983): 212–17.

Mercer Limited, William M. *International Benefit Guidelines.* Dallas/London. Annual.

Highlights of social security and private benefit practice in 60 countries.

Mercer International, William M. *Country Reference Guides.* Updated regularly.

Separate reports on about 25 countries including an overview, customary private pension practice, mandatory benefits, social security, and taxation of benefits.

Modigliani, Franco and Richard Hemming, eds. *The Determinants of National Saving and Wealth.* Proceedings of a conference held by the International Economic Association in Bergamo, Italy. London: St. Martin's, 1983.

Includes papers on the savings behavior of several countries.

Mok, Leo, ed. *International Handbook on Pension Law and Similar Employee Benefits.* London: Graham and Trotman, 1989. 705 pp.

Replies to questionnaires on the legal aspects of private pension systems in seventeen countries (Australia, Belgium, Colombia, Czechoslovakia, Denmark, Finland, Federal Republic of Germany, Ireland, Israel, Netherlands, New Zealand, Poland, Portugal, Sweden, Switzerland, United Kingdom, and United States). Brief social security information. Also articles on a variety of countries covering labor law, pension regulations, surplus assets, predator proofing, sale of companies, expatriate benefits, pensions upon divorce, sex discrimination in benefits, and stock option plans.

Munnell, Alicia H. "The Impact of Public and Private Schemes on Saving and Capital Formation." In *Conjugating Public and Private: The Case of Pensions,*

International Social Security Association, pp. 215–36. Geneva, 1987.
Mainly discusses the U.S., but includes a brief discussion of existing international studies on the effect of social security systems on savings.

––––––. "Public Pension Surpluses and National Saving: Foreign Experience." *New England Economic Review* (March/April 1989): 16–38.
Canada, Japan, Sweden, and the United States are analyzed.

Murdock, Burt and Lorna Dailey. "Termination Indemnities." *Benefits & Compensation International* (June and July 1983) (2-part article).
Terms and conditions for payment of termination indemnities in 23 Latin American, Asian and European countries.

Organisation for Economic Co-operation and Development. *Ageing Populations: The Social Policy Implications.* Paris, 1988. 90 pp. (Demographic Change and Public Policy)
Includes statistical tables on the elderly population and social expenditures of industrialized countries.

––––––. *Labour Force Statistics.* Paris, Annual. 500+ pp.
Comparative labor force statistics on all industrialized countries for 20-year period. 1968–88 data published in July 1990.

––––––. *OECD Economic Surveys.* Paris. Annual.
Overview of economic, financial, and employment situation. Statistical tables; includes household savings rate. Separate booklets on each of the 24 OECD countries.

––––––. *Reforming Public Pensions.* Paris, 1988. 154 pp.
An analysis of the social security and mandatory pension systems of industrialized countries.

––––––. *Social Expenditure 1960–1990.* Paris, 1985.

Pampel, F. C. and J. A. Weiss. "Economic Development, Pension Policies, and the Labour Force Participation of Aged Males; a Cross-national, Longitudinal Approach," *American Journal of Sociology* 89 (1983): 350–72.
International study on the impact of supply and demand factors on retirement behaviors.

The Review of Income and Wealth. New Haven, CT: International Association for Research in Income and Wealth. Quarterly.

Rosa, Jean-Jacques et al. eds. *World Crisis in Social Security.* San Francisco: Institute for Contemporary Studies, 1982.
Includes papers on several countries.

Schmahl, Winfried, ed. *Redefining the Process of Retirement: An International Perspective.* Berlin: Springer, 1989.

Torrey, Barbara Boyle, Kevin G. Kinsella, and Cynthia M. Taueber. *An Aging World.* Washington, DC: U.S. Government Printing Office, 1987. (Published for the U.S. Bureau of the Census)
Extensive comparative statistics on demographics, retirement income, etc. covering all industrialized countries.

Tout, Ken. *Ageing in Developing Countries.* Oxford/New York: Oxford University Press, 1989. 334 pp.

Turner, John A. and Lorna M. Dailey, eds. *Pension Policy: An International Perspective.* Washington, DC: U.S. Government Printing Office, 1991.
Papers from the Department of Labor International Conference on Private Pension Policy and Statistical Analysis held February 21–23, 1990, in Washington, DC. Authors from Canada, Japan, the Netherlands, the United Kingdom, and the United States discuss pension portability, indexation, financing, and sources of pension and labor statistics.

Turvey, Ralph et al. *Consumer Price Indices: An ILO Manual.* Geneva, 1989. 196 pp.
> Comprehensive manual covering the construction of Consumer Price Indices. Explains different national practices and gives examples from various countries.

U.S. Department of Health and Human Services. Social Security Administration. *Social Security Programs Throughout the World.* Washington, DC: U.S. Government Printing Office. Biennial. 285 pp.
> Brief tables on the social security systems of 141 countries and territories. Contributions, benefits, laws, administrative organizations.

Von Furstenberg, George M., ed. *Social Security Versus Private Savings.* Cambridge, MA: Ballinger Press, 1979.
> Includes papers on Canada, France, Germany, Sweden, the United Kingdom, and the United States.

Walters, Cathy. *Policies Affecting the Labour Participation of Older Workers Overseas.* Woden, ACT: Department of Social Security, September 1988. (Social Security Review, Background/Discussion Papers No. 24)

Wolff, E. N., ed., *International Comparisons of the Distribution of Household Wealth.* Fairlawn, NJ: Oxford University Press, July 1987.

The Wyatt Company/ECS. *Benefits Report: Europe/USA.* Brussels/Fort Lee, NJ. Annual.
> Description of the social security and private pension systems in 17 European countries plus the United States, including financing and taxation of benefits.

Databases

Bedford Index. Falls Church, VA: Bedford Research Consultants.
> Bibliographic references with abstracts on foreign pension and social security systems, compensation, labor laws, health care, and taxation of benefits. Covers all countries of the world with an emphasis on countries with private pension systems. Designed for international benefits professionals. Predominantly English-language sources. Available to clients of Bedford Research Consultants.

LaborDoc. Geneva, Switzerland: International Labour Office.
> Bibliographic references to sources of foreign labor law, industrial relations, social security, and pensions. Somewhat oriented to publications of international organizations, legislation, and government documents. Multilingual. Available online through Orbit Search Service, a Division of Maxwell Online, Inc.

Luxembourg Income Study (LIS) Database. Walferdange, Luxembourg.
> The LIS database is located at the Center for Population, Poverty and Policy Studies in Walferdange, Luxembourg. It includes income microdata sets prepared to a common plan, based on common definitions of income sources and family and household characteristics. Countries included are Australia, Canada, France, Federal Republic of Germany, Israel, Netherlands, Norway, Sweden, Switzerland, United Kingdom, and United States. Luxembourg has committed to participate. Income of retirees and pension benefits information available if included in original country data. Available to researchers worldwide through EARN-BITNET computer network. Further information in "LIS User Guide."

Sample diskettes available. U.S. contact is Dr. Timothy Smeeding, Vanderbilt University, Nashville, Tennessee.

NIA/CIR International Data Base on Aging. Washington, DC.

The National Institute of Aging (NIA) and the U.S. Bureau of the Census, Center for International Research (CIR) have developed this database containing detailed demographic and socioeconomic information on thirty-one countries. National censuses, surveys, and population projections are included from 1950 on, divided into five-year age cohorts. Also includes marital and educational status, labor force participation, occupations, mortality rates, and related information. Further information from the Center for International Research, U.S. Bureau of the Census.

Comments by Robert L. Clark

In many developed countries, private, employer-provided pensions have evolved into important financial and labor market institutions. As an important component of total employee compensation, pensions have been shown to influence hiring, turnover, and retirement decisions. The build-up of cash reserves may increase national savings, and their preferential tax status introduces an additional element of interest by national policymakers.

During the last decade, there has been a rapid growth of economic and financial studies examining various aspects of employer pensions. These research projects have been conducted using the various sources of available data. Appropriate data have been very difficult to obtain either because the data have not been collected, are available only with a long time lag, or have not been released by the government. Further progress on understanding the economic effects of pensions depends on improving the data available for analysis.

To date, less attention seems to have been paid to determining the economic consequences of employer pensions in other countries. This may be attributed to greater data problems arising in these countries. Dailey and Turner provide a useful review of data sources in Australia, Canada, France, Japan, the Netherlands, Switzerland, the United Kingdom, and West Germany. In addition, they compare known pension statistics for these countries.

I strongly endorse their basic premise that international comparisons of private pensions is an important method of understanding the economic effects of pensions and is very useful for considering modifications in existing public policies. By examining pension policies in other countries, we can observe how workers and retirees in these countries respond to different forms of pension regulations and tax policies.

Analysts seeking to examine pensions across a series of countries face many hurdles. Dailey and Turner point out some of these problems in their paper. I want to emphasize some of their comments, disagree with their treatment of several issues, and extend the discussion in a few areas.

1. The objective of any study of private pensions must be clearly defined. For example, if one is concerned with retirement income, high pension coverage rates and high benefits do not necessarily imply that one country has higher average retirement income than another. In this case, the role of social security and private savings must be considered along with pension benefits. The development of employer pensions depends on the magnitude of the national social security system. Relatively high replacement ratios from social security sharply limit the role of private pensions.

2. Are public pension plans included in the analysis? In many countries, one or more social security systems cover private workers plus a separate program for government workers. In general, the social security system for private workers will provide a lower replacement ratio than the public plan. As a result, private workers may be covered by an employer pension plan in addition to social security. By contrast, the plan for government employees may be sufficiently generous that there is no need for further pension coverage. The relevant question is whether the plan for government workers is to be treated as an employer pension in the study of pensions. Including these plans will raise coverage rates, since virtually all government employees will be covered, and increase the average benefit, since the pension for government employees will tend to be more generous than that for private employees. Dailey and Turner note that some countries include government plans in their pension statistics while others do not.

3. What is a pension? In cross-national comparisons, this is not such an easy question to answer (even in the U.S. the answer may not be so obvious). An example is Japan where the traditional method of retirement income payments are lump-sum severance payments. Workers accumulate credits with each year of work and are paid a benefit when they leave the firm either at retirement or prior to retirement. Including these plans as pensions, 90 percent of the firms with thirty or more workers in Japan offer some type of pension. Dailey and Turner cannot seem to decide if they want to include the lump-sum plans as a pension. They are excluded from the coverage statistics but are frequently described in other sections of the paper.

4. Special care must be given to international comparisons of time series financial data. Dailey and Turner present such a series on pension assets. They convert local currency to U.S. dollars and then adjust for consumer prices. While these adjustments are useful for comparing values across countries at a point in time, using them as a measure

of change within a country can produce misleading conclusions. For example, Table 3 indicates that pension assets in Japan increased from $69.9 billion in 1985 to $115.9 billion in 1986. Much of this increase is due to the sharp decline of the dollar as opposed to an actual increase in the yen value of reserves.

5. There are major barriers of language or jargon as well as translation problems that arise in understanding pensions. Analysts must be careful that words have the same meaning to the writer and the reader. Different translations of the same texts may yield alternative English words and hence give the reader a different interpretation of what is meant.

6. When comparing the generosity of benefits across countries, the research must know whether the benefit is a life annuity or a fixed-term annuity. In Japan, many pension benefits are paid only for a fixed period of time, typically ten or fifteen years. A related issue is whether the benefits are a joint and survivor benefit, or cease at the death of the worker.

7. The treatment of book reserves is an important concept for evaluating pension assets. Book reserves are widely used in West Germany and in Japan for the lump-sum severance payments. Should these claims be treated as assets? What is their legal standing?

8. I am unsure why the authors want to concentrate on the world-wide pension universe. Why is it important to know that 44 percent of pension participants are in the United States? The authors spend considerable time on this and other such statistics in this paper and in their earlier work.

An international data base on pension statistics would be very useful for policy and economic analysis. However, my comments indicate that considerable care must be given to the management of these data in order to make them consistent across countries. Dailey and Turner state that "Rather than focusing on the complexities of the different pension institutions, this analysis focuses on the outcome of the institutions as described in their statistics." My primary concern is that, without considerable knowledge of the national pension systems, an examination of the statistics may be meaningless and lead to inappropriate policy conclusions.

9. The authors begin their chapter with the assertion that "comparative statistics for social security have been available for decades." It is true that certain social security aggregates are regularly published along with general benefit and coverage rules. However, these data are insufficient for policy analysis on many important issues including determination of average benefits and often coverage itself. It would

be very useful if any effort to collect and maintain an international data base on employer pensions would be linked to information on the national social security programs.

In summary, I strongly endorse the study of international pension statistics and comparative analysis of pension policies. By examining pension coverage and policies in other countries, we can learn much about possible effects of proposed policy initiatives in the United States. By encouraging the collection and maintenance of an international data base on pension statistics, the Pension Research Council plays an important role in assisting future comparative studies of employer pensions.

Appendix: Sources of Data on Pensions

This report describes sources of data on pensions, focusing primarily on information compiled by government agencies. One private data collector is included, the Employee Benefit Research Institute (EBRI), because it compiles data that complement those of the government agencies. Because the focus is on private pensions, sources of data on publicly provided old-age, survivors, and disability insurance—that is, Social Security benefits—are excluded. Limited information is included on pension systems for federal government civilian and military employees and state and local government employees.

The information is arranged by the agency with primary responsibility for the data series. In addition to the data source, the following categories of information are given (if applicable) for each entry: data items, coverage, frequency, historical data, references (including publications in which the data series appear), and a contact person. Notes providing background information are included where appropriate.

List of Sources

Bureau of Labor Statistics
    Employment Cost Index—Rates of Change
    Employment Cost Index—Levels
    Employee Benefits Survey
Pension and Welfare Benefits Administration
    Form 5500 Series

This report is based on information supplied by various government agencies and EBRI. It was prepared by Eugene P. Seskin, Bureau of Economic Analysis, U.S. Department of Commerce, for the 1990 Spring Symposium, "Pensions and the U.S. Economy: The Need for Good Data," March 22–23, 1990, Philadelphia.

Federal Reserve Board
  Flow of Funds Accounts
  Survey of Consumer Finances
Employee Benefit Research Institute
  EBRI Quarterly Pension Investment Report
Pension Benefit Guaranty Corporation
  Premium Payment System
  Case Administration System
  Benefit Payment System
Office of Personnel Management
  Civil Service Retirement and Disability Fund
Internal Revenue Service
  Employee Plans Master File
Railroad Retirement Board
  Railroad Retirement System
Bureau of the Census
  Current Population Survey
  Pension Supplements to the CPS
  Survey of Income and Program Participation
  Annual Survey of Public Employee Retirement Systems
  Quarterly Survey of Public Employee Retirement Systems
Social Security Administration
  New Beneficiary Survey
  Private Social Welfare Expenditures
  Public Employee Retirement
  Income of the Population 55 or Older
Department of Defense
  Military Retirement System

Bureau of Labor Statistics (BLS), U.S. Department of Labor

Source: Employment Cost Index (ECI)—Rates of Change
Note: The ECI measures the rate of change in employee compensation, which includes wages, salaries, and employers' cost for employee benefits. The ECI is designed as a Laspeyres, fixed-weight index at the industry and occupational level, thus eliminating the effects of employment shifts among industries and occupations. The index is computed from data on compensation by occupation collected from a sample of establishments and occupations weighted to represent the universe of establishments and occupations in the economy. In 1987, the ECI was expanded making it possible to produce estimates of compensation cost levels (see below). These cost levels are calculated by applying current, rather than fixed, employment weights to wage and salary and benefit cost data collected from the establishments.
Data items: *Changes* in employer costs for *aggregate* employee benefits, including paid leave, supplemental pay, insurance benefits, retirement and savings

benefits, legally required benefits, unemployment insurance, workers' compensation, and other benefits; pension and retirement benefits are not identified separately.

Coverage: All employees in private. industry (except farm and household workers and the self-employed) and in state and local governments.

Frequency: Quarterly. (Payroll reference periods in March, June, September, and December, published in the month following the reference month.)

Historical data: Information on total compensation beginning with 1979 is available.

References: *BLS Handbook of Methods*, Bulletin 2285, U.S. Department of Labor, BLS, 1988; Nathan, Felicia. "Analyzing Employers' Costs for Wages, Salaries, and Benefits," *Monthly Labor Review*, U.S. Department of Labor, BLS, October 1987; Wood, G. Donald. "A New Measure of the Cost of Compensation Components," *Survey of Current Business*, U.S. Department of Commerce, Bureau of Economic Analysis, November 1988; and *Employment Cost Indexes and Levels, 1975–89*, Bulletin 2339, U.S. Department of Labor, BLS, October 1989.

Contact person: Albert Schwenk, Division of Employment Cost Trends, BLS, U.S. Department of Labor, Washington, DC 20212; (202) 523–1220.

* * *

Source: Employment Cost Index (ECI)—Levels

Data items: *Levels* of employer costs for employee compensation per hour measured as a rate at a point in time. Provides a detailed breakdown of benefits including pension and retirement benefits and savings and thrift plans.

Coverage: All employees in private industry. Coverage of employees of state and local governments to begin in 1991. The 1987 estimates were based on data collected for 16,000 jobs from about 3,200 establishments in the private nonfarm sector.

Frequency: Annually. (March reference date, published in mid-summer.)

Historical data: Information beginning with 1987 is available.

References: *BLS Handbook of Methods*, Bulletin 2285, U.S. Department of Labor, BLS, 1988; Nathan, Felicia. "Analyzing Employers' Costs for Wages, Salaries, and Benefits," *Monthly Labor Review*, U.S. Department of Labor, BLS, October 1987; Wood, G. Donald. "A New Measure of the Cost of Compensation Components," *Survey of Current Business*, U.S. Department of Commerce, Bureau of Economic Analysis, November 1988; and *Employment Cost Indexes and Levels, 1975–89*, Bulletin 2339, U.S. Department of Labor, BLS, October 1989.

Contact person: Albert Schwenk, Division of Employment Cost Trends, BLS, U.S. Department of Labor, Washington, DC 20212; (202) 523–1220.

* * *

Source: Employee Benefits Survey (EBS)

Note: The EBS provides data on employee work schedules and develops information on the incidence and detailed characteristics of employee benefits, including lunch and rest periods, holidays, vacations, and personal, funeral, jury-duty, military, parental, and sick leave; sickness and accident, long-term disability, and life insurance; health care; and private retirement/capital accumulation plans. The coverage of the survey has changed over time (see below).

Data items: Percent of employees covered in benefit plans paid for, at least in part, by the employer—reported separately for defined benefit pension plans and defined contribution plans. Tabulations show percent of workers covered by various provisions of the plans.

Coverage: 1979—Test survey.

1980 to 1986—Full-scale survey of medium and large private sector establishments with at least 50, 100, or 250 employees (depending on the industry) for most industries.

1987—State and local governments with 50 or more employees in the forty-eight contiguous states.

1988—Private-sector survey covering full-time employees in medium and large establishments (those with 100 or more employees) in all nonfarm industries.

1990—New multi-year project combining the EBS and the ECI. Will expand EBS coverage to that of the ECI, as well as bring together information on the details of benefit plans with their cost to employers. Medium and large private establishments will be surveyed in odd years, and small establishments (from 1 to 99 employees) and governments will be surveyed in even years.

Frequency: Annually (see **Coverage**). News releases in the spring following the survey year and in an annual BLS Bulletin. More detailed information on the survey's data base is available on computer tapes.

Historical data: See **Coverage.**

References: *BLS Handbook of Methods*, Bulletin 2285, U.S. Department of Labor, BLS, 1988; *Employee Benefits in State and Local Governments, 1987*, Bulletin 2309, U.S. Department of Labor, BLS, May 1988; *Employee Benefits in Medium and Large Firms, 1988*, Bulletin 2336, U.S. Department of Labor, BLS, August 1989; and Meisenheimer II, Joseph R., and Wiatrowski, William J. "Flexible Benefit Plans: Employees Who Have a Choice," *Monthly Labor Review*, U.S. Department of Labor, BLS, December 1989.

Contact person: William Wiatrowski, Division of Occupational Pay and Employee Benefit Levels, BLS, U.S. Department of Labor, Washington, DC 20212; (202) 523–9444.

Pension and Welfare Benefits Administration (PWBA), U.S. Department of Labor

Note. The PWBA and the Internal Revenue Service (IRS) share responsibility for administering the Employee Retirement Income Security Act of 1974 (ERISA). IRS is responsible for the receipt and validation of Form 5500 series return data. The return information is subsequently extracted from the Employee Plans Master File (EPMF) and sent to PWBA on a monthly basis. (See also **Internal Revenue Service.**)

*   *   *

Source: Form 5500 Series Annual Return/Report of Employee Benefit Plan (With 100 or more participants), Schedule A Insurance Information, Sched-

ule B Actuarial Information, Schedule C Service Provider and Trustee
Information; Form 5500-C Return/Report of Employee Benefit Plan (With
fewer than 100 participants), filed at least once every three years; Form
5500-R Registration Statement of Employee Benefit Plan (With fewer than
100 participants), filed the other two years; and Form 5500 EZ Annual
Return of One-Participant (Owners and Their Spouses) Pension Benefit
Plan.

Data items: Characteristics of private employee pension benefit plans, including information on participants, as well as financial and actuarial data. (See
also **Frequency.**)

Coverage: Private employee pension benefit plans. (See **Source.**)

Frequency: Annual tabulations produced by the Department of Labor, but not
published on a regular basis. Minimum three-year lag before data for an
individual year are available. Examples of tabulations (based on edited
sample of Form 5500 records, weighted to represent universe); number of
private pension plans by type; number of participants in private pension
plans by type; amount of assets in private pension plans by type; number of
private pension plans by type and asset size; income, expenses, and changes
in net assets of private pension plans; and market value of assets and
liabilities of private pension plans.

Historical data: Information beginning with 1975 is available.

References: Turner, John A., and Daniel J. Beller, editors. *Trends in Pensions*,
U.S. Department of Labor, PWBA, 1989. Washington, DC: U.S. Government Printing Office.

Contact person: Daniel Beller, Office of Research and Economic Analysis,
PWBA, U.S. Department of Labor, Washington, DC 20210; (202) 523–
9505.

Federal Reserve Board (FRB)

Source: Flow of Funds Accounts

Data items: Financial assets for private pension funds (includes Federal Employees' Retirement Thrift Savings Fund) and state and local government
pension funds, including year-end outstanding assets, quarterly unadjusted
flows, and quarterly seasonally adjusted flows.

Coverage: Sample data for *private pension funds* provided by Trust Universe
Comparison Service compiled by Wilshire Associates, weighted to represent
the universe based on benchmarks from tabulations of Forms 5500 and
5500-C (see **Pension and Welfare Benefits Administration**). Data for *state
and local government pension funds* from the Bureau of Census (Governments
Division) survey of 100 largest state and local government retirement funds,
which account for approximately 85 percent of the total assets of such funds
(see **Bureau of the Census**).

Frequency: Outstanding assets data available annually; unadjusted and seasonally adjusted flows available quarterly. Preliminary estimates published
in FRB Z.1 release of the FFA, about two months after the end of the
quarter. Major revisions coincide with autumn publication of annual outstanding assets in *Flow of Funds Accounts: Financial Assets and Liabilities*. (Quarterly outstanding assets available on request.)

Historical data: Annual data begin with 1946; quarterly data begin with 1952.
(Data before 1982 were compiled mainly from the Securities and Exchange
Commission and the Department of Labor.)

Contact person: Albert Teplin, Flow of Funds Section, Division of Research and Statistics, Federal Reserve System, Washington, DC 20551; (202) 452–3482.

*   *   *

Source: Survey of Consumer Finances
Data items: Survey participants are asked about structure of their pension plans and perceptions of their rights.
Coverage: In 1983, interviews of 4,103 households were conducted. Employers were contacted to provide technical information about pension plans, including Form 5500. Data on 1,012 plans were obtained; pension providers were not identified by name. A 1989 Survey of Consumer Finances was also conducted; the corresponding survey of pension providers awaits funding.
Frequency: Conducted on a three-year cycle. However, the 1986 survey consisted of only a telephone followup to the 1983 households; only minimal data on pensions were collected.
Historical data: Only data for 1983 are currently available.
Contact person: Arthur Kennickell, Monetary and Financial Studies Section, Division of Research and Statistics, Federal Reserve System, Washington, DC 20551; (202) 452–2247.

Employee Benefit Research Institute (EBRI)

Source: *EBRI Quarterly Pension Investment Report (QPIR)*
Data items: Assets (levels and net flows) in the pension system and performance of pension investments; provides greater detail than the figures published by the Federal Reserve Board in the Flow of Funds Accounts (FFA). (See also **Federal Reserve Board.**) Part I of the *QPIR* presents estimates of asset allocation, net contributions, and earnings for private trustee pension plans. Estimates in Part I come from the combined efforts of EBRI, the Federal Reserve Board's FOF, Wilshire Associates, and SEI and are based on data from the Department of Labor and the Trust Universe Comparison Service. Part II of the *QPIR* presents estimates of financial assets for private trusteed and insured pension plans, and for state and local government pension plans. (Data come from the FOF and from the American Council of Life Insurance.)
Coverage: Private trusteed, private insured, and state and local government pension plans.
Frequency: Quarterly. Published three months following the reference quarter.
Historical data: Part I of the report shows asset levels for the most recent four quarters and end-of-year levels from 1982 through the most recent year end. The flows in this section are also shown for the most recent four quarters; annual data are shown from the year 1983 through the most recent complete year. Part II shows annual estimates for selected years beginning in 1950 through the most recent year end.
References: *EBRI Quarterly Pension Investment Report*, Third Quarter 1989, EBRI, December 1989.

Contact person: Jennifer Davis, EBRI, 2121 K Street, NW, Suite 600, Washington, DC 20037–2121; (202) 659–0670.

Pension Benefit Guaranty Corporation (PBGC)

Note. Pursuant to Title IV of the Employee Retirement Income Security Act of 1974 (ERISA), the PBGC, a U.S. government agency, administers two insurance programs for private pensions. One program is for single-employer defined benefit plans, and the other is for collectively bargained multiemployer plans. To facilitate administration of these programs, the PBGC collects and maintains data on covered plans, participants, and sponsors. These data are maintained in one of the following three automated systems.

* * *

Source: Premium Payment System (PPS)
Data items: Information from PBGC Form 1 Annual Premium Payment on plan type, participant count, and premium paid to the PBGC. Supplement Schedule A Single-Employer Plan, Variable Rate Portion of the Premium, was added in 1988 when a variable rate premium was introduced.
Coverage: 107,000 ongoing private *defined benefit* plans (with approximately 40 million participants); 104,500 single-employer and 2,500 multiemployer plans. (Excludes defined benefit plans of professional service employers with no more than 25 participants, church plans, and those not qualified for favorable tax treatment as well as *defined contribution* plans.)
Frequency: Annually. Payment reports must be filed within eight months following the beginning of the plan year.
Historical data: Information from PBGC Form 1 for plan years 1976 to 1987 is currently available.
References: Some statistical data summarized in PBGC's *Annual Report to Congress*. Quarterly summaries of reversions of pension assets have been released since 1980. See also *Federal Insurance of Private Pension Benefits*, Congress of the United States, Congressional Budget Office, October 1987.
Contact person: John Thompson, PBGC, 2020 K Street, NW, Washington, DC 20006–1860; (202) 778–8851.

* * *

Source: Case Administration System (CAS)
Data items: Information from PBGC Form 500 Standard Termination Notice Single-Employer Plan Termination and PBGC Form 600 Distress Termination Notice of Intent to Terminate. Data include general plan information (reason for termination, changes in employer, number of participants), as well as information on disposition of residual assets of the plan.
Coverage: Data on 110,000 standard terminations and more than 1,500 distress terminations; about 9,000 to 10,000 plans are terminated each year.
Frequency: Updated continuously as termination notices are filed.
Historical data: The CAS contains information on terminations that the PBGC has processed since its inception in 1974; however, only information for recent years is on-line.

References: Some statistical data summarized in PBGC's *Annual Report to Congress.* Quarterly summaries of reversions of pension assets have been released since 1980. See also *Federal Insurance of Private Pension Benefits,* Congress of the United States, Congressional Budget Office, October 1987.

Contact person: John Thompson, PBGC, 2020 K Street, NW, Washington, DC 20006–1860; (202) 778–8851.

*   *   *

Source: Benefit Payment System (BPS)

Data items: Characteristics of payees (and future payees) receiving benefits from the PBGC including: type of recipient (retiree, beneficiary), recipient's status (current participant, "future" participant), age and sex of retiree (or beneficiary), type of retirement (normal, early, disability), age at retirement, months of service, benefit amount, deductions, amount of retirement check, form of payment, form of annuity, state or country of residence, frequency of payment. Characteristics of associated plans including: employer identification number and plan number (EIN-PN), plan name, effective date of plan, date of plan termination, date of PBGC trusteeship, total participants in plan, active participants, active non-vested participants, separated but vested participants (or their beneficiaries), number of retirees (or beneficiaries) in pay status. (At present, these data are not linked with other data sources such as Form 5500; however, the PBGC is setting up a research library and a new Pension Data Center that will maintain data for analytical and research needs, including linkage to data from other sources and periodic release of statistics.)

Coverage: Information on over 109,000 participants in plans for which the PBGC has assumed trusteeship, and on another 120,000 participants who will become eligible for benefits in the future.

Frequency: Updated continuously as the PBGC assumes trusteeship of pension plans and responsibility for benefit payments.

Historical data: The BPS contains information on payees for whom the PBGC has assumed responsibility since its inception in 1974; however, only information for recent years is on-line.

References: Some statistical data summarized in PBGC's *Annual Report to Congress.* Quarterly summaries of reversions of pension assets have been released since 1980. See also *Federal Insurance of Private Pension Benefits,* Congress of the United States, Congressional Budget Office, October 1987.

Contact person: John Thompson, PBGC, 2020 K Street, NW, Washington, DC 20006–1860; (202) 778–8851.

Office of Personnel Management (OPM)

Source: Civil Service Retirement and Disability Fund

Note: The Civil Service Retirement and Disability Fund (CSRDF) is comprised of two tiers of defined pension benefits, the Civil Service Retirement System (CSRS) and the Federal Employees' Retirement System (FERS). FERS, which was implemented on January 1, 1987, covers most federal employees who were hired after 1983. It is a three-part pension program designed along the lines of private-sector plans. Using Social Security as a base, it provides an additional basic benefit as well as a Thrift Savings Plan. The Thrift Savings Plan is administered by a separate, independent agency and financed through a separate trust fund.

Data items: The 1987 *Annual Report* presents detailed descriptions of the two retirement systems as well as information on the financial statistics of the two systems for the period 1983–87 including: additions (income), deductions (expenses), and net assets; cost-of-living adjustments since 1977; plan investments; past and projected flows of plan assets (1979–2065); underlying economic and actuarial assumptions; aggregate information on employee and survivor annuitants, including mean and median monthly annuity, age distribution, and distribution by state of residence (periods covered for annuitant data vary: 1978–87, 1983–87, and fiscal year 1987 only).

Coverage: For the year ending September 30, 1987, plan participants numbered 2,880,000 active employees, 125,000 separated employees entitled to deferred benefits, and 2,090,000 annuitants (1,546,000 retired annuitants and 544,000 survivor annuitants).

Frequency: Annually. Public Law 95 requires that all federal government retirement systems submit annual financial and actuarial reports to the Congress and Comptroller General of the United States. (See also **Historical data**.)

Historical data: The CSRS was established on May 22, 1920; FERS was established on June 6, 1986. Annual reports for years previous to that referenced below are available.

References: *Civil Service Retirement and Disability Fund Annual Report* (September 30, 1987); the annual report for September 30, 1988, is forthcoming.

Contact person: Douglas Groft, Retirement and Insurance Group, U.S. Office of Personnel Management, Washington, DC 20415; (202) 632–5496.

Internal Revenue Service (IRS), U.S. Department of the Treasury

Source: Employee Plans Master File (EPMF)

Note: The EPMF file system contains virtually all of the items from the Form 5500, approximately 80 percent of those from the Form 5500-C, and 90 percent from the Form 5500-R, plus most of the items from the Form 5500 EZ. IRS abstracts approximately 80 percent of the items available from Schedules A and C for the Department of Labor and 50–60 percent of the items from Schedule B. (See **Pension and Welfare Benefits Administration** for a description of the forms.)

Data items: "Standard" information for each pension plan includes the employer identification number (EIN), the plan number (PN), and the name and address of the employer (sponsor). Other information includes: business code, plan assets, number of participants, amount of contributions, type of plan (defined benefit, defined contribution), type of plan entity (single employer, multiemployer), initial date of plan, and date of latest plan amendment.

Coverage: Private employment pension benefit plans (see **Pension and Welfare Benefits Administration**).

Frequency: File updated monthly.

Historical data: Information beginning with 1975 is available. Information from the EPMF may be requested on computer tape or in printed form.

Requests must be by Form Number. In addition to the standard information listed above, a limited number of additional items may be chosen with each request.

References: *Employee Plans Master File Handbook*, IRM 7810, July 1989. A study was undertaken based on Form 5500 series returns filed for plan year 1977, that evaluated data on type of plan, funding arrangement, balance sheet, income statement, plan terminations, plan amendments, and PBGC coverage. See, Greenia, Nicholas. "Employee Benefit Plans, 1977," *SOI Bulletin*, U.S. Department of the Treasury, IRS, Spring 1982.

Contact person: Katherine Millikin (ISM:T:I), IRS, U.S. Department of the Treasury, Washington, DC 20224; (202) 535–9579.

Railroad Retirement Board

Source: Railroad Retirement System

Note: The Railroad Retirement Act provides retirement and disability annuities for qualified railroad employees, spouse annuities for their wives or husbands, and survivor benefits for families of deceased employees who were insured under the Act. These benefit programs are administered by the U.S. Railroad Retirement Board, which also administers the Railroad Unemployment Insurance Act and has administrative responsibilities under the Social Security Act for certain benefit payments and railroad workers' medicare coverage.

Data items: The *Informational Conference Handbook* and the *Annual Report* referenced below contain information compiled annually on such areas as the financial status of the system, the average amount of benefits by type of annuitant, and benefits paid by state of residence. In addition, monthly financial and benefit statistics are compiled on the retirement and survivor programs. Three microdata bases also exist: the master benefit file, containing detailed information on employees, spouses, and survivors; the service and compensation file, containing detailed information on service history and earnings; and the checkwriting integrated computer operation file, containing detailed information pertinent to the actual writing of payment checks.

Coverage: Through September 30, 1988, benefits under the railroad retirement system have been awarded to 1,700,000 retired employees, 900,000 spouses, and 2,100,000 survivors. At the end of September 1989, the number of beneficiaries on the rolls was about 904,000, and benefits were being paid at the rate of about $7 billion annually. (There were an average of 304,000 persons employed in the railroad industry in 1989.)

Frequency: Annual report to Congress. Monthly benefit statistics are published approximately three months following the reference month.

Historical data: Monthly statistics have been published since 1968. The microdata bases also contain historical information; for example, data on service and compensation begin with 1936.

References: *Informational Conference Handbook*, January 1990, U.S. Railroad Retirement Board; *Railroad Retirement Board 1988 Annual Report*; and *Railroad Retirement and Survivor Benefits for Railroad Workers and Their Families*, Railroad Retirement Board, March 1989.

Contact person: LeRoy Blommaert, Information Management Section, Railroad Retirement Board, 844 Rush Street, Chicago, IL 60611; (312) 751–4548.

Bureau of the Census (Census), U.S. Department of Commerce

Source: Current Population Survey (CPS)

Note: The monthly CPS deals mainly with questions relating to labor force participation that are asked about each member 14 years old and over in every sample household. In March, supplementary questions are asked about money income, noncash benefits, and work experience for the previous year.

Data items: Number of persons with employer- or union-provided pension plan coverage, by wage or salary income with industry and demographic breakdowns. Census does not publish detailed estimates of pension and retirement income from the CPS. Unpublished estimates of aggregate retirement income and number of recipients are available. The CPS recently incorporated a new processing system that provides more detailed unpublished estimates (for 1987–88) of the number of persons with retirement income by detailed type (private pensions, federal retirement, military retirement, state or local government retirement, railroad retirement, annuities, IRA or KEOGH, and other).

Coverage: The March CPS sample covers the civilian noninstitutional population of the United States, and members of the Armed Forces living off post or with their families on post; it excludes all other members of the Armed Forces. In the March 1986 sample, approximately 60,500 occupied households were eligible for interview; of these, about 2,500 interviews could not be obtained.

Frequency: Annually. Data are collected in the March supplement to the CPS and refer to coverage during the previous calendar year. Estimates are released approximately 6 months after the survey date.

Historical data: Estimates of pension plan coverage were published in the *Consumer Income* Series P-60 for the years 1980–85; unpublished estimates are available for 1986 and 1987.

References: Current Population Reports, Series P-60, No. 155, *Receipt of Selected Noncash Benefits: 1985*, U.S. Department of Commerce, Census, January 1987.

Contact person: Charles Nelson, Income Statistics Branch, Census, U.S. Department of Commerce, Washington, DC 20233; (301) 763–8576.

* * *

Source: Pension Supplements to the CPS

Note: Several CPS pension supplements have been conducted. The latest was in 1988 and is described below.

Data items: Pension coverage rates for 1988 (separately for defined benefit and defined contribution plans) by age, sex, race, job tenure, industry, firm size, and union representation. Comparisons of 1988 coverage rates with those from the earlier supplements (see **Historical data**) are also presented.

Coverage: The 1988 interviews were conducted with persons in one-half the CPS sample who were currently employed for pay. Among those persons aged 16 or older, 27,496 interviews were completed, representing an estimated 113.7 million workers.

Frequency: Intermittently (see below).

Historical data: Similar supplements were conducted in 1972, 1979, and 1983.

References: Woods, John R., "Pension Coverage Among Private Wage and

Salary Workers: Preliminary Findings From 1988 Survey of Employee Benefits," *Social Security Bulletin*, U.S. Department of Health and Human Services, SSA, October 1989.

Contact person: Ronald Tucker, Current Population Survey Branch, Census, U.S. Department of Commerce, Washington, DC 20233; (301) 763–2773.

* * *

Source: Survey of Income and Program Participation (SIPP)

Note: The SIPP is a longitudinal sample survey designed to provide comprehensive information that reflects the financial situation of persons, families, and households in the United States (excluding persons in institutions). Sample members are interviewed at 4-month intervals for a period of about 2½ years. A new sample (panel) is introduced each year, so that panels overlap. In any month, at least two panels are simultaneously being interviewed, and, for part of each year, three panels are interviewed. Each interview elicits information covering the prior 4-month reference period. Each sample is divided into four groups (called rotation groups), and one rotation group is interviewed each month. Each 4-month round of interviewing is called a wave.

The SIPP questionnaire includes two main sections. In the first, called the core, questions are asked about topics that require continuous monitoring. In the second, called the topical module, questions are asked about topics that can be covered less frequently. The fourth wave topical module to the 1984 SIPP contained supplemental questions on both pension eligibility of the working population and on characteristics of persons receiving retirement income.

Data items: Pension coverage and vesting rates by worker characteristics (age, sex, monthly earnings, industry, firm size, and participation in IRA and 401(k) plans). Retirement income—pension income, total household income, and Social Security income—by characteristics of retirees (age, sex, marital status, years since retirement, former industry, current work status, and education); information on the presence of a COLA (cost-of-living adjustment) was also obtained.

Coverage: The SIPP sample design for the 1984 panel consisted of 26,000 housing units selected to represent the noninstitutional population of the United States; 20,900 were occupied and eligible for interview. (A new panel of smaller size was introduced in February 1985 and has been introduced in February of each succeeding year.)

Frequency: Estimates for 1985 and 1986 have not been published, but are available through SIPP microdata public use files.

Historical data: Not applicable.

References: Current Population Reports, Series P-70, No. 12, *Pensions: Worker Coverage and Retirement Income, 1984*, U.S. Department of Commerce, Census, September 1987.

Contact person: Charles Nelson, Income Statistics Branch, Census, U.S. Department of Commerce, Washington, DC 20233; (301) 763–8576.

* * *

Source: Annual Survey of Public Employee Retirement Systems

Note: Before 1951, public employees were not eligible to participate in the federal Social Security program. Changes in federal laws after that allowed state and local governments at their option to provide Social Security coverage for their employees, including those who also participated in retirement systems of those governments. The Social Security Amendments of 1983 eliminated the option of state and local governments to withdraw from the federal system effective January 1, 1984.

Data items: Financial aspects of the systems including receipts, payments, and assets, as well as membership and number of beneficiaries. Data are shown for the nation, for states, and for individual retirement systems if they had cash and investment holdings of $20 million or more.

Coverage: Public employees in retirement systems sponsored by a recognized unit of government as defined by the Bureau of the Census; employees must be compensated with public funds. In addition to state governments, Census defines five types of local governments: county, municipal, township, school district, and special district. (Excludes systems that use the following three methods of supplying retirement benefits: (1) funds supported entirely by employee contributions; (2) direct payments to retired or disabled individuals from appropriations of general funds; and (3) payments to a private trustee or insurance carrier that administers the investments and benefit payments.)
A mail file representing the universe of approximately 2,500 retirement systems exists; financial information for each individual retirement system in the universe is available.

Frequency: Annually. The latest available *published* information is for 1987 (see **References**); computerized data for 1988 are also available.

Historical data: Information beginning with 1959 is available in printed format.

References: 1987 Census of Governments, Volume 4, Government Finances, Number 6, *Employee Retirement Systems of State and Local Governments*, Department of Commerce, Census, December 1989.

Contact person: Henry Wulf, Finance Branch, Governments Division, Census, U.S. Department of Commerce, Washington, DC 20233; (301) 763–7664.

*   *   *

Source: Quarterly Survey of Public Employee Retirement Systems

Data items: Receipts, benefit and withdrawal payments, and composition of assets of major public employee retirement systems.

Coverage: Public employee retirement systems with the largest amount of assets (cash and security holdings). The 104 systems in the panel account for slightly more than 87 percent of total assets of the approximately 2,500 systems identified in the Census of Governments. Usable replies are received each quarter from about three-fourths of the panel.

Frequency: Quarterly. Available 100–120 days after the end of each quarter (see **References**). A microcomputer spreadsheet with individual system information in detail for each quarter is available.

Historical data: Data in published summary format are available on a quarterly basis beginning with 1968.

References: *Finances of Selected Public Employee Retirement Systems*, U.S. Department of Commerce, Census.

Contact person: Henry Wulf, Finance Branch, Governments Division, Census, U.S. Department of Commerce, Washington, DC 20233; (301) 763–7664.

Social Security Administration (SSA),
U.S. Department of Health and Human Services

Note. The vast majority of data compiled by SSA relates to publicly provided old-age, survivors, and disability insurance (OASDI). Since the focus here is primarily on private pensions, only information compiled by SSA that includes items on private pensions, military pensions, or state and local government pensions is covered below.

* * *

Source: New Beneficiary Survey (NBS)

Data items: Information on household composition, employment history, job characteristics (including pension status), health, sources of income, and asset holdings.

Coverage: Nationally representative sample of men and women who began receiving retired-worker benefits during the 12-month period June 1980–May 1981. (18,600 personal interviews were conducted.)

Frequency: Conducted in 1982; a reinterview, the New Beneficiary Followup (NBF), with NBS respondents or their survivors began in the fall of 1990. Pensions are addressed in several sections of the NBF survey instrument (pensions related to current or most recent employment, the effect of widowhood or divorce on receipt of pensions, current income from pensions, and detailed questions on pension amounts over time).

Historical data: Not applicable. However, NBS data are available on computer tape.

References: Maxfield, Linda D. "The 1982 New Beneficiary Survey: An Introduction," *Social Security Bulletin*, U.S. Department of Health and Human Services, SSA, November 1983; and *The 1982 New Beneficiary Survey: Users' Manual*, U.S. Department of Health and Human Services, SSA, April 1986.

Contact person: Martynas Ycas, Office of Research and Statistics, SSA, Department of Health and Human Services, 4301 Connecticut Ave., NW, Washington, DC 20008; (202) 282–7089.

* * *

Source: Private Social Welfare Expenditures

Data items: Information on private social welfare expenditures (including payments under private pension plans) and their relationship to the gross national product (GNP). This series complements data available on public social welfare expenditures.

Coverage: Total expenditures in the United States.

Frequency: Annually. Data for 1987 are currently available.

Historical data: Information beginning with 1972 is available.

References: Kerns, Wilmer L., and Milton P. Glanz, "Private Social Welfare Expenditures, 1972–87," *Social Security Bulletin*, U.S. Department of Health and Human Services, SSA, November 1989.

Contact person: Bill Kerns, Office of Research and Statistics, SSA, U.S. Department of Health and Human Services, 4301 Connecticut Ave., NW, Washington, DC 20008; (202) 282–7223.

* * *

Source: Public Employment Retirement

Data items: Aggregate information on benefits and beneficiaries under federal, state, and local government public employee retirement systems. Data covering state and local employees are from Bureau of the Census publications (see **Bureau of the Census**); data covering federal employees are from reports of the administering agencies and from the *U.S. Budget Appendix.*

Coverage: Federal, state, and local government employees.

Frequency: Biennially. Data for 1986 are currently available.

Historical data: Some information beginning with 1954 is available.

References: Bixby, Ann K. "Benefits and Beneficiaries Under Public Employee Retirement Systems, Calendar Year 1986," *Social Security Bulletin*, U.S. Department of Health and Human Services, SSA, May 1989.

Contact person: Ann Bixby, Office of Research & Statistics, SSA, U.S. Department of Health and Human Services, 4301 Connecticut Ave., NW, Washington, DC 20008; (202) 282–7222.

$$* \quad * \quad *$$

Source: Income of the Population 55 or Older

Data items: Information on the major sources and amounts of income, including private pensions or annuities, military retirement, other federal government employee pensions, and state and local government employee pensions.

Coverage: Subsample of persons 55 or older created from the March Current Population Survey (see **Bureau of the Census**) arranged in aged units— married couples living together (at least one of whom is 55 or older) and nonmarried persons 55 and older; married persons living apart are classified as nonmarried persons. This source focuses on the income of the aged population separately, whether or not they live with other relatives. In contrast, the Bureau of the Census publications using CPS data classify aged persons living with a younger relative who is considered the householder as in "families under 65."

Frequency: Biennially. Data for 1988 are currently available; calendar year 1990 data will be available in summer 1992.

Historical data: The first report in the series is based on 1976 data.

Reference: Grad, Susan. *Income of the Population 55 or Older, 1986.* U.S. Department of Health and Human Services, SSA, June 1988.

Contact person: Susan Grad, Office of Research and Statistics, SSA, U.S. Department of Health and Human Services, 4301 Connecticut Ave., NW, Washington, DC 20008; (202) 282–7094.

Department of Defense (DoD)

Source: Military Retirement System

Note: The military retirement system applies primarily to the Armed Forces, although provisions apply to retirement systems for certain other groups (see **Coverage**). The system is a funded noncontributory defined benefit plan that includes nondisability retired pay, disability retired pay, retired pay for reserve service, and survivor annuity programs. There is no vesting before retirement. Retiree and survivor benefits are automatically adjusted annually to protect the purchasing power of initial retired pay.

Data items: The Statistical Report (see **References**) contains numerous tables including information on: number of retired military personnel by year; annual DoD obligations or expenditures for military retired pay; status of funds and other data for retired pay (by service); number of military retirees and monthly retirement benefits by service and three-digit zip code, state, or country; retirees by salary or rank and current (or retired) age; retirees by rank and years of service, survivor-related data, and more.

Coverage: The military retirement system applies to the Army, Navy, Marine Corps, and Air Force. Most provisions also apply to retirement systems for members of the Coast Guard (administered by the Department of Transportation), officers of the Public Health Service (administered by the Department of Health and Human Services), and officers of the National Oceanic and Atmospheric Administration (administered by the Department of Commerce).

Frequency: Annually. Public Law 95 requires that all federal government retirement systems submit annual financial and actuarial reports to the Congress and Comptroller General of the United States.

Historical data: Time periods of available information vary by data item; some information beginning with 1900 is available.

References: *FY 1988 DOD Statistical Report on the Military Retirement System*, Office of the Actuary, Department of Defense, and *Valuation of the Military Retirement System*, September 30, 1988, Department of Defense, Office of the Actuary.

Contact person: Harry Richardson, Office of the Actuary, Department of Defense, 1600 N. Wilson Blvd., Suite 434, Arlington, VA 22209–2593; (202) 696–5865.

Contributors

EMILY S. ANDREWS is Associate Professor of Labor and Industrial Relations at the Labor Research Center of the University of Rhode Island (URI) and a Fellow of the Employee Benefit Research Institute (EBRI). Prior to her academic appointment at URI, she served as EBRI's research director. Dr. Andrews held policy research positions at the Social Security Administration, the Labor Department, and the President's Commission on Pension Policy. Her publications include "Pension Policy and Small Employers: At What Price Coverage?" and "The Changing Profile of Pensions in America." She holds a Ph.D. in economics from the University of Pennsylvania.

ROBERT B. AVERY is an Associate Professor in the Department of Consumer Economics at Cornell University and a Research Associate at the Federal Reserve Bank of Cleveland. Prior to his arrival at Cornell he was a Senior Economist at the Board of Governors of the Federal Reserve System (1981–1988) and an Assistant Professor of Economics in the Graduate School of Industrial Administration at Carnegie Mellon University (1975–1981). He received his undergraduate degree from the University of Pennsylvania and his Ph.D. in Economics from the University of Wisconsin. While at the Federal Reserve Board, he served as Project Director of the 1983, 1986, and 1989 Surveys of Consumer Finances. His current research interests center on the use of these data to study issues related to wealth and saving. He is also working on problems associated with the deregulation of the banking system.

ZVI BODIE is Professor of Finance and Economics at Boston University, School of Management. He holds a Ph.D. in economics from the Massachusetts Institute of Technology and has served on the finance faculty at MIT's Sloan School of Management. He is a Research Associate of the National Bureau of Economic Research in Cambridge, Massachusetts, where he was Director of the NBER Project on Financial Aspects of the U.S. Pension System from 1979 to 1985. He is also a member of the Pension Research Council of the Wharton School, University of Pennsylvania, and the Financial Accounting Standards Board Task Force on Interest Methods. His previous edited volumes include *Pensions in the U.S. Economy*, *Issues in Pension Economics*, and *Financial Aspects of the U.S. Pension System*, all published by the University of Chicago Press. His textbook, *Investments*, was published by Richard D. Irwin, Inc.

GARY BURTLESS is a Senior Fellow in the Economic Studies program at Brookings, where he does research on labor markets, income redistribution, and the economic effects of taxes. Since receiving his Ph.D. from the Massachusetts Institute of Technology in 1977, he has written and published numerous articles on applied econometrics and microeconomics, including recent papers on the effects of Social Security, welfare, unemployment insurance, and manpower training.

Before coming to Brookings in 1981, Dr. Burtless served as an economist in the Policy and Evaluation offices of the Secretaries of Labor and Health, Education, and Welfare. His responsibilities in those offices included technical monitoring of several large-scale social experiments, including manpower and training projects and the two largest of the negative-income-tax experiments.

Dr. Burtless has written numerous books and papers. His books include *A Future of Lousy Jobs? The Changing Structure of U.S. Wages* and *Can America Afford to Grow Old? Paying for Social Security* (with Henry Aaron and Barry Bosworth, Brookings, 1989).

ROBERT L. CLARK is Professor, Department of Economics and Business, North Carolina State University. He earned his Ph.D. in Economics from Duke University in 1974. His research has examined the economic effects of employer pensions focusing on the influence of pensions on job turnover, retirement, and the economic well-being of the elderly. He has analyzed the incidence and magnitude of post-retirement increases of pension benefits and the role of government regulation in the trend toward greater use of defined contribution plans. Forthcoming publications include *Retirement Systems in Japan*, the Pension Research Council; *The Choice of Pension Plans in a Changing Regulatory Environment*, American Enterprise Institute, with Ann McDermed; and *Retirement Income Plans in the United States*, to be published in Japanese by the Japan Foundation for Research and Development of Pension Schemes. His other research examines issues associated with the economics of individual and population aging.

LORNA M. DAILEY is a research consultant with more than twelve years experience researching international pension and social security issues. In 1986, she established Bedford Research Consultants, an international research and information services firm serving the employee benefits and pensions fund investment industries. The firm maintains its own international library and bibliographic database on foreign pension and social security systems. In conjunction with the U.S. Department of Labor, she has conducted a study of comparative pension statistics covering nine countries. She has a Master of Library Studies degree from the University of Hawaii and a Master of International Management degree from the American Graduate School of International Management.

ALAN L. GUSTMAN is currently Loren M. Berry Professor of Economics at Dartmouth College, which he joined in 1969, and a Research Associate for the National Bureau of Economic Research. In 1976 and 1977, Dr. Gustman served as a Special Assistant for Economic Affairs for the U.S. Department of

Labor. He holds a doctoral degree from the City College of New York and a Bachelor's degree from the University of Michigan. His areas of research are labor economics and economics for aging.

MICHAEL D. HURD is Professor of Economics at the State University of New York at Stony Brook and a Research Associate at the National Bureau of Economic Research. He holds an M.S. (Statistics) and a Ph.D. (Economics) from the University of California, Berkeley. His research on the economics of aging includes studies of the determinants of retirement, the measurement of the economic status of the elderly, and the effects of mortality risk on the saving and consumption behavior of the elderly. His most recent paper is a survey of the research in these three areas.

LAURENCE J. KOTLIKOFF is Professor of Economics at Boston University and a Research Associate of the National Bureau of Economic Research. He received his Ph.D. in Economics from Harvard University in 1977 and subsequently taught at the University of California, Los Angeles and at Yale University. In 1981–82 he served as a Senior Economist with the President's Council of Economic Advisers. Dr. Kotlikoff has served as a consultant to the International Monetary Fund, the World Bank, and the Organization for Economic Cooperation and Development. He is author of *What Determines Savings?*, co-author (with Alan Auerbach) of *Dynamic Fiscal Policy*, co-author (with Daniel Smith) of *Pensions in the American Economy*, and co-author (with David Wise) of *Pension Backloading and Retirement Incentives: The Wage Carrot and the Pension Stick*, and has published extensively in professional journals, newspapers, and magazines on issues of deficits, the tax structure, social security, pensions, saving, and insurance.

DAVID C. LINDEMAN is Director of the Corporate Policy and Research Department of the Pension Benefit Guaranty Corporation (PBGC), a self-financing government corporation established under Title IV of the Employee Retirement Income Security Act of 1974. Before joining PBGC, he was a principal analyst in the Tax Division of the Congressional Budget Office (CBO) and served as Acting General Counsel. At CBO, he authored papers and studies on tax policy, pension funding, and social security.

Previously, he held positions at the Office of Management and Budget and the Department of Health and Human Services. Mr. Lindeman earned a Bachelor's degree *cum laude* in Government from Columbia College. He also received his J.D. degree from Columbia Law School and is a member of the D.C. Bar.

OLIVIA S. MITCHELL is a Professor of Labor Economics at Cornell University's Industrial and Labor Relations School. She specializes in labor economics, evaluation analysis, and public finance. Dr. Mitchell also directs the Labor Force Demographics Program for the Cornell/ILR Institute for Labor Market Policies, works with the ILR/Cornell Center for Advanced Human Resource Studies, and is Associate Editor of the Industrial and Labor Relations Review. She is concurrently a member of the National Academy of Social Insurance and a Research Associate at the National Bureau of Economic Research. Dr. Mitchell holds the B.S. degree (1974) in Economics from

Harvard University, and M.A. (1976) and Ph.D. (1978) degrees in Economics from the University of Wisconsin-Madison. She is co-author of *Retirement, Pensions, and Social Security* and many other published studies.

ALICIA H. MUNNELL is Senior Vice President and Director of Research for the Federal Reserve Bank of Boston. In addition to her responsibilities as Director, Ms. Munnell conducts research in the areas of tax policy, social security, and public and private pensions. Prior to joining the Boston Fed in 1973, Ms. Munnell earned her doctorate in Economics from Harvard University. She began her studies in economics at Wellesley College, earning her B.A. in 1964. She then earned an M.A. from Boston University, where she is currently a member of the Academy of Distinguished Alumni.

A member of many advisory committees and task forces, Ms. Munnell has served as Staff Director for the National Planning Association's Joint Committee on Public Pensions and as a member of the Carnegie Corporation's Commission on College Retirement. She is currently a member of the Institute of Medicine, the National Academy of Public Administration, and the Pension Research Council of the Wharton School of Finance and Commerce.

Ms. Munnell has written numerous articles on the subjects of tax policy, social security and pensions, and her books include *The Economics of Private Pensions* (Brookings Institution) and *The Future of Social Security* (Brookings Institution, 1977).

LESLIE E. PAPKE is Assistant Professor of Finance/Economics at the Boston University School of Management. She holds a Ph.D. from the Massachusetts Institute of Technology and has served on the Applied Economics faculty at the Sloan School of Management. She is a Faculty Research Fellow in the Taxation Program of the National Bureau of Economic Research. She is a recipient of the NBER Fellowship in Aging for 1990–91. Her published research focuses on state and local public finance and business taxation.

ROBERT P. PARKER is Associate Director for National Economic Accounts of the Bureau of Economic Analysis, U.S. Department of Commerce. In this position, which he has held since 1982, he is responsible for the development, planning, and preparation of the national income and product, wealth, and input-output accounts of the United States. At BEA, he previously served as Chief and Assistant Chief of the National Income and Product Division. Before joining BEA, he was at the Bureau of the Census for nine years where he directed the *Enterprise Statistics* publication program and worked on the development of the Standard Statistical Establishment List. He received a B.A. in Mathematics from Duke University in 1961 and did graduate work in Economics at The American University. He is a fellow of the American Statistical Association.

ANNA M. RAPPAPORT is a Managing Director of William M. Mercer Meidinger Hansen, Incorporated. She is an actuary and futurist with 30 years of business experience and has a broad background in pension and benefits consulting, corporate research, and life insurance company management. Her special interest has been social and economic change and how it affects the benefits and human resources management. She has taught graduate and undergraduate courses at the College of Insurance in New York, spoken at many professional meetings, and appeared in numerous seminars for Mercer Meidinger Hansen clients. She is the author of many articles and papers, and was a recipient of the ACME award for Literacy Excellence in 1987. She is frequently quoted and has been quoted in the *New York Times*, the *Wall Street Journal*, *Chicago Tribune*, *Business Week*, and *Fortune*. She serves as a consultant to major clients of the firm.

Rappaport is a graduate of the University of Chicago with a Master of Business Administration degree. She is a Fellow of the Society of Actuaries, a member of the American Academy of Actuaries, and an Enrolled Actuary.

SYLVESTER J. SCHIEBER is Vice President of The Wyatt Company and Director of its Research and Information Center in Washington, DC. He received a Ph.D. in Economics from the University of Notre Dame in 1974. During his professional career he has specialized in the analysis of public and private retirement policy and health policy issues. He has been responsible for the development of a number of special ongoing survey programs focusing on these issues. Prior to joining The Wyatt Company in 1983, he served as the first Research Director of the Employee Benefit Research Institute in Washington, DC. Before that, he served as the Deputy Director, Office of Policy Analysis, Social Security Administration, and Deputy Research Director, Universal Social Security Coverage Study, Department of Health and Human Services.

IRWIN TEPPER specializes in the financial analysis of employee benefit programs. He consults with plan sponsors and governmental agencies on planning and policy issues, including asset allocation, funding, reporting, and plan design. He has also developed a microcomputer-based software system that is used by sponsors to facilitate asset/liability management. Dr. Tepper is active in executive education. He lectures and leads case discussions on employee benefit issues to a wide variety of audiences.

The work of Dr. Tepper, an active researcher in the field, has been published in leading journals, including the *Harvard Business Review*, the *Journal of Finance*, and the *Financial Analysts Journal*. His contributions have been cited in *Fortune*, *Institutional Investor*, *Forbes*, and *Pensions and Investments Age*.

Dr. Tepper was previously an Associate Professor at the Harvard Business School, where he taught Corporate Finance and Investments. He has lectured at the Massachusetts Institute of Technology. He holds a doctoral degree from the Wharton School, a master's degree from the University of Maryland, and a bachelor's degree from Rensselaer Polytechnic Institute.

LAWRENCE H. THOMPSON currently serves as Assistant Comptroller General in charge of the Human Resources Division of the U.S. General Accounting Office (GAO). The General Accounting Office undertakes, on behalf of Congress, a broad range of studies focusing primarily on the evaluation of federal agency operations and the impacts of federal programs. The Human Resources Division is responsible for studies that involve health, education, labor, and income security issues and programs.

Dr. Thompson served as the Chief Economist of GAO from 1983 until the beginning of 1988, when he assumed his current position. Prior to joining GAO, he worked for nine years on income security issues in the Department of Health and Human Services (HHS). This included service as Director of Social Security Planning in the Office of the Secretary of HHS, Executive Director of the 1979 Advisory Council on Social Security, and Associate Social Security Commissioner for Policy.

Dr. Thompson received a Bachelor of Science degree from Iowa State University, a Master of Business Administration from the Wharton School of the University of Pennsylvania, and holds a Ph.D. in Economics from the University of Michigan. He is a career civil servant who has worked for the federal government since 1970. His first years with the federal government were spent working on intergovernmental financing issues and urban poverty problems in the policy research division of the Office of Economic Opportunity and on school finance problems with the National Institute of Education.

JOHN A. TURNER directs pension and health benefits research at the Pension and Welfare Benefits Administration, U.S. Department of Labor. He has written a number of publications concerning private pensions and social security, including recently co-editing the books *Trends in Pensions* and *Pension Policy: An International Perspective* (forthcoming). Before coming to the Labor Department in 1980, he worked in the research office of the Social Security Administration. He received his Ph.D. in Economics from the University of Chicago.

KATHLEEN P. UTGOFF, before joining the law firm of Groom and Nordberg in September 1989, was Executive Director of the Pension Benefit Guaranty Corporation (PBGC), the federal corporation responsible for insuring defined benefits pension plans. As Executive Director, Dr. Utgoff was the architect of major changes in the federal pension insurance program. She is credited with returning the PBGC to financial stability after a period of rising claims and a growing deficit. Before becoming Executive Director, she served as a Senior Economist at the Council of Economic Advisers from 1983 to 1985. She received her Ph.D. from the University of California, Los Angeles.

FREDERICK O. YOHN received undergraduate degrees in Engineering and Economics from MIT. After graduate training in Economics at Princeton University, his doctoral research on credit rationing and fixed investment was carried out at France's INSEE. He joined the Federal Reserve Board in 1977 as an Economist in the Capital Markets section. After transferring to the Flow of Funds section, he was responsible for numerous data development projects, including the Fed-EBRI private pension fund data. In 1989, he joined the Corporate Economics Department of Aetna Life and Casualty. In addition to monitoring economic activity, he continues to be involved in the analysis of financial market developments and the investigation of households' and businesses' financial behavior.

Index

Pension Research Council Publications

Concepts of Actuarial Soundness in Pension Plans. Dorrance C. Bronson. 1957.

Continuing Care Retirement Communities: An Empirical, Financial and Legal Analysis. Howard E. Winklevoss and Alwyn V. Powell, in collaboration with David L. Cohen and Ann Trueblood-Raper. 1983.

Corporate Book Reserving for Postretirement Healthcare Benefits. Edited by Dwight K. Bartlett. 1990.

An Economic Appraisal of Pension Tax Policy in the United States. Richard A. Ippolito. 1990.

The Economics of Pension Insurance. Richard A. Ippolito. 1989.

Employer Accounting for Pensions: Analysis of the Financial Accounting Standards Board's Preliminary Views and Exposure Draft. E. L. Hicks and C. L. Trowbridge. 1985.

Fundamentals of Private Pensions, Sixth Edition. Dan M. McGill and Donald S. Grubbs. 1988.

Inflation and Pensions. Susan M. Wachter. 1987.

It's My Retirement Money, Take Good Care of It: The TIAA-CREF Story. William C. Greenough. 1990.

Joint Trust Pension Plans: Understanding and Administering Collectively Bargained Multiemployer Plans under ERISA. Daniel F. McGinn. 1977.

Pension Asset Management: An International Perspective. Edited by Leslie Hannah. 1988.

Pension Mathematics with Numerical Illustrations. Howard E. Winklevoss. 1977.

Pensions and the Economy: Sources, Uses, and Limitations of Data. Edited by Zvi Bodie and Alicia H. Munnell. 1992.

Pensions, Economics and Public Policy. Richard A. Ippolito. 1985.

Proxy Voting of Pension Plan Equity Securities. Planned and edited by Dan M. McGill. 1989.

Retirement Systems for Public Employees. Thomas P. Bleakney. 1972.

Retirement Systems in Japan. Robert L. Clark. 1990.

Search for a National Retirement Income Policy. Edited by Jack L. VanDerhei. 1987.

Social Investing. Edited by Dan M. McGill. 1984.

Social Security and Private Pensions: Competitive or Complementary. Planned and edited by Dan M. McGill. 1977.

This book was set in Baskerville and Eras typefaces. Baskerville was designed by John Baskerville at his private press in Birmingham, England, in the eighteenth century. The first typeface to depart from oldstyle typeface design, Baskerville has more variation between thick and thin strokes. In an effort to insure that the thick and thin strokes of his typeface reproduced well on paper, John Baskerville developed the first wove paper, the surface of which was much smoother than the laid paper of the time. The development of wove paper was partly responsible for the introduction of typefaces classified as modern, which have even more contrast between thick and thin strokes.

Eras was designed in 1969 by Studio Hollenstein in Paris for the Wagner Typefoundry. A contemporary script-like version of a sans-serif typeface, the letters of Eras have a monotone stroke and are slightly inclined.

Printed on acid-free paper.

DATE DUE

AUG 04 1998		DEC 11 1999
SEP 10 1997		DEC 30 1998
APR 07 1998		
APR 07 1998		
OCT 22 1997		
DEC 26 1997		MAY 15 2006
FEB 13 1998		
MAY 21 1998		
JAN 03 1998		
AUG 01 1999		